Essentials of Management Accounting in Business

D1350634

Michael Bendrey is a Chartered Management Accountant, a Chartered Certified Accountant and holds an MSc in Business Administration. He has held a variety of financial appointments in the Chemical, Electrical, Printing, Packaging and Newspaper Industries, and since 1976 has been engaged in education and training at all levels.

He has taught on professional, undergraduate and postgraduate programmes at the Universities of the West of England (where he was Faculty Chairman at Bristol Business School), Bristol, Bath, Exeter and Ballarat (Australia). Michael has combined this academic career with consultancy activities, and advised on the appraisal and financing of large infrastructure projects in the Middle East (Syria, Jordan and Oman), Africa (Ethiopia, Zambia, Tanzania and Mozambique), and old Eastern Bloc countries (Latvia, Poland and Russia). He has also worked in Cyprus and Turkey on similar projects, and acted as a consultant to UK companies.

Roger Hussey is Dean of the Odette Business School at the University of Windsor, Canada, and Visiting Professor at Bristol Business School, University of the West of England. His first career was as an accountant in industry, and he is still a Fellow of the Association of Chartered Certified Accountants. He went on to study for an M.Sc in Industrial Relations at Bath University, and followed this with a Ph.D. in Management at the same university.

On leaving Bath, Roger went to St Edmund Hall, Oxford University, as Director of Research into Employee Communications for 6 years. This was followed by 15 years at Bristol Business School before moving to Canada in 2000.

Also available in the series

Essentials of Financial Accounting in Business: Mike Bendrey, Roger Hussey and
    Colston West
Management Accounting 5th Edition: Terry Lucey
Accounting and Finance 5th Edition: Alan Pizzey

Essentials of Management Accounting in Business

Mike Bendrey, Roger Hussey
and Colston West

continuum
LONDON • NEW YORK

Continuum

The Tower Building, 11 York Road, London SE1 7NX

370 Lexington Avenue, New York NY 10017-6503

British Library Cataloguing-in-Publication data

A catalogue record for this book is available from the British Library.

ISBN: 0-8264-6303-7 (paperback), 0-8264-6304-5 (hardback)

Typeset by RefineCatch Limited, Bungay, Suffolk

Printed and bound in Great Britain by MPG Books Ltd, Bodmin, Cornwall

CONTENTS

Preface   vii

PART I: INTRODUCTION   1

1.   The role of management accounting   3

PART II: PLANNING AND CONTROL   13

2.   Cost classification   15
3.   Cost behaviour   32
4.   Cost prediction techniques   49
5.   Budgetary control   67

PART III: COSTING AND PRICING   89

6.   Cost allocation and apportionment   91
7.   Absorption costing   106
     Assignment – Brisbane Briefcases Ltd   125
8.   Marginal costing   127
9.   Activity-based costing   140
10. Process costing   154
11. Other costing methods   167
12. Standard costing   177
13. Cost collection and recording   196
     Assignment – Westbank Foods Ltd   208

PART IV: DECISION MAKING   211

14. Cost-volume-profit analysis   213
15. Limiting factors   235
16. Relevant costs and revenues   251
17. Payback and accounting rate of return   269

18. Discounted cash flow   282

     Assignment – Aussie Woollen Products Ltd   308

     Assignment – Wight Mineral Water Co Ltd   310

     Answers   312

     Appendix – Discounted cash flow tables   326

     Index   329

PREFACE

This edition has been developed from the very successful *Accounting and Finance in Business*, and concentrates on the management accounting aspects covered in previous editions.

We have maintained the easy style which has encouraged the use of the book on a range of courses including Higher National Diploma and Certificates programmes, undergraduate and postgraduate degrees, Royal Society of Arts and London Chamber of Commerce programmes and elements of some professional programmes. It is on the reading lists of many higher and further educational institutions both in the UK and abroad.

The current edition provides the basic level of knowledge which is becoming increasingly called for in programmes not directly related to accounting and business studies. As examples, engineering degrees now often require knowledge of management accounting techniques, and the study of marketing also calls for a level of financial knowledge in the practitioner. Indeed, it is hard to find any business activity where some understanding of finance is not an advantage, and this edition continues to cover the appropriate basics of management accounting.

At the same time, the opportunity of producing the new edition has been taken to expand some of the existing chapters, such as that on standard costing, and to cover more advanced aspects in the new chapters introduced. These new chapters have been added for those who wish to extend their understanding of the subject. A chapter has been introduced on cost prediction techniques, including the use of linear regression and learning curves, as has one on integrated accounts.

We hope that lecturers, students and others who are familiar with earlier editions will agree that we have achieved our aim in providing a comprehensive introduction to management accounting in business, while at the same time touching on some of the more advanced techniques which will continue to make the book useful to both the student and the practitioner.

Mike Bendrey
Roger Hussey
Colston West

PART I

INTRODUCTION

CHAPTER 1

The role of management accounting

1 | OBJECTIVES

At the end of this chapter you should:

- understand what management accounting is;
- understand how it fits into the management information system;
- appreciate how management accounting has developed;
- understand the role of management accounting within organizations;
- appreciate the differences between management accounting and financial accounting.

2 | INTRODUCTION

As businesses and other organizations developed in size from small, owner-managed enterprises to large multinational groups, it was realized very quickly that the managers of those organizations would require data and information about the parts of the business for which they were responsible, so as to enable them to carry out their roles in an effective manner.

A small business, such as a sole trader, has little need for a complex management information system. The owner is often able to plan and control the business with the existence of very few formal, written systems. The business plan may be in the owner's head and the owner is able to control all the activities of the business on a day-to-day basis.

As the business grows it becomes necessary to split the business into functions, such as production, marketing, personnel, engineering and finance, with the appointment of a manager responsible for each functional area. It then becomes necessary to formalize the approach to planning and control by having a flow of information appropriate to each manager's responsibilities.

Yet larger businesses, such as large groups, face the same problems, and their response is to divide the organizations into divisions, so that each separate activity is the responsibility of its own management.

The information which is provided to the internal management of an organisation is known as *management accounting*.

3 | A DEFINITION OF MANAGEMENT ACCOUNTING

Management accounting may be described as the determination, presentation, interpretation and application of financial and quantitative information to the internal management of an organization at all levels. It is used for:

- formulation of the organization's strategy;
- planning the organization's activities;
- measuring and controlling the organization's performance;
- facilitating decision making;
- ascertainment of costs and income;
- establishing prices.

4 | DEVELOPMENT OF MANAGEMENT ACCOUNTING

The precursor to management accounting is regarded as cost accounting, which dates from a period when the emphasis was on the ascertainment of product costs. Undoubtedly cost accounting and management accounting existed from the early times of the Industrial Revolution, but in the UK there developed a need during the First World War for the provision of costing information for the negotiation and charging of government contracts for the provision of war materiel.

A formal recognition of the distinct nature of cost accounting was achieved by the formation of distinct and separate professional bodies. The Institute of Cost and Works Accountants (ICWA) was incorporated in the UK in 1919, and in the same year a similar management accounting body was formed in the USA.

The emphasis was initially applied to manufacturing organizations and, indeed, even to this day much of the science and art of costing and management accounting is applied to production-based enterprises. In common with the traditional approach, this book covers management accounting largely, although not exclusively, in a production environment. However, it should be appreciated that management accounting is applied also to such varied organizations as banks, retail organizations, service enterprises, not-for-profit organizations, local authorities, universities and hospital trusts.

As an illustration of the further development of management accounting, the ICWA later became the Institute of Cost and Management Accountants, and currently is the Chartered Institute of Management Accountants (CIMA), whose members are now known as Chartered Management Accountants.

5 | PLANNING

The role of management accounting in planning includes both the long-term and the short-term aspects. Long-term plans cover strategic planning, which may span a period of three to five years, and is the responsibility of the top management of the organization. Short-term planning usually involves the preparation of plans or budgets for each area of the business, providing steps in the achievement of the long-term plans. Short-term plans are often produced in the form of *functional budgets*, and usually cover the period of a year.

6 | CONTROL

The budgets also form part of the control process within organizations, to ensure that organizations are given direction, and that each function is operating in conformity with the overall business plan. This is achieved by collecting actual performances of costs and revenues on the same basis as the business plan, comparing those actuals with the plan, and establishing differences from the plan, known as *variances*. If those variances are unacceptable to a degree, then action is taken to correct the situation. By operating budgets in this way, each functional area of the business is aware of what is expected of it to conform to the business plan, and is also aware to what extent it is, or is not, conforming to that plan. This is essentially the *scorekeeping* role of management accounting.

7 | ASCERTAINMENT OF COSTS AND INCOME

One of the major reasons for maintaining a management accounting system is for the ascertainment of costs and income. Management accounting endeavours to ascertain the costs incurred by the organization of:

- Materials used in production and for other activities, such as maintenance and administration.
- Other resources used, such as labour and various categories of overheads.
- Products, jobs and contracts produced by the organization.
- Services provided by the organization for customers.
- Sub-assemblies manufactured as part of the final product.
- Functional areas of the business.
- Divisions, departments and sections of the business.
- Processes through which the production may pass.
- Services provided by one section to other areas of the organization.
- Getting work in progress and finished goods to their location and condition.

A management accounting system may not be required to ascertain all of these in any one particular organization, but the management accountant, in conjunction with the other management, will determine which of the above costs should be ascertained by the system. This will be determined by the type of products and services produced, the methods of production, the structure of the organization and the financial information which is required by the various levels of management to assist them in carrying out their activities.

The system will also trace income to products and sections of the business, such as *profit centres*. These are sections of the business to which both costs and income can be traced.

8 | DECISION MAKING

Management accounting has a crucial contribution to make in the decision making aspects of management. In business there are many decisions which have to be made, both on a regular basis, daily, weekly or monthly, and on a long-term basis, where strategic decisions affect the future direction of the organization in a fundamental way.

Decision making is about the future of the organization, and decision-making information has special characteristics which make it fundamentally different from the financial information which is used for planning, control and cost ascertainment. In order to be effective in decision making, management requires projected financial information which is relevant to the decision being made. Decision making requires what are known as *relevant costs and revenues*, and long-term decisions often require one-off or ad hoc reports.

Examples of the kinds of decisions which are often required to be made, each requiring its own projected information specific to that decision, are as follows:

- *Make or buy decision*

Whether a particular product or component should be made within the company or whether its manufacture should be sub-contracted to be made outside the organization. Consideration by management of the different costs which are likely to be incurred in each case is necessary to enable the most cost-effective decision to be made.

- *Increase output decision*

Whether it is profitable to increase output. Consideration by management of the additional costs which may be incurred, compared with the additional revenue which may be generated, may be required in this case.

- *Setting up a new production line*

The investment costs may need to be projected, along with the running costs incurred and the income generated, so as to determine whether it would be financially worthwhile to set up a new production line.

- *Close down or suspend activity decisions*

Consideration may need to be given to the costs which would be avoided by this action and also those which would continue to be incurred, together with the effects on income in both cases.

- *Choosing between competing products*

Consideration may need to be given to the respective costs and revenues which would be incurred and generated by each product, and whether they are *mutually exclusive products*, that is, only one or the other may be produced and sold, but not both.

- *Changing production methods*

Consideration needs to be given to the costs which will be incurred for each production method.

- *Optimal use of scarce resources*

It is sometimes possible to identify a scarce resource or constraint which must be used in the most effective way in order to optimize its use and maximize profits. It may be a particular material which is in limited supply, or alternatively skilled labour or production capacity. Whichever it is, management will need the kind of information which will enable it to make the most profitable decision.

- *Lowest cost financing decision*

For any activity which requires finance, the lowest cost alternative over time commensurate with the resources available may need to be chosen. This may involve the management accountant considering the various alternatives, such as leasing, deferred payment or immediate payment.

9 | PRICING

Management accounting has an important role to play in the establishment of prices charged for the goods and services sold by the organization. In some cases, having built up the total cost of a product or service by using the costing or management accounting system, a *profit margin*, or a *mark-up*, can be added, perhaps as a percentage, so as to fix a selling price chargeable to the customer. This is known as *cost-plus pricing*.

This approach might be adopted when dealing with a one-off job to a specific specification for a customer, such as the production and sale of a specialized piece of machinery. This is known as jobbing production.

In most cases, however, the price of a product or service is more likely to be fixed by competitive market considerations and not necessarily set by reference to the cost of production. Unless the organization is a monopoly or oligopoly, it is likely to be a price taker rather than being able to set prices based on cost. Even in the case of the jobbing producer set out above, the price is still likely to be set based on what the market will bear rather than a simple cost-plus approach. The management accounting system may be used to give guidance only for price setting in circumstances where it is ultimately set by the market.

Even where the price is set by market considerations, the management accounting system is able to give some important product or service cost information to determine whether the organization is able to produce the product within the price range set by the market, and earn an adequate profit.

Alternatively, if actual cost is higher than market prices, then the technique of *target costing* may be applied so as to seek ways of producing the product or service within cost levels which will still yield a profit to the firm.

10	MANAGEMENT ACCOUNTING AND FINANCIAL ACCOUNTING COMPARED

We have seen that *management accounting* is the aspect of accounting which deals with the provision of financial information to the internal management of an organization to enable them to carry out their various managerial roles. The other aspect of accounting is *financial accounting*, which deals with the provision of financial information to outside parties such as shareholders, government agencies, creditors and investors generally, in order to account to the owners of the business and others for the directors' stewardship of resources entrusted to their care.

The content, presentation and uses of management accounting and financial accounting differ considerably, and the major differences may be summarized as follows.

- *Recipients*

As we have seen, management accounting statements are received by the internal management of an organization, whereas financial accounting statements are used by groups outside the organization, such as shareholders (owners), creditors (loan capital providers), government agencies (taxation authorities and Companies' House), and the market generally (investors and investment advisors).

- *Reporting periods*

The reporting requirements of financial accounting in the UK are covered by legal requirements, accounting standards and, for those companies listed on the Stock Exchange, the Stock Exchange Listing Agreement. Generally, limited companies are required to report annually, with listed companies required to report their results half-yearly in interim statements. Some companies, such as British Airways, report quarterly.

Management accounting reporting requirements are determined by the organization itself. Some aspects may be reported monthly (management accounts) and others quarterly (a detailed balance sheet). However, daily reporting of cash balances may be regarded as necessary and appropriate, with weekly reporting for such items as payroll costs. The regularity of each reported item is determined by the internal management of the organization.

- *Content*

The content of financial accounting statements is determined and controlled by legislation, accounting standards and other organizations, such as the Stock Exchange, to which a listed organization subjects itself. There are also *Generally Accepted Accounting Principles* (GAAP) applicable in whichever country the company reports, and the accounts usually also conform to these requirements. Statements such as the profit and loss account (the income statement), the balance sheet and the cash flow statement have their contents and layout specified in detail, and there is relatively little deviation from those specifications.

On the other hand, the content of management accounting statements is left to the discretion of the management of an organization, therefore different organizations will have their own content and layout in their management accounting statements.

In some areas, however, there is a strong linkage between the management accounts and the financial accounts. For example, the valuation of stocks and work in progress may be obtained from the management accounting activity and then be incorporated into the published financial accounts. The valuation of such stocks for financial accounting purposes must conform to accounting standards (currently Statement of Standard Accounting Practice 9), and although there is no control over the method of stock valuation for management accounting purposes, it makes sense to use the same valuation basis (SSAP 9) for both management and financial accounting activities.

The principle of the common treatment of items both in financial and management accounting is a general one for reporting purposes. If different treatments are used, then this may cause different profits to arise from each system and these differences would have to be explained to the management.

- *Function*

We have seen that the main reasons for producing management accounting statements is to enable the management to carry out the managerial activities of planning, decision making and control. Financial accounting, on the other hand, does not effectively facilitate any of those activities but is more concerned with accounting for the directors' stewardship of the resources entrusted to their keeping.

- *Time dimension*

Financial accounting is concerned with reporting *past* activities to the organization's outside stakeholders, whereas management accounting not only reports past performance but is also concerned with *future* budgets, plans and investment alternatives.

- *Audit*

Financial accounting is normally subject to audit where, in some limited companies for example, the external auditors are appointed by the shareholders who then have powers to carry out such work within the firm to enable them to prepare a report on the accounts annually to the shareholders. Management accounting statements are not legally subject to audit, although the auditors would be concerned in so far as the management accounting system provides information for the financial accounts, such as the example of stock values referred to earlier.

- *Accuracy*

Because of the requirement to audit published financial accounting statements there is a necessity for them to conform to levels of accuracy that are not necessarily applied to management accounting statements. In many circumstances the provision of management accounting statements speedily after the accounting period may be more important than delaying their issue to make them 100 per cent accurate. Speed may be achieved at the expense of accuracy.

- *Detail*

As previously described, the content of financial accounts is controlled by legislation and accounting standards. The result is that financial accounts contain the required record of the entity's results essentially in summary form. There is virtually no analysis of the total performance into that of each department, subsidiary or division making up the firm. In management accounting, however, one of the essential aspects is to provide the detailed performance information appropriate to each part of the business. In addition, financial accounting summarizes income and expenditure whereas management accounting statements present costs in greater detail, such as material, wages and overheads by product or service.

11 | SUMMARY

Management accounting is the determination, presentation, interpretation and application of financial information to all levels of management of an organization. It is mainly concerned with providing regular information internally for planning, decision making, control, costing and pricing.

Financial accounting, however, provides audited statements to external users such as shareholders, creditors and the investing community, primarily accounting for the directors' stewardship of resources. In comparison with management accounting, its form and content is heavily prescribed by legislation, accounting standards and the appropriate GAAP.

STUDENT ACTIVITIES

Task 1.1
Collect samples of management accounting statements and reports from within the organisation where you work. List them by title, and against each one state to which manager and function it is directed and the regularity of its submission, whether it is reported daily, weekly, monthly, quarterly or is an ad hoc report.

Task 1.2
Obtain a copy of a published annual report and accounts of a listed company. This may be obtained from the organization's company secretary at its registered office, a local, college or university library, or in some cases from the internet.

Make yourself familiar with the content and layout of each of the financial statements included in the report, such as the profit and loss accounts, the balance sheets and the cash flow statement. Go through the notes to the accounts, which are an integral part of the accounts, and trace how the notes provide analyses of some of the items contained in the financial statements. Look for the accounting policies which have been applied by the company in preparing the accounts.

Task 1.3

Compare and contrast the information you have collected in Tasks 1 and 2 above. Look at the content, level of detail, the regulations which govern the statements and the recipients.

Consider how the management accounting and financial statements you have collected are able to be used by their respective recipients for the activities of scorekeeping, planning, decision making, control, costing and pricing.

Question 1.4

Draw up a table which lists and compares the major differences which exist between the activities of management accounting and financial accounting.

Question 1.5

Summarize each of the major management activities for which management accounting information provides assistance within an organization. Consider to what extent financial accounting statements may also be used for the same activities.

Question 1.6

Management accounting information is essential in assisting managers to carry out their role of decision making. Describe in detail ten decisions which might be made by managers within an organization, and describe the financial information which they would require to help them make each decision.

OBJECTIVE TEST* *(tick the appropriate box)*

i) Financial accounting is useful for:

   a) planning ☐

   b) decision making ☐

   c) both ☐

   d) neither ☐

ii) The content of management accounting statements is controlled by:

   a) auditors ☐

   b) accounting and reporting standards ☐

   c) legislation ☐

   d) all of these ☐

   e) none of these ☐

iii) The content of financial accounting statements may be determined by:

   a) legislation ☐

   b) accounting and reporting standards ☐

    c)   the Stock Exchange ☐

    d)   none of these ☐

    e)   all of these ☐

iv) Financial accounting statements:

    a)   show how each business segment has performed ☐

    b)   show information about past and future performance ☐

    c)   show only the past performance of an entity ☐

    d)   publishes budget comparisons against each item ☐

v) Financial accounting statements are used by:

    a)   long-term creditors ☐

    b)   owners of the business ☐

    c)   potential investors and their advisors ☐

    d)   none of these ☐

    e)   all of these ☐

PART II

PLANNING AND CONTROL

CHAPTER 2

Cost classification

1 | OBJECTIVES

At the end of this chapter you should be able to:

- understand what costs are;
- classify costs in a number of ways;
- understand the pricing of materials;
- understand the valuation of stocks;
- draw up a simple product cost statement;
- calculate a simple product selling price based on cost.

2 | INTRODUCTION

It is easier to understand and deal with things in everyday life if we identify items with common characteristics, group them together, and treat all of them in the group in a similar way. For example, children in school are grouped according to age and/or ability, and therefore it is convenient to teach them in classes. This is not to say that all members of a class are treated in exactly the same way, as there will be some variations within a group. However, these variations are not regarded as major, otherwise the children with these different characteristics would be put into a different group.

Businesses are also classified, sometimes according to size, sometimes according to business type. Thus we have some differences in legislation for sole traders, partnerships, private limited companies and public limited companies.

Accountants group expenditure and revenue according to common characteristics in order to ease their understanding, processing and presentation to both internal managers and the outside users of annual reports and accounts. This is known as *cost classification*.

3 | FIXED ASSETS AND CURRENT ASSETS

Any business needs *resources* to enable it to operate. These *resources* may be classified as *fixed assets* or *current assets*. *Fixed assets* are those resources which the business owns and means to keep in the longer term, usually for longer than a year, out of which the business derives a benefit in being able to use them in operating the business for that period of time. Examples include:

- *premises* which the business owns and from which it operates; these might include *factories*, *offices*, and *stores*;

- *plant and machinery* which the business owns and operates to enable production to take place;

- *furniture and office equipment* used by the administration, selling and distribution departments of the business;

- *motor vehicles* such as trucks to collect *raw materials* and deliver the *finished goods*, and cars used by the salesmen to collect orders.

Current assets are those *resources* which the business owns and which are used up in the day-to-day activities of the business and which are part of the trading cycle of purchasing and converting the *raw materials* into *finished goods*. Examples include:

- *stocks of raw materials* which are purchased either for *cash* or on *credit*, for conversion into finished goods;

- *stocks of finished goods* which have been manufactured or alternatively purchased for sale to customers;

- *stocks of work-in-progress* occur in a manufacturing business where, at any point in time, partly finished goods exist which require further work on them to convert them into *finished goods* for sale to the customer;

- *debtors* are the balances owing to the business by those customers who have purchased *finished goods* on credit;

- *bank balances* are those balances of cash held at a bank;

- *cash balances* are balances of cash held at the office either as petty cash, or as cash waiting to be banked.

> You should now be able to attempt question 2.4 at the end of this chapter.

4	CAPITAL AND REVENUE EXPENDITURE

The *resources* known as *current assets* can be converted into other *current assets*. For example, *cash in hand* or *bank balances* can be used to purchase *raw material stocks*, or *debtors* are converted into *cash* or *bank balances* when they pay the amounts which they owe.

Similarly, *current assets* can be used to create *fixed assets*. For example, *cash* or *bank balances* can be used to purchase land and buildings. Expenditure on *fixed assets* is known as *capital expenditure*.

In addition to *capital expenditure*, any business also incurs day-to-day expenditure on other items which are necessary to carry out the purchasing, production, administration, selling and distribution activities of the organization. These other items of expenditure are known as *revenue expenditure* and share the characteristic that the benefit derived from the expenditure arises in the same period as the costs are incurred. Examples include:

- *raw materials consumed*, otherwise known as *direct materials*, are those materials which are used in the product or products manufactured by the organization: although most businesses purchase raw materials to be kept in store until needed, they do not represent a charge against profits, and therefore become a cost, until they are consumed;

- *production department wages* are wages paid to machine operators and other personnel engaged in the production process;

- *other wages and salaries* are wages and salaries paid to personnel in the stores, administration, sales, distribution and other departments of the business;

- *electricity* which may be the expenditure on power for operating the machines, *lighting* for the factory, stores and offices, and *heating*;

- *sub-contract work*, sometimes called *outwork*, is work that is carried out by another business which is engaged in providing a service or expertise in the production of the product; this may be in the form of a *sub-assembly* or partly finished part of the main product, or in extreme cases the production of the whole product may be sub-contracted in order, for example, to enable the business to satisfy a level of demand for the product which cannot be met from its own capacity;

- *lubricating oil* used for the production machinery;

- *running expenses* of the *salesmen's* motor cars such as *oil*, *petrol*, *tyres*, *repairs and maintenance*, and *licences*;

- although the expenditure on *fixed assets* of the business is classified as *capital expenditure*, the action of *writing off* or *amortizing* the cost of the *fixed assets* against the profits of the business over their effective lives is known as *depreciation* and is classified as *revenue expenditure*.

Some items, which by all normal definitions should be classified as *capital expenditure*, nevertheless are treated as *revenue expenditure* if they are of low value. For example, an office calculator which cost only £5 would be treated as *revenue expenditure* even though it possesses all the characteristics of an item of *capital expenditure* in that it has an extended life and would be used by the business for a period exceeding a year.

The definition of a *small value item* is a decision which would be made by each individual business and may be dependent on its size. It is quite common for a business to decide not to treat as *capital expenditure* any item which costs less than £50, but the precise limit will vary between businesses.

> *You should now be able to attempt question 2.5 at the end of this chapter.*

5 | COST CLASSIFICATIONS

Items of *revenue expenditure* are known as *costs*. Some *costs* are not charged against profits as soon as they are incurred, but are held in abeyance until they are actually used up in the manufacture of a product. An example of these costs is *raw material* which goes into a store when purchased and is used to manufacture a product at a later stage. When it is subsequently issued to production is the time when the raw material becomes a cost for accounting purposes. Other costs are charged against profits as soon as they are incurred. Examples are wages, salaries, insurances, light and heat, telephone and depreciation.

In order to help us deal with costs in a logical way, we group costs under a number of different headings relating to how costs are incurred in the manufacture or production of a product or service. This process of grouping costs is known as *cost classification*.

Costs incurred in the manufacture of a product, known as *product costs*, can be classified either as *direct costs* or *indirect costs*. *Indirect costs* may also be described as *overhead costs* or *overheads*, and if a particular product cost cannot be described as a *direct cost* it is automatically classified as an *overhead*.

A *direct cost* is a cost which can be traced or identified relatively easily to the product or products which are being produced, and is a cost which is incurred specifically for the production of those products.

An *overhead cost* is a cost which is incurred to enable the organization to carry out its operations of purchasing, manufacturing, selling and distribution, but nevertheless such costs cannot be easily traced to or identified with particular products.

Although most of the examples in this chapter are concerned with the classification of costs as applied to the manufacture of products, the approach can also be applied to the service sector and delivery of services such as banking, transport and accountancy.

6 | PRODUCT DIRECT COSTS

Direct costs can be classified as *direct materials*, *direct wages* and *direct expenses*.

- *Direct materials* are those materials which are used in the production of, and feature in the final form of, the products which are produced by the enterprise. Although for ease of expression and description they are described as materials, they are not restricted to *raw materials*, as they may also include *parts* and *partly finished sub-assemblies* which are purchased from an outside supplier and form part of the final products.

Example

Product	Direct material
Desks	Wood, screws, handles
Books	Paper, glue, ink
Shoes	Leather, glue, rubber/plastics, laces
Motor vehicles	Steel, tyres, glass
China	Clay, transfers, glaze

An allowance is usually made for the normal levels of wastage incurred in the production process, such waste also being treated as direct material.

It should be noted that some materials which are used in the manufacture of the products do not come under the classification of *direct materials*. For example, lubrication and cooling oil for the production machinery, cleaning materials used by the factory cleaners, and maintenance and repair materials used for maintaining the production machinery, are all treated as *indirect materials* or *overheads*, as none of these items feature in the final products which are being produced.

Even some small-value items which are really *direct materials* are often treated as *overheads* because their cost is difficult to measure when costing individual products. An example is sewing cotton when making clothing and glue in making boxes.

- *Direct wages* (or *direct labour*) are those wages paid to the personnel who are directly involved in the production of each of the items produced. This will include wages paid to operators of the machinery used to manufacture the products, wages paid to personnel who assemble the products, and wages paid to those personnel who finish them, such as painting, polishing and testing.

- *Direct expenses* are those costs which can also be directly traced to the products which are being manufactured, but cannot be classified under the headings of *direct materials* or *direct wages*. For example, in the manufacture of furniture, if the operation of French polishing is sub-contracted to an expert, the resultant cost is neither direct material, the French polish is never owned by the manufacturer, nor direct wages, as the expert is not on the payroll of the manufacturer. Nevertheless, the cost is clearly a product direct cost and would therefore be charged to direct expenses of the product on which the French polisher worked.

You should now be able to attempt question 2.6 at the end of this chapter.

7 | TREATMENT OF MATERIALS

When *materials* are purchased they are often put into stock before being issued to production when needed for that purpose. There are a number of alternative costing approaches available when charging these materials to production, and we will now examine the major pricing alternatives.

- *First-in-first-out* (FIFO) prices the issues to production in the same order as those unit prices were incurred and charged into the stores. Thus the earliest prices are used up first until the quantities at that price are exhausted, then the next price received is used, and so on. This is a very common and acceptable method of pricing issues mainly because it charges material costs against the profits in the same order in which those prices are incurred.

- *Last-in-first-out* (LIFO) prices the issues to production using the latest prices received into store first until all the units at that price are exhausted, then the next latest price is used and so on. Although this method is acceptable in some overseas countries, it is not allowed in the UK for computing profits for taxation purposes. One effect of using this method is that the earliest prices incurred may never be used if the stock level is not allowed to fall to zero.

- *Average cost* (AVCO) calculates a weighted average price for the stock each time a consignment is received and uses that price to charge the units issued to production until another consignment is received, when a new issue price is calculated. This method is a very common one which is particularly appropriate to computerized stock control systems where the average prices may be easily recalculated each time a new consignment of stock is received. It also has the attribute of smoothing out the impact of changes of prices in the profit and loss account.

Although these methods are described as methods for *pricing* the issues, they can also be described as methods of *stock valuation*. This is because the stock remaining is valued based on the value of the opening stock plus the stock received less the stock issued, and therefore the use of the different pricing methods affects the value of closing stock. It is also stressed that FIFO and LIFO refer to the order in which the *prices* are used, not necessarily the order in which the *physical stock* is issued.

Example

The following quantities of material were received and issued by the stores of *Samara Simulations Ltd* for the month of June. There was an opening stock at the beginning of the month of 50 units valued at £150.

Date	Receipts quantity	Unit price £	Issues quantity
June 2			25
June 3	100	3.50	
June 6			50
June 8			50
June 10	25	4.00	
June 15			25
June 20	50	3.20	
June 30			40

Required

Record the entries in the stock account using each of the FIFO, LIFO and AVCO methods of pricing issues and summarize the charges against profits for the month and the value of closing stocks for each method.

Solution

FIFO method

Date	Receipts			Issues			Balance	
	Units	Rate	£	Units	Rate	£	Units	£
June 1							50	150.00
June 2				25	3.00	75.00	25	75.00
June 3	100	3.50	350.00				125	425.00
June 6				25	3.00	75.00		
				25	3.50	87.50	75	262.50
June 8				50	3.50	175.00	25	87.50
June 10	25	4.00	100.00				50	187.50
June 15				25	3.50	87.50	25	100.00
June 20	50	3.20	160.00				75	260.00
June 30				25	4.00	100.00		
				15	3.20	48.00	35	112.00
						648.00		

LIFO method

Date	Receipts			Issues			Balance	
	Units	Rate	£	Units	Rate	£	Units	£
June 1							50	150.00
June 2				25	3.00	75.00	25	75.00
June 3	100	3.50	350.00				125	425.00
June 6				25	3.50	87.50		
				25	3.50	87.50	75	250.00
June 8				50	3.50	175.00	25	75.00
June 10	25	4.00	100.00				50	187.50
June 15				25	4.00	100.00	25	75.00
June 20	50	3.20	160.00				75	235.00
June 30				25	3.20	80.00		
				15	3.20	48.00	35	107.00
						653.00		

AVCO method

Date	Receipts			Issues			Balance	
	Units	Rate	£	Units	Rate	£	Units	£
June 1							50	150.00
June 2				25	3.00	75.00	25	75.00
June 3	100	3.50	350.00				125	425.00
June 6				25	3.40	85.00		
				25	3.40	85.00	75	255.00
June 8				50	3.40	170.00	25	85.00
June 10	25	4.00	100.00				50	185.00
June 15				25	3.70	92.50	25	92.50
June 20	50	3.20	160.00				75	252.50
June 30				40	3.37*	134.80	35	117.70
						642.30		
					* rounded			

Summary:

	Charge against profits £	Value of closing stock £	Total £
FIFO	648.00	112.00	760.00
LIFO	653.00	107.00	760.00
AVCO	642.30	117.70	760.00

> You should now be able to attempt question 2.7 at the end of this chapter.

8 | PRODUCT INDIRECT COSTS OR OVERHEADS

If a cost is not a *product direct cost*, that is one that can be treated as *direct material*, *direct wages* or *direct expenses*, it is classified as a *product indirect cost* or an *overhead*. Overheads are those items of *revenue expenditure* which cannot be traced directly to the production of particular products where a range of products is manufactured, these costs often having the characteristic of being shared by all the output. Overheads can be classified as follows.

- *Production overheads* (or *manufacturing* or *factory overheads*) are incurred as part of the cost of manufacture, but cannot be traced to the products produced as direct costs. Examples are factory rent, business rates, factory cleaning costs (cleaners' wages and cleaning materials used), depreciation of machinery, power, light and heat, and salaries and wages paid to supervisory personnel.

- *Administration overheads* are those costs which are incurred by the administrative function, which is necessary for the running of any business.

These overheads mainly involve office costs and examples are office salaries, postage, stationery, rent, business rates, lighting and heating of the offices, and secretarial expenses. The accounting department is often treated as an administration overhead.

- *Selling overheads* are those costs incurred by the selling function of the business. Examples are advertising, salesmen's salaries and commission, and salesmen's travel costs such as car depreciation, petrol, oil and maintenance costs.

- *Distribution overheads* are those costs incurred in getting the finished product into the hands of the customer. Examples are final packing costs, transportation and/or postage depending on the mode of distribution, and all the costs of operating a fleet of distribution vehicles, i.e. trucks and vans would be classified under this heading.

- *Research and development* overheads are experienced by some organizations where costs are incurred in the researching and development of new products and processes. The costs of carrying out these activities often have to be borne by the income from the existing product range, as some time will elapse before income will be generated by the products or processes under development.

Example

Product cost classification

		Product cost (£)
Direct costs:	Direct materials	X
	Direct wages	X
	Direct expenses	X
	Prime cost	X
Indirect costs or overheads:	Production	X
	Production cost	X
	Administration	X
	Selling	X
	Distribution	X
	R & D	X
	Total cost	X

Notes

The term *prime cost* is applied to the total of the *product direct costs*. The term *production cost* is applied to the *prime cost* plus *production overhead*. *Production costs* exclude all non-production expenses such as *administration, selling, distribution* and *research overheads*. This is particularly important when a valuation of *work in progress* or *finished goods* is required as, in general, these are valued at *production cost*.

You should now be able to attempt tasks 2.1, 2.2 and 2.3 and question 2.8 at the end of this chapter.

9 PROBLEMS OF COST CLASSIFICATION

Each organization needs to make its own decisions about how particular items of revenue expenditure should be classified according to product cost classification. There are no hard and fast rules, but there are general guidelines which help to define approaches. For example, one organization may treat the wages paid to the supervisors of operators as a direct product cost in the same way as the operators' costs are treated. A similar organization, however, may classify the wages of all supervisors as an indirect cost and thus treat them as a production overhead. Both approaches may be regarded as acceptable.

You will appreciate that as production becomes more automated and production personnel become more remote from the product itself, then the more difficult it becomes to classify such costs as direct wages. An example of this is the highly automated chemical process industry where, by its very nature, few operators actually handle the products which are being produced. In some cases such wages may be treated as production overhead.

> *You should now be able to attempt questions 2.8 and 2.9 at the end of this chapter.*

10 SUMMARY

The expenditure or costs of a business can be classified as either *capital expenditure* or *revenue expenditure*. Capital expenditure is made up of costs, usually of a substantial nature, incurred in the procurement of assets which the business intends to keep in the longer term and from which it derives the benefit from being able to use them over a period of time. These assets are known as *fixed assets* and may be further classified into such categories as *land and buildings*, *plant and machinery*, *fixtures and fittings* and *motor vehicles*.

Revenue expenditure represents the costs of operating the business on a day-to-day basis where the benefit derived from the expenditure arises within the same period as the costs are incurred. Revenue expenditure is usually classified according to *product costs*.

> *You should now be able to attempt the objective test at the end of this chapter.*

STUDENT ACTIVITIES (* denotes questions with answers at the end of the book)

Task 2.1
Select an everyday manufactured product of your choice. List as many costs which are incurred in the production, sale and distribution of that product as

possible. Now classify the costs you have listed according to the normal way in which product costs are classified for costing purposes.

Task 2.2

Using your own organization, whether it is the college where you are studying or your place of work, make a list of all the capital expenditure items you consider may be treated as revenue expenditure because they are of low value.

Task 2.3

See how many cost classifications you can apply to your personal expenditure for the last three months.

Question 2.4

Complete the columns below to analyse the *assets* into *fixed assets* and *current assets* respectively. Tick the appropriate column.

Asset	Fixed assets	Current assets
Office furniture		
Factory building		
Work in progress		
Cash in building society		
Trade debtors		
Fork-lift truck		
Goods awaiting delivery to customers		
Land		

Question 2.5

Complete the columns below to analyse the items of *expenditure* into *capital* and *revenue expenditure* respectively. Tick the appropriate column.

Expenditure	Capital expenditure	Revenue expenditure
Purchase of land		
Payment of pension premiums		
Payment of storeman's wages		
Payment of sales manager's salary		
Repairs to factory roof		
Cost of factory extension		
Paint for product's finish		
Paint for factory windows		
Factory rent and rates		
Stationery for office use		

Question 2.6

i)   List two direct materials appropriate to each of the following products.

Product	Direct materials
Desks	
Books	
Shoes	
Motor vehicles	
China	

ii) For the following products give *three* examples of direct materials used in their production:

Product	Direct materials
Canned beans	
Boxes of corn flakes	
Computers	
Diesel locomotives	
Men's suits	

Question 2.7

From the following information prepare the entries in the stock account to record the receipts and issues for the month of September using each of the first-in-first-out (FIFO), last-in-first-out (LIFO), and average cost (AVCO) methods of pricing issues. The opening balance of stock on 1 September was 324 units valued at £2 per unit.

Date	Receipts quantity	Unit price £	Issues quantity
Sept 2			200
Sept 3	200	2.20	
Sept 5			300
Sept 10	110	2.50	
Sept 15			100
Sept 20			20
Sept 25	200	3.00	
Sept 30			150

Question 2.8

Poole Furniture Ltd manufactures desks and chairs. Indicate the correct cost classification of the following revenue expenditure items using the code below. The first one has been done for you.

Revenue expenditure item	Cost classification code
Direct wages	1
Direct materials	2
Direct expenses	3
Production overheads	4
Administration overheads	5
Selling overheads	6
Distribution overheads	7

Cost	Classification
Pre-formed chair legs purchased from a supplier	2
Factory rent	
Office business rates	
Depreciation on salesmens' cars	
Maintenance wages	
Power	
Factory lighting	
Lubrication oil for sawing machine	
Maintenance of truck used to send finished goods to customers	
Factory cleaners' wages	
Foreman's wages	
Factory manager's salary	
Canteen costs	
Consignment of timber	
Consignment of nails, screws and hinges	
Cleaning materials	
Depreciation of factory machinery	
Packing materials	
French polisher's wages	
Depreciation of office computer	

Question 2.9*

Brixham Garden Furniture manufactures garden gnomes, and plans to produce 2,000 units over the next month. Each variety takes the same amount of materials and time to produce, and *Brixhams* is keen to determine the following:

i)   prime cost
ii) production cost
iii) administration overheads
iv) selling overheads
v)   distribution overheads
vi) total cost

Brixham's costs for the month are:

Rent	
factory:	£500
office:	£100
Business rates	
factory:	£300
office:	£100
Sand:	£1,000
Power:	£700
Light and heat	
factory:	£2,000
office:	£1,300

Wages
    operators: £10,000
    maintenance: £1,500
    canteen: £2,500
Cement: £5,000
Depreciation
    office equipment: £500
    moulds: £2,200
    fixtures and fittings: £800
Salesmen's salary and commission: £2,200
Delivery expenses: £500
Office salaries: £1,800
Cement-mixer repairs: £900
Salesmen's car expenses: £1,100
Finishing paint: £200
Packing: £800

vii) If *Brixhams* wishes to add 50 per cent to total costs as a mark-up, what should the selling price be, per gnome?

viii) Calculate the profit margin as a percentage of sales.

Question 2.10

Classify the items of expenditure for *Oman Engineering Ltd* into revenue and capital expenditure using sub-categories for revenue expenditure and tick the appropriate columns.

DM = Direct materials
DL = Direct labour
DE = Direct expenses
P = Production overhead
A = Administration overhead
S = Selling overhead
D = Distribution overhead

Oman Engineering Ltd

Expenditure item	Revenue							Capital
	DM	DL	DE	P	A	S	D	
Factory business rates								
Machinery depreciation								
Cleaners' wages								
Sheet steel for product								
Machinists' wages								
Canteen costs								
Fabrication wages								
Factory paint								
Salesmen's salaries								
Maintenance wages								

Expenditure item	Revenue							Capital
	DM	DL	DE	P	A	S	D	
Electric motors (product)								
Power								
Gatehouse wages								
Heating								
Packing materials								
Delivery costs								
Insurance (factory)								
Stationery								
Office machinery								
Telephone								
Postage								
Sub-contract work (product)								
Chucks (work-holding equipment)								
Paint (product)								
Electric motors (machinery)								
Pension premiums								
Welding equipment								
Plant and machinery								
Salesmen's car depreciation								
Office desks								
Factory extension								
National Insurance								
Welding gas or rods								
Rent of equipment								
Grinding discs								
Jigs and tools								
Nuts and bolts								

OBJECTIVE TEST* *(tick the appropriate box)*

i) In a business which trades in buying and selling motor vehicles, an example of a fixed asset would be:

   a) A hand drill ☐

   b) A motor car ☐

   c) A computer ☒

   d) None of these ☐

ii) Day-to-day expenditure on items necessary to carry out the functions of purchasing, production, administration, selling and distribution are known as:

a) Current assets ☐

b) Payments ☐

c) Income expenditure ☐

d) Revenue expenditure ☒

iii) An example of capital expenditure would be:

a) Repairs to office windows ☐

b) Repairs to factory windows ☐

c) A new Jaguar car for the managing director ☒

d) None of these. ☐

iv) An example of a direct cost would be:

a) Sub-contract work ☒

b) Factory foreman's wages ☐

c) Electricity to power a grinding machine ☐

d) None of these ☐

v) An example of a production overhead would be:

a) Sub-contract work ☐

b) Outwork ☐

c) Depreciation of managing director's Jaguar car ☐

d) Factory cleaning costs ☒

The following costs apply to a product called Severn Blocks referred to in (vi)–(ix):

Direct materials: £654
Direct wages: £456
Direct expenses: £123
Factory indirect costs: £321
Administration costs: £789
Selling and distribution costs: £987
The profit margin on selling price: 10 per cent

vi) Product prime cost of Severn Blocks is:

a) £1,431 ☐

b) £1,554 ☐

c) £1,110 ☐

d) £1,233 ☒

vii) Product production cost of Severn Blocks is:

a) £1,431 ☐

b) £1,554 ☒

c) £1,110 ☐

d) £1,233 ☐

viii) Product selling price of Severn Blocks is:

a) £2,587 ☐

b) £3,663 ☐

c) £4,033 ☐

d) £3,700 ☒

ix) The total overhead costs of Severn Blocks are:

a) £2,097 ☒

b) £1,110 ☐

c) £1,776 ☐

d) None of these ☐

x) Which, as far as direct or indirect cost classification is concerned, is the odd one out:

a) Paper to wrap the product to protect it during production ☐

b) Paper for office typewriter ☐

c) Paper for cleaning machinery ☐

d) Paper serviettes for works canteen ☐

CHAPTER 3

Cost behaviour 成本性态

1 | OBJECTIVES

At the end of this chapter you should be able to:

- understand why costs are classified according to cost behaviour;
- understand what fixed costs are;
- understand what variable and semi-variable costs are;
- understand how cost behaviour is shown graphically.

2 | INTRODUCTION

In Chapter 2 we gave an an explanation of two ways in which expenditure may be classified. It is first possible to classify expenditure into *capital* and *revenue* (revise Question 2.5), and thereafter revenue expenditure or costs may be classified according to *direct* and *indirect product costs* (revise Question 2.8). A further method of classifying costs is according to the way in which they *behave* as production or sales increase or decrease.

3 | COST BEHAVIOUR

This method of classifying costs, according to *cost behaviour*, is a very important one in management accounting, in that, as we shall see in later chapters, it has implications in the areas of budgeting, decision making, costing and pricing.

Example

Tom Torquay rents a workshop in which he assembles buckets for children for use on the beach. Each bucket consists of a moulded plastic shape to which a metal handle is attached, and finished off with colourful transfers stuck around the outside. All three parts are bought in from outside. Tom's expected costs are as follows:

Bucket mouldings: 35p per bucket

Bucket handles: 15p per bucket

Bucket transfers: 5p per bucket

Rent: £200 per month

Business rates: £50 per month

Insurance: £50 per month

Packaging: £10 per 1,000 buckets

The buckets are assembled by Tom and his wife, as Tom reasons that this enables him to avoid the cost of wages as he and his wife are rewarded by the profits of the business created when they sell the buckets at £1 each. In a poor month they can assemble and sell 500 buckets, but at the peak of the season they manage 2,000 buckets. What are his respective profits in a poor and a good month?

Solution

First it is necessary to determine how the costs behave according to the different levels of production. Some of the costs which are incurred move up and down in total as production changes. These are the costs which are expressed as a rate per unit, of which an example is bucket mouldings: produce one bucket and the moulding cost incurred is 35p; produce two buckets and it is 70p, and so on. This relationship applies also to bucket handles, bucket transfers and also packaging. Although packaging costs are expressed as a rate per 1,000 buckets, its total cost will also rise and fall according to the total number produced and sold.

Having identified all the costs which behave in this way, it is possible to determine what their total would be for each level of production:

		Poor month		Good month
Monthly production (buckets)		500		2,000
Total costs:		£		£
Mouldings	500 × 35p	175	2,000 × 35p	700
Handles	500 × 15p	75	2,000 × 15p	300
Transfers	500 × 5p	25	2,000 × 5p	100
Packing	$\dfrac{500 \times 1p}{1,000}$	5	$\dfrac{2,000 \times 1p}{1,000}$	20
Total		280		1,120

Because each of these costs varies in total with the level of production they are known as *variable costs*. Notice that the production in a good month is four times that in a poor month, and the variable costs also increase in sympathy (4 × £280 = £1,120).

There are also other costs which behave in a different way. Tom is required to pay rent of £200 per month irrespective of the number of buckets produced and sold. Even if he produces no buckets at all, he would be obliged to pay this monthly rent charge. Other costs which also behave in the same way are business rates and insurance, and if these costs are grouped together for the two levels of production they would be as follows:

	Poor month	Good month
Monthly production (buckets)	500	2,000
Total costs:	£	£
Rent	200	200
Business rates	50	50
Insurance	50	50
Total	300	300

Because each of these costs remains constant in total irrespective of the level of production they are known as *fixed costs*. Notice that each of these costs in total is uninfluenced by production levels and, unlike the variable costs above, does not increase as production rises.

It is now possible to determine T. Torquay's profits for each of the monthly production levels by comparing total costs with total sales revenue generated by sales at £1 per bucket. His income (profit and loss) statements become:

T. Torquay
Profit and loss statements

		Poor month		Good month
Production and sales (buckets)		500		2,000
		£		£
Sales revenue	500 × £1	500	2,000 × £1	2,000
Total variable costs		280		1,120
Total fixed costs		300		300
Total costs		580		1,420
Profit/(loss)		(80)		580

Torquay makes a loss when the production and sales are as low as 500 buckets mainly due to the fact that costs which it has to bear whatever the activity level, the fixed costs, become a high cost per unit due to the lower volumes. Thus when sales are 500 units, the fixed costs per unit are:

$$\frac{£300}{500} = 60\text{p per unit}$$

which, when added to the variable costs of

$$\frac{£280}{500} = 56\text{p per unit}$$

gives a total unit cost of £1.16, which exceeds the selling price of £1 per unit by 16 pence. Hence the total loss of 500 units × 16p per unit = £80 at that level of production.

When 2,000 buckets are produced, however, the fixed costs of £300 are spread over 2,000 units to give a fixed cost per unit of:

$$\frac{£300}{2,000} = 15\text{p per unit}$$

which, when added to the variable costs of

$$\frac{£1,120}{2,000} = 56\text{p per unit}$$

gives a total unit cost of 71p, which, when compared to the selling price of £1, gives a profit of 29p per unit. Hence the total profit of

$$2,000 \text{ units} \times 29\text{p per unit} = £580$$

at that level of production.

Notice that the total variable costs per unit remain constant irrespective of the level of production, i.e. 56p per unit, whereas total variable costs change according to activity levels, i.e. £280 when 500 buckets are produced and £1,120 when 2,000 buckets are produced. Conversely, total fixed costs per unit change according to the number of units produced, i.e. 60p per unit when 500 buckets are produced, and falls to 15p per unit when production is 2,000 buckets. However, the fixed costs in total remain constant at £300 irrespective of the production levels.

4 | DEFINITIONS

From the solution to *Torquay* we can draw some general definitions as follows. A *variable cost* is a cost which, in total, increases or decreases in direct proportion to the volume of production or sales. Thus, an increase in production and sales of 20 per cent would also be accompanied by a 20 per cent increase in variable costs. Examples are direct materials and direct wages paid as a rate per item produced (known as piecework), both of which vary with production levels, and salesmen's commission and packing materials, both of which tend to vary with sales revenue and sales volume respectively. Variable costs behave like this:

Production (units)	1	5	10	15	25	38
Variable cost per unit	£1	£1	£1	£1	£1	£1
Total variable costs	£1	£5	£10	£15	£25	£38

Notice that this definition narrowly defines a variable cost as one which varies with activity, i.e. production or sales. However, this does not exclude the possibility that other factors may cause costs to vary such as inflation, management decisions to spend more money on advertising, and the negotiation of volume discounts on material purchases. These other cost changes, however, do *not* come under this definition of variable costs.

A *fixed cost* is a cost which, in total, remains constant and is uninfluenced by changes in the volume of production and/or sales in the short term. Examples are rent, rates, insurances, factory manager's salary and many administration overheads. Fixed costs behave like this:

Production (units)	1	5	10	15	25	38
Total fixed costs	£50	£50	£50	£50	£50	£50

Notice that this definition also narrowly defines fixed costs in relation to production or sales, but total fixed costs may change due to other factors such as a management policy to increase expenditure on, for example, research and development.

In the longer term no cost is entirely fixed as considerable changes in activity levels would necessarily be accompanied by changes to total fixed costs. For example, to increase production beyond the capacity of the present plant and machinery would necessitate further investment which would increase fixed costs such as depreciation and maintenance as a consequence.

> *You should now be able to attempt question 3.4 at the end of this chapter.*

5 | GRAPHICAL PRESENTATION OF COST BEHAVIOUR

In presenting the way in which variable and fixed costs behave in a *graphical* manner, three conventions are normally adopted.

1. The total fixed and variable costs respectively are plotted as opposed to the fixed and variable costs per unit of production.

2. Total fixed and/or variable costs in financial terms (e.g. £s) are shown on the vertical or y axis of the graph.

3. Because our definitions of fixed and variable costs are based on how they behave in relation to production or sales, activity is shown on the horizontal or x axis of the graph. Activity is usually expressed in units or sales value (£s), but may also be expressed as a percentage of total capacity of the business. Sales and production are regarded as equal.

Variable costs are shown as a straight-line graph, commencing at zero cost and production to illustrate that no variable costs are incurred at zero activity. To construct a variable cost graph, we calculate the total variable costs for a particular level of production and plot that point on the graph. Because it is a straight-line graph, we can draw the line from the point which represents the costs when production is zero, the origin, through the point, and all the points which are along this line represent the variable costs at each production level.

Taking the example of variable costs in the previous section where the variable cost for 25 units is £25, the variable cost graph would look like this:

Example

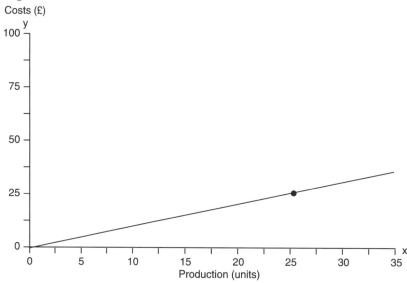

You should now be able to attempt question 3.5 at the end of this chapter.

Fixed costs may be shown as a horizontal straight line which demonstrates that a given level of fixed costs are incurred whatever the activity level. This representation of fixed costs also shows that even at zero production level such costs will be incurred and cannot be avoided.

Taking the example in the previous section where fixed costs are £50 in total for all levels of activity, the fixed cost graph would look like this:

Example

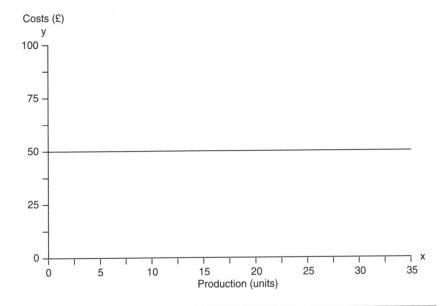

You should now be able to attempt question 3.6 at the end of this chapter.

Because *total costs* are equal to the addition of total variable costs and total fixed costs, it is possible to combine the effects of the total variable and total fixed cost lines onto a single graph, to produce a total cost line.

There are two possible presentations. In the first example the total variable cost line is plotted first, and the total fixed cost line is plotted above it to give the total cost line. Using the data from the previous example the graph would look like the first of the two examples that follow.

Notice that this presentation results in the total cost line being parallel to the total variable cost line due to the fact that the fixed costs are the same at all levels of activity.

In the second example the total fixed cost line is plotted first and the total variable cost line is plotted above it to give the total cost line.

Example 1

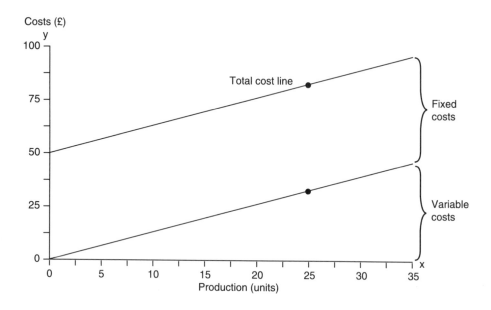

Example 2

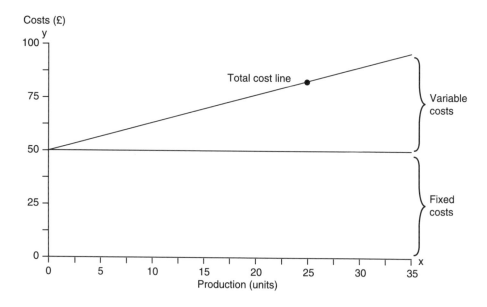

Both presentations should result in the same total cost line from a given set of data, therefore the choice of presentation to obtain total cost is simply a matter of preference at this stage in your studies. Example 1 does, however, enjoy an advantage which will be explained later in Chapter 14.

> *You should now be able to attempt question 3.7 at the end of this chapter.*

6   SOME PROBLEMS OF COST BEHAVIOUR

Identifying costs according to their cost behaviour characteristics and treating them as either fixed or variable, although a useful approach, tends to be an oversimplification, and some costs do not lend themselves easily to this treatment. Two particular examples which are met are those of classifying direct wages and semi-variable costs.

Direct wages costs – There is little doubt that both *direct materials* and *direct expenses* may be regarded as true *variable costs*, a test being that both these costs are avoidable if production ceases. Although *direct wages* are regarded as a variable cost, present labour laws and agreements with trade unions do not allow employers to dismiss labour easily. It is difficult, therefore, to reduce direct labour cost in line with falling production, and in these circumstances, particularly in the short term, labour behaves more like a fixed cost.

In costing the products manufactured, however, only the time actually spent on producing the output is regarded as a direct wages cost, and where operators are idle but remain employed because they cannot be dismissed in the short term, then their idle time is charged to production overheads rather than as direct wages. In this way, direct wages assume the characteristic of being a variable cost, any fixed unavoidable element being treated as an overhead. For this reason, unless there are clear indications to the contrary, all *product direct costs* making up the *prime cost* should be regarded and treated as *variable* in terms of cost behaviour.

Semi-variable costs – Some items of cost are a mixture of fixed and variable costs, and this causes such costs to behave in a special way. The total cost changes as activity changes, but not in strict proportion as would happen if they were straightforward variable only costs.

An example of such a cost is power from electricity. Many businesses pay for electricity on a two-part tariff made up of a standing charge and a rate per unit or kilowatt-hour. The standing charge has all the characteristics of a fixed cost as it is payable whether production takes place or not, furthermore the same amount is payable whatever the production level. The unit charge, however, tends to vary with production levels, and no unit charge would be payable where zero production causes no electricity consumption to take place.

Example

The following is a list of total costs for *Auckland Products* at two different levels of activity. The first three costs have already been classified into variable (V), fixed (F) and semi-variable (SV). The explanations that follow on after the list of total costs, under the heading 'Solutions', show how this has been done.

Production/sales levels (units)	2,000	5,000	Cost
	Total costs		behaviour
	£	£	
Supervision	20,000	20,000	F
Direct materials	100,000	250,000	V
Storage and handling	10,000	17,500	SV
Maintenance	30,000	60,000	
Direct wages	90,000	225,000	
Electricity	10,000	19,000	
Rent	26,000	26,000	
Insurance	8,000	8,000	
Salesmen's salaries			
(including commission)	50,000	65,000	
Packaging	27,500	68,750	
Staff salaries	80,000	80,000	
Distribution	30,000	52,500	
Rates	20,000	20,000	
Depreciation	40,000	40,000	

Solution

Supervision
The total cost of supervision remains constant at £20,000 for both levels of activity which is characteristic behaviour for a fixed cost.

Direct materials
The total cost of direct materials increases with output which is characteristic behaviour for a variable cost. Furthermore, the total direct material cost increases proportionately with activity – a production increase from 2,000 units to 5,000 units, an increase of 2.5 times, is accompanied by an increase in direct material costs also of 2.5 times, thus confirming that total direct material costs are variable.

An alternative approach is to calculate the direct material cost per unit at each level of production. At 2,000 units, the direct material cost per unit is:

$$\frac{£100,000}{2,000} = £50 \text{ per unit}$$

At 5,000 units the direct material cost per unit is:

$$\frac{£250,000}{5,000} = £50 \text{ per unit}$$

Where there is a constant cost per unit at both activity levels, this is an indication of a variable cost. (See the explanation of variable costs in section 3.4.)

Storage and handling
Clearly this cost is not a fixed cost as it increases in total as activity rises. At first sight, therefore, this cost appears to behave in a way similar to a variable cost. However, as production increases by 2.5 times if it were a variable cost it would also increase by 2.5 times, i.e. from £10,000 when 2,000 units are produced to

£25,000 at the 5,000 unit level. The actual increase has been somewhat less than this due to a fixed cost element in total storage and handling costs. Therefore storage and handling in this case is a semi-variable cost.

> *You should now be able to attempt question 3.8 at the end of this chapter.*

7 ANALYSIS OF SEMI-VARIABLE COSTS INTO THEIR FIXED AND VARIABLE ELEMENTS

In addition to recognizing a cost as a semi-variable one, it is also necessary to determine the fixed and variable elements of cost which make up a semi-variable cost. To achieve this analysis there are five basic steps in what is sometimes called the *high–low method.*

1. Establish the total cost levels of a particular item at two levels of activity. In the example in Section 3.6 storage and handling costs have already been established for production levels of 2,000 units and 5,000 units as £10,000 and £17,500 respectively.

2. Calculate the change in cost which arises due to the change in production, sometimes known as the *differential cost.* For storage and handling this may be set out as follows:

Example

	Production units		Cost £
	5,000		17,500
	2,000		10,000
Change in production	3,000 units	Change in cost	7,500

3. Calculate the cost per unit arising from the change in cost and the change in production. For storage and handling this becomes:

$$\frac{\text{change in cost (£)}}{\text{change in production (units)}} = \frac{£7,500}{3,000} = £2.50 \text{ per unit}$$

Because the change in total cost arising from the change in production is brought about by changes in the total variable cost element only (remember, the total fixed cost element will not change as a result of increasing or decreasing activity), then the £2.50 represents the variable cost per unit of production.

4. Calculate the total variable costs for each level of production. For storage and handling this becomes:

Example

Production units		Variable cost per unit		Total variable costs
	×	£	=	£
5,000		2.50		12,500
2,000		2.50		5,000

5. Subtract the total variable costs from the total costs at each production level to obtain the total fixed costs at each production level. This becomes:

Example

Production units	Total costs		Total variable costs		Total fixed costs
	£	−	£	=	£
5,000	17,500		12,500		5,000
2,000	10,000		5,000		5,000

Notice that for any truly semi-variable cost this procedure should give the same total fixed costs for each level of activity, which agrees with the characteristics associated with fixed costs described earlier.

> *You should now be able to attempt question 3.9 at the end of this chapter*

8 | REASON FOR ANALYSIS OF SEMI-VARIABLE COSTS

The analysis of semi-variable costs into their fixed and variable elements enables all costs to be treated as either fixed or variable for the purposes of the graphical presentation referred to earlier. The fixed and variable elements of the semi-variable costs being added to the other fixed or variable costs of the organization as appropriate.

The analysis of costs into fixed and variable according to their cost behaviour enables us to determine the way in which total costs change as activity changes. Nevertheless, some costs do not behave in these simple ways, and when shown graphically depict a more complex form of cost behaviour.

Example

Newlyn Engineering has graphed the behaviour of some of its costs. The descriptions of each cost behaviour have become detached from the original graphs. Match each description to the graph which depicts its behaviour. As usual, cost is depicted on the 'y' axis and activity on the 'x' axis.

i) Gas – The invoice from British Gas is made up of a fixed, so-called service charge, plus a rate per unit of gas consumed. Gas consumption varies with production levels.

ii) Consultancy fee – The firm has to pay a fixed sum as a consultancy fee irrespective of the level of production up to a certain production level. Thereafter, if the consultants succeed in achieving higher production levels, the fee is paid as a rate per unit produced in order to reflect the success of the consultancy assignment.

iii) Supervision – The firm needs one supervisor on a fixed salary irrespective of whether production takes place or not. However, as production rises to a certain level it requires a second supervisor, and as production rises yet further it requires a third.

Solution

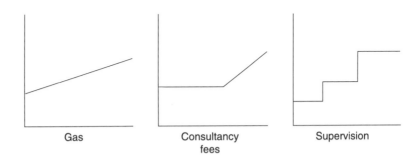

| Gas | Consultancy fees | Supervision |

You should now be able to attempt questions 3.5, 3.6 and 3.10 at the end of this chapter.

9 | MORE COMPLEX COST BEHAVIOUR

It will be appreciated that the approach described in this chapter is based on the assumption that, when considering total fixed and variable costs, all cost behaviour is linear. This assumption is clearly an oversimplification when compared to the way some costs behave in practice. Where more complex cost behaviour is experienced, attempts are made to convert that behaviour into a linear function, and this aspect will be covered in the next chapter on cost prediction techniques. In addition, some aspects of curvilinear cost behaviour will be covered in the next chapter.

10 | SUMMARY

In addition to the way in which costs may be classified as set out in Chapter 2, costs can also be classified according to the way in which they *behave* in total relative to activity levels, i.e. production or sales. A cost is described as a *variable cost* if it increases or decreases, in total, in proportion to changes in the level of activity. Examples are direct materials, direct wages and power. A cost is described as a *fixed cost* if, in total, it remains constant irrespective of the level of activity. Examples are rent, rates and insurances.

In general, variable costs are avoidable if activity does not take place, and fixed costs are unavoidable in that they are incurred whether or not production is carried out. Some items of expenditure are *semi-variable* costs as they have both a fixed and a variable element in their make up. Examples of these may be gas, electricity and salesmen's remuneration where a commission based on sales is added to a basic salary. An analysis of semi-variable costs into their fixed and variable elements enables all costs to be classified as either fixed or variable.

The method of classifying costs according to *cost behaviour* is a very useful one which helps in providing management information for planning, decision making, pricing and control. Some costs, however, behave in a more complex way than the comparatively straightforward manner of either fixed, variable or semi-variable costs based on activity levels.

> *You should now be able to attempt the objective test at the end of this chapter.*

STUDENT ACTIVITIES (*Denotes questions with answers at the end of the book)

Task 3.1
Cost behaviour may be portrayed in graphical form, a technique which is very often used in business as 'a single picture is worth a thousand words'. Review a number of quality newspapers and business magazines for a period, and prepare a collection of the different types of graphs used by the publication to present to their readers changes in various items such as share prices, production or costs over time.

Task 3.2
Working individually, draw up a list of industries where you consider the distinction between fixed and variable costs is important and a list of industries where it is not important. Compare your lists and explain any differences.

Task 3.3
A friend who is a member of a trade union has asked you to help her with a problem. During wage negotiations with her company she was told that in times of recession the management cannot regard labour as a fixed cost. She does not know what the implications of this statement are. Write her a letter of explanation.

Question 3.4
Brixham Kits Ltd operates a factory which produces kits for self-assembly kitchen cupboards. Determine which of its costs are variable or fixed:

Cost	Variable	Fixed
Door hinges		
Chipboard panels		
Depreciation of cutting machine (straight line)		
Screws		
Depreciation of factory building (straight line)		
Factory manager's salary		
Salesmen's salaries		
Salesmen's commission		
Boxes for final product		
Advertising		
Office salaries		
Stationery and printing		
Factory heating		
Wages of operators		
Factory insurance		

Question 3.5

Newquay Pens Ltd operates a business producing ball-point pens. Its variable costs per pen, i.e. the metal, plastic and assembly costs, amount to 55p. Its maximum capacity is 100,000 pens per annum.

Required

i) Plot Newquay's variable cost graph to cover all possible levels of production.

ii) Read off from the graph the total variable costs which Newquay will incur at the 60 per cent activity level.

Question 3.6

In addition to the variable costs per pen of 55p set out in the above question, Newquay Pens expects to incur some fixed costs. These will be, per annum:

	£
Rent	4,000
Rates	3,000
Depreciation	6,000
Administration	5,000
Light and heat	2,000
Salaries	10,000
	30,000

Required

Plot Newquay's fixed cost line to cover all possible levels of activity.

Question 3.7

Using the data already given concerning Newquay's cost levels set out in Questions 3.5 and 3.6, draw up graphs using the two alternative presentations discussed in the chapter, showing on each graph:

- the total cost line
- total variable costs
- total fixed costs
- total costs at 60 per cent activity level

Question 3.8*

The following is a list of total costs for *Auckland Products* at two different levels of activity. The first three costs have already been classified into variable (V), fixed (F) and semi-variable (SV), with explanations in the 'Solution' in Section 3.6 about how this has been done. Read the notes again carefully and classify the other costs in the same way:

Production/sales levels (units)	2,000	5,000	Cost behaviour
	Total costs		
	£	£	
Supervision	20,000	20,000	F
Direct materials	100,000	250,000	V
Storage and handling	10,000	17,500	SV
Maintenance	30,000	60,000	
Direct wages	90,000	225,000	
Electricity	10,000	19,000	
Rent	26,000	26,000	
Insurance	8,000	8,000	
Salesmen's salaries			
(including commission)	50,000	65,000	
Packaging	27,500	68,750	
Staff salaries	80,000	80,000	
Distribution	30,000	52,500	
Rates	20,000	20,000	
Depreciation	40,000	40,000	

Question 3.9

Analyse the other costs which you have identified for *Auckland Products* as semi-variable in the above question into their fixed and variable elements using the five steps discussed in the chapter.

Question 3.10

Newlyn Engineering has charted the behaviour of some of their costs. The descriptions of each cost behaviour have become detached from the original graphs. Match each description to the graph which depicts its behaviour. As usual, cost is depicted on the y axis and activity on the x axis. The first three costs have already been identified in Section 3.8

iv) Direct material – Newlyn Engineering has an agreement for the purchase of direct material under which it has to pay a certain rate per unit until its production reaches a certain level, after which it is given a discount per unit. A further discount per unit is earned when a yet higher production level is attained.

v) Direct wages – The firm simply pays its operators a rate per item produced (piecework). There is no guaranteed minimum payment when production is low or zero.

vi) Water rates – The firm has an arrangement with the water authority whereby it pays a rate per litre consumed up to a maximum charge, after which level it pays the same total sum irrespective of consumption levels. Water consumption is based on activity levels.

vii) Other rates – It pays a certain sum completely unrelated to production levels.

viii) Salesmen's salaries – The salesmen, who are entitled to a fixed basic salary plus a variable commission based on sales levels, are increased in number as sales rise.

ix) Royalty – Newlyn Engineering has a royalty agreement whereby it pays a rate per unit produced, up to a certain production level, when a maximum royalty is paid which remains constant for a further rise in production. At a yet higher production level, the royalty again becomes payable as a rate per unit produced.

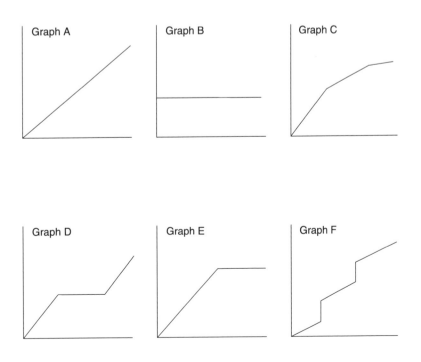

OBJECTIVE TEST* *(tick the appropriate box)*

i) Whether a cost is fixed, variable or semi-variable depends on its behaviour in relation to the volume of:

   a) production ☐

   b) sales ☐

   c) both ☐

   d) either ☒

ii) If a cost is described as fixed, when activity doubles its cost per unit:

   a) remains constant ☐

   b) doubles ☐

   c) halves ☒

   d) neither ☐

iii) If a cost is described as variable, when activity doubles its cost per unit:

   a) remains constant ☒

   b) doubles ☐

   c) halves ☐

   d) neither ☐

iv) If a cost is described as semi-variable, when activity doubles its total cost:

   a) doubles ☐

   b) less than doubles ☒

   c) more than doubles ☐

   d) remains constant ☐

v) Analysing the following semi-variable costs into fixed and variable elements,

Production (units)	Semi-variable costs
4,000	£14,000
10,000	£29,000

results in:

	Fixed costs	Variable costs	
a)	£19,000	£1.00 per unit	☐
b)	£6,000	£2.00 per unit	☐
c)	£10,000	£2.50 per unit *	☐
d)	£4,000	£2.50 per unit	☒

CHAPTER 4

Cost prediction techniques

1 OBJECTIVES

At the end of this chapter you should:

- understand the techniques used to predict costs and cost behaviour;
- be aware of the limitations of linear cost behaviour assumptions;
- be able to use linear regression to fit a straight line to a scattergraph;
- understand the use and application of learning curves;
- be able to calculate b-index for different learning curve percentages;
- be able to calculate times allowed for cumulative levels of output.

2 GRAPHING COSTS

We have seen in the previous chapter how fixed and variable costs are graphed together so that a total cost line may be plotted. You are advised to revise those graphs which show the total cost line before continuing with this chapter. You may remember that on the horizontal axis (the x axis) production is plotted, and on the vertical axis (the y axis) cost is plotted. Because, in general, cost depends on production levels, rather than the other way around, cost is known as the *dependent variable* and production is known as the *independent variable*. It is usual to plot the dependent variable on the y axis.

3 LINEAR COST FUNCTION 线性成本法

The formula for a linear cost function is:

$$y = a + bx$$

where y = total cost, i.e. total fixed costs plus the total variable costs

a = fixed cost or the intercept where the total cost line meets the y axis

b = variable cost per unit or the slope of the total cost line

x = production or number of units produced

There are a number of ways which accountants use to analyse, estimate and predict linear cost behaviour and so graph the total cost line. You must bear in mind that these are methods which give estimates only, so the use of each method will give different derived estimates of fixed and variable costs.

4 | COST ESTIMATION METHODS

There are a number of methods which can be used in order to construct a graph showing cost behaviour. They are:

- engineering approach or synthetic cost construction;
- historical cost observation;
- scattergraph method;
- high–low method;
- visual fit method;
- linear regression;
- learning curve approach.

5 | ENGINEERING APPROACH OR SYNTHETIC COST CONSTRUCTION

This is a method which can be applied where unit and total costs are calculated prior to the production having taken place. It can be used, therefore, at the commencement of a business, when launching a new product or when budgeting for costs to be incurred in a new budget year. It is useful for repetitive processes where input and output are clearly defined and it is essentially the application of logic to building up product costs.

The steps are:

- determine the physical quantities of the units of input required for each product in terms of direct labour, direct material and machine and/or labour time for overheads;
- analyse the behaviour of those costs into fixed, variable, semi-variable and stepped;
- estimate unit and total costs for each unit of input;
- convert into cost estimates for various levels of output.

6 | HISTORICAL COST METHOD

This method looks at the costs which have been incurred in the past at alternative levels of activity or production to use as a basis for predicting future cost levels. It involves the inspection of each cost item compared to activity levels and its classification according to fixed, variable, semi-variable or stepped behaviour.

The following problems can arise in using past observations in order to predict future cost levels.

- There may be changes to cost levels between the historical and future time periods due to inflation and other changes. This may require adjustments to the historical data to bring them to future cost levels.

- Exceptional or one-off elements of cost may be included in the historical data, which will need to be adjusted in order to provide a basis for future cost levels.

- Adjustments may be required for the leads and lags of accounting practice. For example, a bonus paid to operators may be made a week after the production on which it is based occurs. Care must be taken to ensure that the cost levels incurred are associated with the appropriate production levels achieved.

7 SCATTERGRAPH METHOD

This method plots past observations of cost levels against the activity levels associated with those costs. This creates a *scattergraph*, as the resultant plots are almost certain to be non-linear.

Example

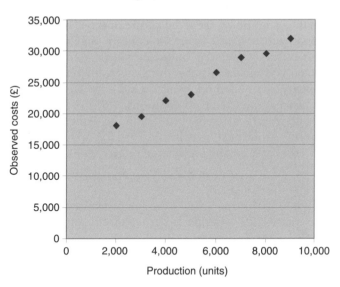

Scattergraph of observed costs

An estimate of cost behaviour is determined by fitting a straight line to the data, which may be achieved in a number of ways. These ways are described in 4.8 to 4.10 below.

8 | HIGH–LOW METHOD

This is achieved by selecting the periods of the highest and lowest activity levels and then establishing the total cost observations for those two activity levels. The differences between the activities and costs for each period are then used to analyse the total costs into fixed and variable elements.

Example

	Activity (units)	Total cost
Lowest	1,000	£16,000
Highest	9,000	£32,000
Difference	8,000	£16,000

Variable costs per unit =

$$\frac{\text{Difference in costs}}{\text{Difference in activity}} = \frac{£16,000}{8,000 \text{ units}} = £2/\text{unit}$$

Fixed costs

If the variable costs are £2 per unit, then the total variable costs are $1,000 \times £2 = £2,000$ or $9,000 \times £2 = £18,000$. The fixed costs are therefore total cost minus variable costs, which is $£16,000 - £2,000 = £14,000$ or $£32,000 - £18,000 = £14,000$, thus confirming the fixed nature of those costs.

This approach is based upon the concept that changes in costs which arise between two activity levels must be due to changes in the variable cost elements only. Calculating the differences, therefore, isolates those variable cost elements. This method tends to simplify cost behaviour and suffers by being influenced by extreme observations.

The resultant values may be inserted in the straight line equation $y = a + bx$ so that values of y (total cost) may be obtained for values of x (production). Thus the estimated total cost for the production of, say, 8,000 units would be:

$$y = £14,000 + (£2 \times 8,000 \text{ units}) = £30,000$$

and for 6,250 units

$$y = £14,000 + (£2 \times 6,250 \text{ units}) = £26,500$$

Notice that the calculated costs by this method do not necessary equal the costs actually observed for that level of activity. The calculated costs all appear on the straight line created by this method.

9 | VISUAL FIT METHOD

The visual fit method is an approximate method of fitting a line to a scattergraph whereby a straight line is drawn freehand on the graph, which appears to reflect the trend of the data plotted. Because it is a freehand line drawn visually, it will not possess any mathematical characteristics which could be used in other areas of cost estimation. The value for 'a' is the point where the line intersects the y axis and the value for 'b' is the total variable cost at any point on the line divided by the production level at that point.

10 | LINEAR REGRESSION OR LEAST SQUARES METHOD

Linear regression is a mathematical means of fitting a line of best fit to a set of observations on a scattergraph. It is sometimes known as the least squares method because the line fitted by this method minimizes the squares of the deviations between the observations and the line. Although technically two lines may be fitted to a scattergraph which respectively minimize the deviations vertically and horizontally, it is more usual to fit a line which minimizes the vertical deviations, described as regressing 'y' on 'x'.

In practice a trend line may be calculated using a computer spreadsheet. For example, using Microsoft Excel the *fx* facility in the toolbar calls up the function category. If 'statistical' is chosen from the list, then 'trend' chosen from the list of function names, a formula for linear regression or least squares method may be entered into a cell. It is important for examination purposes, however, that you understand the manual calculations involved as set out in this chapter.

There are two mathematical approaches to calculating values with which to construct the line. One method uses the following equations:

$$\Sigma y = Na + b\Sigma x$$
$$\Sigma xy = a\Sigma x + b\Sigma x^2$$

the procedure being:

N is the number of paired observations

Collect historical data for x and y and sum each column (Σ)

Calculate x^2 column and sum (Σ)

Calculate x multiplied by y column and sum (Σ)

Substitute in the above equations

Solve the simultaneous equations to obtain values of 'a' and 'b'

Select required values of x (production)

Substitute 'a', 'b' and 'x' in the straight line equation y = a + bx to solve for the selected values of 'y' for each level of 'x'

Example

The following data were observed when maintenance cost behaviour was being considered:

Hours worked (x)	Maintenance costs (y)
	£
100	1,400
220	2,700
260	3,100
300	3,600
340	3,700

a) Calculate values of y from the data using the above formula. These values will be on the line of best fit.

b) Predict the maintenance cost if the hours worked were 200.

Solution

	x Hours worked	y Maintenance costs (£)	xy	x^2
	100	1,400	140,000	10,000
	220	2,700	594,000	48,400
	260	3,100	806,000	67,600
	300	3,600	1,080,000	90,000
	340	3,700	1,258,000	115,600
Total	1,220	14,500	3,878,000	331,600

$N = 5$

Formulae:

$$\Sigma y = Na + b\Sigma x \qquad \text{formula 1}$$
$$\Sigma xy = a\Sigma x + b\Sigma x^2 \qquad \text{formula 2}$$

(a) Substitute in formulae:

$$14,500 = 5a + 1,220b \qquad \text{formula 1}$$
$$3,878,000 = 1,220a + 331,600b \qquad \text{formula 2}$$

Multiply formula 1 by 1,220/5

$$1,220a + 297,680b = 3,538,000$$

Subtract formula 2

$$1,220a + 331,600b = 3,878,000$$
$$= \qquad -33,920b = \qquad -340,000$$
$$b = \qquad £10.02 \text{ (rounded)}$$

Substitute in formula 1

$$5a + 12,224 = 14,500$$
$$5a = \quad 2,276$$
$$a = £455.20$$

(b) Estimate for 200 hours worked:

$$y = a + bx$$
$$y = £455.20 + £10.02 \,(200)$$
$$y = £2,459.20$$

> *You should now be able to attempt question 4.3 at the end of this chapter.*

Alternative equations

An alternative way of calculating 'a' and 'b' is to use the specific equations for those values. Use of these equations avoids the necessity of solving simultaneous equations, but involves solving first for 'b' and substituting the result in the equation for 'a'.

$$a = \frac{\Sigma y}{n} - \frac{b\Sigma x}{n}$$

$$b = \frac{n\Sigma xy - \Sigma x\Sigma y}{n\Sigma x^2 - (\Sigma x)^2}$$

Example

Production units	Costs (£)
3,000	15,000
3,500	18,000
4,000	17,500
4,500	21,000
5,000	20,000

a) Calculate the values of 'a' and 'b' for the line of best fit

b) Calculate the cost levels for the production levels shown, using the formulae

c) Predict cost levels for 4,250 units and 5,200 units

d) Calculate values for 'a' and 'b' using the high–low method

e) Compare the results of the two methods

Solution

Using the alternative formulae:

Production units	Observed costs (£)		
x	y	xy	x²
3,000	15,000	45,000,000	9,000,000
3,500	18,000	63,000,000	12,250,000
4,000	17,500	70,000,000	16,000,000
4,500	21,000	94,500,000	20,250,000
5,000	20,000	100,000,000	25,000,000
Totals 20,000	91,500	372,500,000	82,500,000

a)

$$n = 5$$

$$b = \frac{(5 \times 372,500,000) - (20,000 \times 91,500)}{(5 \times 82,500,000) - (20,000)^2}$$

$$b = \frac{32,500,000}{12,500,000} = \underline{£\,2.60}$$

Substitute in formula for 'a':

$$a = \frac{91,500}{5} - \frac{2.6 \times 20,000}{5}$$

$$a = £\,7,900$$

b)

Production units	Observed costs (£)	Calculated costs (£)	Formula
X	y	y	
3,000	15,000	15,700	£7,900 + (£2.6 × 3,000)
3,500	18,000	17,000	£7,900 + (£2.6 × 3,500)
4,000	17,500	18,300	£7,900 + (£2.6 × 4,000)
4,500	21,000	19,600	£7,900 + (£2.6 × 4,500)
5,000	20,000	20,900	£7,900 + (£2.6 × 5,000)
Totals 20,000	91,500	91,500	

(c)

4,250		18,950	£7,900 + (£2.6 × 4,250)
5,200		21,420	£7,900 + (£2.6 × 5,200)

(d) Using the high–low method:

High	5,000	20,000
Low	3,000	15,000
Difference	2,000	5,000

$$b = \text{rate per unit} \qquad \frac{5,000}{2,000} = £\,2.50$$

			Variable costs	Fixed costs (a)
High	5,000	20,000	£12,500.00	£7,500.00
Low	3,000	15,000	£ 7,500.00	£7,500.00
Difference	2,000	5,000		

e) Comparison of the two methods:

Production units	Observed costs (£)	Regression Calculated costs (£)	High/Low Calculated costs (£)	Difference (£)
3,000	15,000	15,700	15,000	700
3,500	18,000	17,000	16,250	750
4,000	17,500	18,300	17,500	800
4,250	0	18,950	18,125	825
4,500	21,000	19,600	18,750	850
5,000	20,000	20,900	20,000	900
5,200	0	21,420	20,500	920

> *You should now be able to attempt tasks 4.1 and 4.2 and questions 4.4 and 4.5 at the end of this chapter.*

11 | LEARNING CURVES

Non-linear cost behaviour

We have seen that the accountant's view of cost behaviour is usually to consider costs as linear. However, this approach may be considered to be an over simplification of how some costs behave in practice and it has been recognised that in some circumstances the time taken to produce a unit of product falls as cumulative production increases. This is known as the *learning curve effect*.

12 | DEFINITION OF LEARNING CURVES

Learning curves reflect the fact that the unit time taken or time allowed, and hence the unit variable cost, will tend to fall as experience and familiarization with the products and processes increase as cumulative production rises. Although the learning curve effect is essentially applied to time, in some circumstances the effect can be extended to take into account variable costs. Hence, the marginal or variable cost of producing each additional unit falls as production increases.

Examples of learning curves are available in many industrial and commercial enterprises. It has been recognized as particularly appropriate in the aircraft industry where the time taken to construct each additional airframe reduces as cumulative production increases, but the phenomenon is applied to motor vehicle production and virtually any circumstance where labour intensive repetitious activities take place.

13 | FORMULAE

A typical formula for the behaviour of the learning curve is:

$$y = ax^{-b}$$

where:

> y = the average time or variable cost per unit of production
>
> a = the time taken or cost incurred for the first unit
>
> x = the cumulative production
>
> b = a learning curve index

The learning curve is a geometric function and typically creates a downward sloping curvilinear graph. As a consequence, b is a negative figure. However the normal rules of algebra can be applied to convert the formula so that b becomes a positive figure, and the formula becomes:

$$y = \frac{a}{x^b}$$

The value of 'b' will vary according to the characteristics of the particular learning curve.

Example

If we assume that b = 0.5 and it takes 100 hours to produce the first unit of a product, then it is possible to calculate the average time allowed per unit of production (y) for various levels of production by substituting the values into the equation:

Production	Substitution	Average time (hours)	Total time (hours)
5 units	$100/5^{0.5}$	44.72	223.60
7 units	$100/7^{0.5}$	37.97	265.79
9 units	$100/9^{0.5}$	33.33	299.97
10 units	$100/10^{0.5}$	31.62	316.20

The total time is the product of the average time and the number of units; notice from the table that the average time allowed per unit of production falls as production increases, while the total time increases, but at a reducing rate.

14 | PERCENTAGE LEARNING CURVES

Learning curves are expressed as an 'x% learning curve' where each time output is doubled, average hours per unit falls to x% of its previous level. Thus the average time for 10 units is, in the above case, 70 per cent of the average time for 5 units, and therefore can be described as a 70 per cent learning curve. Thus:

$$\frac{31.62 \times 100}{44.72} = 70\%$$

In the above example the percentage calculation is based on the doubling of production from 5 to 10 units, but the calculation may be based on the average times at any points where output doubles.

We can further conclude that the value of the b-index for a 70 per cent learning curve is 0.5. Notice that the description of the learning curve as a percentage is based on the *average* time per unit and not the *total* time.

For any percentage learning curve it is possible to construct a table which shows the data which would arise at points where the output doubles. For example, if the first unit takes, say 150 hours, and an 80 per cent learning curve applies, the times would be as follows:

Cumulative units	Additional units	Total hours	Average hours per unit
1	1	150	150
2	1	240	120
4	2	384	96
8	4	614.4	76.8

Graphically, an 80 per cent learning curve would adopt the following curve:

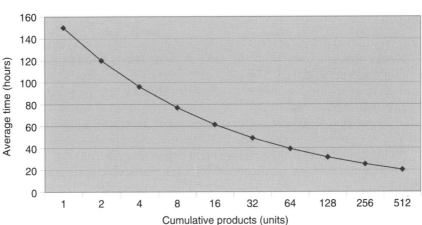

An 80 per cent learning curve

You should now be able to attempt questions 4.6 at the end of this chapter.

---

15 **CALCULATION OF THE B-INDEX**

While the above table can be used to calculate the time allowed for output levels that double at each stage, 1, 2, 4, 8, 16, 32 and so on, it may also be necessary to calculate times allowed for intermediate levels of output such as, for example, 7, 26 and 419 units. The values of the b-index are required for each learning curve percentage in order to be able to calculate the time allowed for any level of output by substituting in the formula, as we did earlier.

The values of b may be calculated in two ways. One method, using the data above, is to substitute the values where output doubles in the table into the learning curve formula, and then solve for b:

Increase from 1 to 2 units   Increase from 4 to 8 units

$$120 = \frac{150}{2^b}$$ $$76.8 = \frac{150}{8^b}$$

$$2^b = \frac{150}{120}$$ $$8^b = \frac{150}{76.8}$$

using logarithms:

$$b \times \log 2 = \log 1.25 \qquad\qquad b \times \log 8 = \log 1.953$$

$$b = \frac{\log 1.25}{\log 2} \qquad\qquad\qquad b = \frac{\log 1.953}{\log 8}$$

$$b = 0.322 \qquad\qquad\qquad\qquad b = 0.322$$

Notice that the data from the table may be taken at any points where output doubles, and in the calculations above the increase from 1 to 2 and from 4 to 8 have been used in order to illustrate this aspect. In practice only a single calculation is needed.

Logarithms (logs) are used as a method of detaching a power from its number. You may remember that you add logs for multiplication and multiply logs for taking powers, which is what we are using in this case.

Once the b-index is calculated for each particular percentage learning curve this may be used in order to calculate a time or cost allowance for any cumulative production level. In the above case the b-index for an 80 per cent learning curve is 0.322, and the time allowance for any level of output may now be calculated for this percentage learning curve.

Another way of calculating the b-index is to use the formula:

$$\frac{\log \text{ of learning curve percentage as a decimal}}{\log 2}$$

$$\text{Thus for a 70\% learning curve: } \frac{\log 0.7}{\log 2} = -0.515$$

$$\text{For an 80\% learning curve: } \frac{\log 0.8}{\log 2} = -0.322$$

Notice that the use of this method gives negative answers for the b-index, which conforms to 'b' being negative as included in the original equation shown at the commencement of this learning curve section. Allowing for rounding, the answers obtained from this method confirm the b-index used earlier for these percentage learning curves.

When calculating allowed times for units of production in interim periods, the calculations must always go back to the time taken for the first unit. So, for example, to find the time allowed for 350 units of production after 1,225 units have already been produced, the time allowed for the cumulative production to the beginning of the period, 1,225 units, must be deducted from the time allowed for the production to date, 1,575 units. The result will give the time allowed for the 350 units for the period. Note that it is not possible for the correct calculation to be obtained by simply substituting 350 units in the basic formulae shown at the beginning of this section.

Example

Electro Ltd manufactures electronic equipment which requires highly skilled labour. Allowed times used for bonus payments have been based on the time taken for the first item produced, but problems have arisen as a learning curve effect has been detected and efficiency gains and shorter times taken have caused bonus payments to soar.

Production times have been recorded as follows:

Cumulative production units	Cumulative time (hours)	Average time per unit (hours)
1	200	200
2	340	170
4	170	144.5

The learning curve follows the general form of:

$$y = \frac{a}{x^b}$$

where:

y = average hours per unit

a = number of labour hours taken for the first unit

x = cumulative number of units produced

b = the learning index

Up to and including March the following performance was recorded:

Cumulative production at 28 February	620 units
Production in March	75 units
Actual hours worked	3,008 hours

Required

a) Determine the percentage learning curve experienced in *Electro Ltd* and calculate the value of the learning curve index (b).

b) Calculate the standard time allowed for the 75 units produced in March.

Solution

a) The percentage learning curve is:

$$\frac{170 \times 100}{200} = 85\% \quad \text{or} \quad \frac{144.5 \times 100}{170} = 85\%$$

an 85% learning curve.

The learning curve index:

$$170 = \frac{200}{2^b} \quad \text{or} \quad 144.5 = \frac{200}{4^b}$$

$$2^b = \frac{200}{170} \qquad 4^b = \frac{200}{144.5}$$

$$2^b = 1.1765 \qquad 4^b = 1.3841$$

61

$$b \times \log 2 = \log 1.1765 \qquad b \times \log 4 = \log 1.2841$$

$$b = \frac{\log 1.1765}{\log 2} \qquad\qquad b = \frac{\log 1.2841}{\log 4}$$

$$\underline{b = 0.234} \qquad\qquad\qquad \underline{b = 0.234}$$

Alternative method:

$$\frac{\log 0.85}{\log 2} = 0.234$$

(b)   *Cumulative units*   *Total hours*

$$695 = \frac{200}{695^{0.234}} \quad \times 695 = \quad 30,060$$

$$620 = \frac{200}{620^{0.234}} \quad \times 620 = \quad 27,542$$

75 units are allowed a standard time of 2,518 hours

16 | SOME PROBLEMS WITH LEARNING CURVES

- Some difficulty may be experienced in defining which percentage learning curve applies in each particular case. The time taken for cumulative production may not fall in the smooth fashion illustrated by the learning curve, but may be more erratic in practice.

- The learning curve assumption assumes that the same percentage learning curve applies over the whole range of output. The basic system does not allow for different learning curve rates over time.

- The fact that the system requires reversion to the time taken for the first unit produced may not be practicable in all circumstances. For example, if production is being considered three years into the production schedule it may not be appropriate to consider the time taken for the first unit made three years previously.

- The assumption that the average time taken or allowed can continue to fall *ad infinitum* is unlikely to occur in practice. At some stage therefore, the learning curve is abandoned in favour of constant times per unit.

- Operators may find it confusing for identical volumes of production to be given different time allowances depending upon when they are produced.

> *You should now be able to attempt questions 4.7 and 4.8 at the end of this chapter.*

17 | SUMMARY

Accountants tend to assume linear behaviour of both fixed and variable costs, and even where historically costs do not behave in a linear fashion, techniques are used to plot cost behaviour linearly.

Engineering or synthetic cost construction methods build up cost behaviour using a logical approach to cost estimation. The scattergraph can be used to plot historical cost or other observations and then straight-line behaviour can be plotted by using the high–low, visual fit and linear regression methods.

In some circumstances curvilinear cost behaviour is represented by considering the learning curve effect in repetitive production where the average time taken, and hence average unit variable cost, falls as cumulative production increases.

> *You should now be able to attempt the objective test at the end of this chapter.*

STUDENT ACTIVITIES (*denotes questions with answers at the end of the book)

Task 4.1

If you have gas central heating in your home, take a series of daily consumption readings from the meter over a representative period of, say, a week or a fortnight. Take outside temperature readings over the same period and against each lowest daily temperature plot the level of gas consumption for that day on a graph. Using linear regression, fit the line of best fit. Compare the calculated consumption figure for each day (the value on the line) and the actual consumption data, and use the data to predict the consumption for an expected temperature given by the weather forecast for a later date.

Is the lowest temperature recorded for each day a good predictor of gas consumption levels?

Task 4.2

Collect data which record the behaviour of a dependent variable (y) compared to the occurrence of a related independent variable (x). Plot the data on a scattergraph and draw a line of best fit to the data by using linear regression. Examples which you may use are sales levels against advertising expenditure, items of cost against production, petrol consumption against miles driven or sales volume against prices.

Clearly identify the respective dependent and independent variables, and use the data as a means of predicting a future level of 'y'.

Question 4.3*

From the following data which shows production in units (x) and direct labour cost (y) calculate the values of 'a' and 'b' by linear regression. Predict the labour cost when production is 9 units.

x	y
2	60
5	100
4	70
6	90
3	80

Question 4.4

The following information relates to an historical analysis of the behavioural pattern of indirect labour cost in relation to production levels for a recent production period.

Production units	Indirect labour cost (£)
20	8,040
40	12,480
100	26,800
160	42,560
120	30,800
30	11,200
60	19,320
100	28,400
130	32,500

Required

a) Use linear regression to estimate the coefficients a and b in the equation for a straight line y = a + bx.

b) Calculate the estimated indirect labour cost for production levels of 140 and 180 units respectively.

c) Calculate values for 'a' and 'b' using the high–low method of cost prediction and predict indirect labour costs for production of 140 and 180 units respectively.

Question 4.5

The following information relates to an historical analysis of the behavioural pattern of maintenance cost in relation to production levels for a recent production period.

Production units	Maintenance cost (£)
20	10,800
41	15,000
101	26,600
161	40,000

121	30,800
20	11,200
61	18,600
101	28,000
120	31,000

Required

a) Use linear regression to determine the terms for a and b in the equation for a straight line y = a + bx.

b) Calculate the estimated indirect labour cost for production levels of 136 and 175 units respectively.

c) Calculate values for a and b using the high–low method of cost prediction and the values for 136 and 175 units respectively.

d) List the comparative strengths and weaknesses associated with the use of each of the two methods of predicting indirect labour cost levels.

e) Briefly describe two other methods of predicting cost behaviour.

Question 4.6

The production of a product took 80 hours for the first item. The management was aware that a 70 per cent learning curve was in operation, and wishes to know how much time to allow for the average and total times for the cumulative production of 16, 64 and 256 units respectively.

Question 4.7

Widget Productions Ltd took 125 hours to produce the first widget and 187.5 hours in total to produce the first two.

a) What percentage learning curve is in operation?

b) Calculate the b-index for this percentage learning curve.

c) Calculate the allowed total time and the average time for 38 and 45 widgets of cumulative production.

Question 4.8

Widget Productions Ltd took 60 hours to produce the first of a special mini-widget and an average of 48 hours to produce the first two.

a) What percentage learning curve is in operation?

b) Calculate the b-index for this percentage learning curve.

c) Having produced 35 items up to the beginning of June, the management wishes to know the total time and the average time it should allow for the next 10 mini-widgets it expects to produce in July.

OBJECTIVE TEST* *(tick the appropriate box)*

i)   The formula for total cost as a linear function is:

   a) $a = y + bx$ ☐

   b) $y = a + bx$ ☐

   c) $b = b + ax$ ☐

   d) $x = a + by$ ☐

ii) The assumption of actual total cost being, in practice, a linear function is:

   a)   always correct ☐

   b)   an oversimplification ☐

   c)   demonstrated by a scattergraph ☐

   d)   borne out by the historical cost method ☐

iii) Identical straight lines on a scattergraph are given by:

   a)   the high–low and the visual fit methods ☐

   b)   the visual fit and the linear regression methods ☐

   c)   the high–low and the linear regression methods ☐

   d)   none of these ☐

   e)   all of these ☐

iv) Linear regression is a method normally used for plotting:

   a)   a curvilinear line for total cost ☐

   b)   a semi-variable total cost line ☐

   c)   a linear cost per unit line ☐

   d)   a total cost per unit line ☐

v)   The percentage learning curve description is based on:

   a)   the relationship where total times allowed double ☐

   b)   the total time relationship where cumulative output doubles ☐

   c)   the relationship where average times allowed double ☐

   d)   the average time relationship where cumulative output doubles ☑

CHAPTER 5

Budgetary control

1 | OBJECTIVES

At the end of this chapter you should be able to:

- understand how budgets are formulated;
- understand how budgetary control helps to run businesses;
- draw up budget statements;
- understand the advantages and problems of budgetary control systems.

2 | INTRODUCTION

Small businesses are relatively easily controlled and directed by one person, usually the owner. He or she may have a very good idea:

- where the business is going (the business plan);
- what cost levels are acceptable (cost control);
- what income levels are required (pricing);
- what volumes of sales should be obtained (motivation);
- what profit levels are adequate (profit planning).

Many of these goals may not be explicitly expressed on paper in a small business, but implicitly pursued as *business objectives*. This is possible and acceptable because most decisions which affect the achievement of these objectives in a business of this size are made by the owner. As the business expands, however, there is a tendency to split the organization into different parts and employ a specialist manager to run each. These parts are known as *functions*. An example of a *functional organization chart* for a limited company engaged in manufacturing is shown below.

The *shareholders* own the business and appoint a *board of directors* to run it on their behalf. The *managing director* or *chief executive* is responsible to the board of directors for the day-to-day operation of the business, and he or she has a number of specialist *functional or line managers* who are responsible for the operation of their own particular functions. Their titles may vary from one organization to another.

In such a complex organization the regular decisions to achieve particular objectives are no longer made by the owner(s). Indeed, there is now no single owner because the company is likely to have many shareholders. Many of the daily decisions are made by the line managers. It is important that these decisions are made within an overall plan which will ensure that the business as a whole will achieve its agreed objectives. This is the *business plan*.

Functional organization chart

It is essential, therefore, that the business develops a formal planning and control system which will state clearly the *objectives* for both the business as a whole and for each functional manager. The business also needs a *reporting system* which will inform the manager and the chief executive when any function is not operating according to the predetermined *plan*, and allow corrective action to be taken. Such a planning, controlling and reporting system is known as *budgetary control*.

3 | FUNCTIONAL BUDGETS

A *budget* is a quantitative and/or financial statement. It is prepared prior to the start of a trading or operating period and sets out the objectives, activities and policies to be carried out during that period by each functional area of the business (*functional budgets*) and for the business as a whole. Budgets are prepared for a specified time period known as the *budget period*. This may be for any length of time, usually a year, in which case it is commonly broken down into shorter control periods of quarters, months, or in some cases, weeks. The longer the period taken for planning purposes, the greater the difficulty in predicting future performance.

Budgets are not only expressed in financial terms, but also in non-monetary measures wherever possible. Thus some budgets are expressed in units of sales or production, direct labour hours, or machine hours to be worked. Some functional financial budgets are expressed in income terms (a *revenue budget*); others in expenditure terms (a *cost budget*) or a combination of the two. For example, a sales income budget is a revenue budget, and the sales cost budget is a cost budget. Both are combined as being the responsibility of the sales or marketing manager.

Budgets are prepared for any part of the business which can be identified as being the responsibility of an individual manager, and therefore a breakdown of the functional budgets into sections is often carried out. For example, the marketing manager may analyse the overall sales revenue budget into sales budgets which would be the responsibility of each area sales manager. Each part of the business for which a budget is prepared is known as a *budget centre.*

Budgets are produced and used in many different types of organization, from manufacturing companies trading for profit, to local and national government bodies, charities and educational establishments. They can also be used to good effect in personal financial planning.

4 | DETAILED BUDGETS

Because one of the aims of producing budgets is to co-ordinate activities and to produce an overall plan which is attainable by the whole organization, some detailed analysis is often required from each budget. For example, when a range of products is produced and sold, co-ordination of production and sales functions is made easier if both managers analyse their annual budgeted volumes by product and by month. This ensures that sales and production volumes are matched by product over time, thus avoiding product shortages or overstocking when production and sales for a period are not co-ordinated.

Although the co-ordination of the sales and production functional budgets may be said to represent the core of the budgeting process in a manufacturing organization, we should not overlook the concept that all budgets must interlock in a feasible way. Some examples of the financial and quantitative budgets normally produced by a manufacturing organization are as follows, together with the detailed analysis which might be expected from the functional manager.

Example

Functional manager	*Financial budgets*	*Quantitative budgets*
Sales/	Sales revenue budget	Sales volume budget
Marketing	Analysed by:	Analysed by:
manager	Product	Product
	Market	Market
	Budget control period	Budget control period
	Sales representative	Sales representative
	Outlet	Outlet
	Sales cost budget	Personnel budget
		Sales vehicles budget
	Advertising and	Television time budget
	promotion budget	Column centimetres
		budget
		Display sites budget
Production	Direct material cost	Material quantities budget
manager	budget	
	Direct wages cost budget	Manpower/Personnel
		direct labour hours
		budget

Functional manager	*Financial budgets*	*Quantitative budgets*
	Direct expenses cost budget	Quantities budget
	Production overheads budget	Direct labour hours budget
		Machine hours budget
	Total production cost budget	Production quantities budget
	Analysed by:	Analysed by:
	Product	Product
	Budget control period	Budget control period
	Factory, department or budget centre	Factory, department or budget centre

Some budgets do not fall under the responsibility of a specific manager, but may require a contribution from a number of managers with the accountant summarizing the data or pulling together information from a number of sources. Some examples of other budgets found in organizations are set out below.

Example

Capital expenditure budget	Details of all projected expenditure on capital projects or assets
	Analysed by:
	Asset
	Project
	Functional responsibility
	Budget period
Budgeted profit and loss account (income statement) and budgeted balance sheet	
Master budget	The combination, co-ordination and integration of all the budgets to produce the master plan for the business as a whole for the budget period.

> You should now be able to attempt question 5.4 at the end of this chapter.

5 BUDGET CO-ORDINATION

Co-ordination of the production and sales budgets enables the *finished goods stocks budget* to be produced. Future policy decisions may be required when budgeted production falls short of budgeted sales for any prolonged period such that stocks are exhausted. Capital expenditure may need to be planned to increase production capacity. Alternatively, sub-contracting of production may be planned.

In the event of budgeted sales falling short of budgeted production, the decisions to mitigate the effect of this by lay-offs, holiday shutdown or increased advertising expenditure all have the effect of influencing other budgets.

The following examples illustrate the responsibilities of certain managers for budgets and identify how these must be *co-ordinated* with the activities of other managers.

Example

Transport/distribution manager

Financial budgets	*Quantitative budgets*
Distribution cost budget	Units budget
	Miles budget
	Tonne/miles budget

Co-ordination must be achieved with the sales quantities budget to determine the distribution cost by market and product.

Example

Purchasing manager

Financial budgets	*Quantitative budgets*
Purchases cost budget	Quantities budget
Purchasing department cost budget	Manpower or personnel budget
	Tonne/miles budget
Analysed by:	Analysed by:
Product	Product
Factory	Factory
Budget period	Budget period

Co-ordination must be achieved with the production and direct material cost budgets to produce the *raw materials stocks budget*.

Example

Accountant/financial manager

Financial budgets	*Quantitative budgets*
Administration cost budget	Personnel budget
Cash flow budget	

Example

Personnel manager

Financial budgets	*Quantitative budgets*
Personnel department cost budget	Personnel budget
	Manpower budget

Financial budgets   *Quantitative budgets*

Analysed by: Analysed by:

Grade   Grade

Skill   Skill

Gender   Gender

Co-ordination must be achieved with all other functional budgets to provide personnel or manpower content.

> You should now be able to attempt task 5.1 at the end of this chapter.

6 | CASH FLOW BUDGET

The *cash flow budget* is a very important budget which co-ordinates with all the other budgets. All functional budgets are produced on an accruals basis. This means that they record expenditure and income when it is incurred or generated, rather than when the cash is paid or received. The cash flow budget is created by converting all the budgeted amounts from the functional budgets into monthly cash flow terms, and including other items not included in the functional budgets such as capital expenditure, dividend and tax payments, and investment income. The cash flow budget helps predict when further cash resources are needed, or alternatively when surplus cash is likely to be available in the budget year. A typical layout is as follows:

Example

Limited company
Monthly cash flow budget

Month	1	2	3	4	etc.
	£	£	£	£	
Cash inflows:					
Cash sales					
Payments by debtors					
Investment income					
Sundry cash receipts	—	—	—	—	
(a) Total cash inflows	—	—	—	—	
Cash outflows:					
Payments to creditors					
Cash purchases					
Wages					
Salaries					
Interest payments					
Capital expenditure					
Dividends payments					

```
           Corporation tax payments
           Other taxation payments, e.g. VAT
           Sundry cash payments            —    —    —    —
    (b)  Total cash outflows               —    —    —    —
    (c)  Net cash flows (a) – (b)
    (d)  Opening cash balance              —    —    —    —
    Closing cash balance (c) + (d)         —    —    —    —
```

> *You should now be able to attempt task 5.3 at the end of this chapter.*

7 THE BUDGET-SETTING PROCESS

The process of setting the functional and other budgets and drawing up the master budget can take a number of months, so preparation commences some time before the start of the period to which the budget refers. It is usual to form a *budget committee* made up of the functional heads chaired by the chief executive. The management accountant usually occupies the role of committee secretary, co-ordinating and assisting in the preparation of the budget data provided by each of the functional heads of the business.

It is usual nowadays for functional and master budgets to be constructed using a computer, either through dedicated planning software or using a computer spreadsheet package, such as *Microsoft Excel or Lotus 1-2-3*. There are considerable advantages to be gained by using such an approach, as a model of the organization's financial and quantitative interrelationships can be formulated using the software. The model can then be used for a 'what-if' approach to budgeting, so that the impact of possible changes to such variables as prices, volumes and costs can be quickly incorporated into the plan and the degree of sensitivity of the budget to these changes ascertained.

Functional and other budgets are received by the budget committee and it is the committee's responsibility to ensure that all budgets have the following characteristics:

- the budgets conform to the organization's policies and goals as established and communicated by the board of directors;

- the individual budgets are reasonable and achievable;

- the budgets are well co-ordinated so that no particular budget is out of phase with the other budgets which make up the master budget;

- the budgets take into consideration the conditions and constraints which are expected to apply during the budget period.

Budgets that do not conform to these requirements are returned for revision to the managers responsible, action which may take place several times before an acceptable budget is submitted. The budget-setting process is therefore said to be an *iterative* approach; that is, each functional budget may go through a series of *iterations*, each time being refined, before being accepted by the budget committee. The final master budget is submitted to the board of directors for approval prior to the commencement of the budget period. After acceptance, the budget becomes the plan adopted by the business as a whole until such time as further amendments are made and approved perhaps later in the year when circumstances change.

In an organization which trades for profit, it is essential that the final budgeted profit is acceptable before the budget is approved by the budget committee and ultimately the board of directors. Therefore the following questions must be answered satisfactorily.

- What is the level of profitability revealed by the budget? This could be established by the use of such measures as *return on capital employed (prime ratio)*, or profit as a percentage of sales revenue (*profit margins*).

- What are the returns achieved by competitors or from alternative investments?

- What is the increase or decrease in budgeted profit compared to last year or to previous years? The shareholders might expect to see a trend of rising profits over time.

- Is the budgeted profit adequate? The profit before taxation is appropriated in three ways: corporation tax is paid to the government, dividends are paid to the shareholders, and the balance of profit is retained in the business to finance future expansion. The adequacy of the profits, therefore, will be determined by the board of directors' policies with regard to the growth of dividends, and also what proportion of future expansion plans should be financed from retained profits.

- Is the level of profit attainable? Consideration should be given to the changes in the market and competitors' and suppliers' actions which might make the budgeted profit unattainable.

Once the master budget is formally accepted and approved by the board of directors it becomes the policy plan for the organization for the budget period. The relevant budgets are then communicated to all budget centre managers, who are encouraged to operate within the approved budgetary framework of costs, sales and performance.

You should appreciate that the foregoing budgets and budget-setting process are based on what might happen in a typical manufacturing company. The approaches may vary considerably from organization to organization.

> *You should now be able to attempt questions 5.5 and 5.6 at the end of this chapter.*

8 | FIXED BUDGETS

A *fixed budget* is one which is prepared for a single level of activity, either production or sales as appropriate, which it is planned to achieve during a budget period. The problem which arises from the use of a fixed budget can be illustrated by the following example of a variable cost, direct materials.

Example

Fixed budget	Budgeted	Actual	Variance
Production units	1,000	1,500	
Direct material costs	£20,000	£28,750	£8,750 (A)*

* A = Adverse variance or overspending 超支

This comparison suggests an adverse variance or overspending of £8,750 in direct material costs. However it does not take into consideration the fact that direct material costs are variable costs, and therefore could be expected to increase in proportion to production increases. Here the actual level of activity differs from the budgeted level of activity, and therefore some proportion of the variance shown is due to the higher activity level.

Based on the budget, the manager is expected to incur direct material cost at a rate of £20 per unit of production. In producing 1,500 units the manager could be expected to incur 1,500 × £20 = £30,000 which is more than the actual expenditure, and yet this approach shows an overspending of £8,750.

The variance shown by a fixed budget comparison fails to provide a useful variance for variable costs where budgeted and actual activity levels differ.

9   FLEXIBLE BUDGETS

A *flexible budget* is one which separates costs according to their different behavioural characteristics. It recognizes that some costs are variable and others fixed. For the variable costs it provides a budget allowance based on the actual level of activity achieved during a budget control period, e.g. a month. This approach then enables useful variances to be calculated which are restricted to those controllable by the manager concerned.

Applying a flexible budgeting approach to the example above, a budget allowance column would be introduced so as to flex the budget for the variable items to accommodate an actual production level of 1,500 units.

Example

Flexible budget	Budgeted	Budget allowance	Actual	Variance
Production units	1,000	1,500	1,500	
Direct material costs	£20,000	£30,000	£28,750	£1,250 (F)*

* F = Favourable variance or under-spending

Because direct material costs are variable, the budget allowance column adjusts or *flexes* the original budget figure to allow for the higher level of production achieved. This is obtained by calculating a budgeted rate per unit, and multiplying by the actual number of units produced:

$$\text{Budgeted rate per unit} = \frac{\pounds 20{,}000}{1{,}000 \text{ units}} = \pounds 20$$

$$\text{Budget allowance} = \pounds 20 \times 1{,}500 \text{ units} = \pounds 30{,}000$$

Notice that in flexible budgeting the variance is always calculated by comparing the actual performance with the budget allowance.

10 | THE TWO APPROACHES COMPARED

Using the fixed budget basis, the overspending or adverse variance is £8,750. This would suggest that the manager in charge of direct materials is required to take some remedial action to bring material costs into line with budgeted levels. Such a conclusion would be wrong. This is because no account has been taken of differing budgeted and actual production levels and their effect on variable costs.

Where the budget allowance is calculated to take into consideration the *variable* nature of direct material costs and the higher level of actual output compared to that budgeted, a favourable variance of £1,250 results. This indicates that instead of corrective action being required, there has been a saving on the expenditure on direct materials after adjusting for higher production levels achieved.

Clearly the variance which arises as a result of the use of a flexible budget is much more useful for control purposes than that shown by a fixed budget because:

- the variance shown by the flexible budget is adjusted for different budgeted and actual activity levels, whereas the variance shown by the use of the fixed budget hides the truly adverse or favourable result;

- the variance shown by the flexible budget shows the variance which may be regarded as controllable by the manager responsible for that item of expenditure.

11 | OTHER COST BEHAVIOUR

The example of the operation of a flexible budgeting system shown above covers direct material costs which are clearly variable in behaviour.

The process of setting up a flexible budget is to consider each cost item individually and determine how it is likely to behave in practice as a result of changes in activity levels. This approach then determines the budget allowance for various activity levels which are likely to be met during the budget period.

Fixed costs – A fixed cost is one which, in the short term, remains unchanged in total irrespective of the level of activity, that is production or sales. We saw in Chapter 3 that fixed costs behave in two main ways.

- They remain unchanged over the whole range of output. For example, working at 50 per cent capacity, the rent payable by a company is £40,000 per annum. At all levels of activity up to 100 per cent the rent will remain at £40,000 and it is only when additional property is rented in order to increase capacity that the rent will increase.

- They change in steps as output changes. For example working at 50 per cent capacity, a company requires one supervisor at £30,000 per annum. If activity increases to 70 per cent, then an additional supervisor is needed at the same rate, and with output at 90 per cent capacity one more supervisor needs to be recruited.

Semi-variable costs – A semi-variable cost is an item of cost which has both a variable and a fixed element in its make-up. For example, each sales representative's remuneration is made up of a fixed basic salary of £25,000, plus a variable element, being commission, which is calculated at 2 per cent of total sales value.

Example

Exmouth Products Ltd operates a system of flexible budgetary control. It has investigated each cost item and wishes to classify it as either fixed (F), variable (V), or semi-variable (SV) from the following costs incurred at two levels of activity, 50,000 units and 80,000 units respectively:

Budget for the year 2002

		50%	80%
Activity level		50%	80%
Production units		50,000	80,000
Direct costs:	Material	140,000	224,000 V
Overheads:	Rent	40,000	40,000 F
	Royalties	6,000	8,400 V

Solution

If direct materials cost £140,000 for 50,000 units of production then, if behaving in a manner typical of variable costs, their cost for 80,000 units would be:

$$\frac{£140,000}{50,000} \times 80,000 = £224,000, \text{ thus confirming their variable nature.}$$

Rent is budgeted at the same level for both levels of activity, thus confirming rent as a fixed cost.

Royalties are clearly not a fixed cost as the total changes as activity changes. If it were a variable cost the cost for production of 80,000 units would be:

$$\frac{£6,000}{50,000} \times 80,000 = £9,600$$

As the royalty cost for 80,000 units is less than £9,600, this cost has a semi-variable characteristic.

Example

Assume that the actual level of activity achieved by *Exmouth Products Ltd* was 60,000 units of production or 60 per cent of capacity and calculate a flexible budget allowance for that activity level for each cost item.

Solution

As direct materials is a variable cost, the budget allowance for 60,000 units would be:

$$\frac{£140,000}{50,000} \times 60,000 = £168,000$$

or

$$\frac{£224,000}{80,000} \times 60,000 = £168,000$$

As rent is a fixed cost over the whole range of output, the budget allowance would be £40,000 for any activity level. As under these circumstances royalties are a semi-variable cost, it is necessary to analyse the cost into its fixed and variable elements using the high–low method Thus:

1) The total cost of royalties for each of the two activity levels is shown.

2) The change in cost which arises due to the change in production:

	Production (units)	Total royalties (£)
	80,000	8,400
	50,000	6,000
Change	30,000	2,400

$$\text{3) Variable cost per unit} = \frac{£2,400}{30,000} = £0.08$$

4) The total variable element for each level of production becomes:

	Production (units)		Total variable costs
	80,000 × £0.08	=	£6,400
	50,000 × £0.08	=	£4,000

5) Fixed cost element becomes:

Production units	Total royalties £	Total variables £	Total fixed £
80,000	8,400	6,400	2,000
50,000	6,000	4,000	2,000

The budget allowance for royalties at the 60,000 units level of output would be therefore:

	£
Fixed cost element	2,000
Variable cost element:	
60,000 units × £0.08 =	4,800
Total budget allowance	6,800

12 OTHER TYPES OF BUDGETS

As we have seen, a very common approach to setting up the individual budgets of an organization is to construct budgets for each functional area of the business and these are known as *functional budgets*. *Non-functional budgets* are budgets which may not necessarily be analysed by function. Examples include the cash flow budget, the capital expenditure budget, the budgeted profit and loss account and the budgeted balance sheet.

Many budgets are produced by taking the current year's levels of revenue and expenditure and adding a percentage to take into consideration changes in price levels between the base year and the budget year. This approach is known as *incremental budgeting*. We will be looking at criticisms of this approach later on in this chapter. An alternative to the production of incremental budgets is to build up a budget for the year starting with a nil or zero budget allowance and only building in a budget figure where this can be justified from the policies and conditions which are likely to prevail during that budget period. This is known as a *zero-base budget*, and the process is known as *zero-base budgeting* or *ZBB*.

It is very common to draw up a budget for a budget period, usually a year, and for the budget to remain unchanged during that period, the actual performance being measured against that budget. This is known as a *fixed budget*, and in a manufacturing environment suffers from the fact that the actual levels of activity achieved may be different from those set out in the fixed budget, causing the variances under this system to be unrepresentative. In a *flexible budget* the budget allowance is adjusted to accommodate the differences between budgeted and actual levels of activity by taking into consideration the fixed and variable nature of costs.

Budgets may be produced for a normal period, for example a year, but where they are regularly updated by adding a further budget period, such as a month or a quarter, while at the same time dropping out the earliest month or quarter, as appropriate, they are known as *rolling budgets*. The production of rolling budgets is a way of ensuring that up-to-date financial plans are used to effect financial control.

13   BUDGETARY CONTROL

Budgetary control is the process of financial control whereby the actual expenditure and income for a period is compared to an appropriate budget allowance for each item for the same period, and the variances established. Control is exercised by taking action to eliminate those variances which are adverse to an unacceptable degree.

An *adverse variance* reduces the budgeted profits and arises where the actual performance is worse than that budgeted for the period. That is, where costs are higher or income is lower than the budget allowance. A *favourable variance* increases the budgeted profits and arises where the actual performance is better than that budgeted. No action is generally required if the variance is either favourable or zero. Budgetary control conforms to the *exception principle of management*, which suggests that action need only be taken when a predetermined plan is not achieved.

14   ADVANTAGES OF BUDGETING

Budgetary control is a very useful control device and the following advantages may arise from its introduction.

- The manager of each budget centre knows in financial and quantitative terms what is expected of him/her for the budget period and therefore is *motivated* to achieve this performance.

- Managers are usually given the opportunity to contribute to the setting of their budgets, which encourages an attitude of *responsibility*.

- The *co-ordination* of all the functions of the business is encouraged at the budget preparation stage.

- By considering the adverse variances only, management is able to determine those functions of the business which are contributing to its failure to achieve the budgeted profit, and also the extent to which they are contributing to that shortfall in financial and quantitative terms. *Control* is facilitated.

- The process of formulating budgets encourages managers to anticipate likely future events well in advance and to consider the options available for the resolution of those future problems well before they occur. This is known as *feed-forward control* and in this way *decision making* is facilitated.

- Producing budgets helps managers to plan the development of their activity or function in a progressive way, but at the same time conform to the overall goals and policies of the organization. *Planning* is encouraged and formalized. In Chapter 7 you will see that cost rates are normally calculated in advance of an operating period, based on budgeted figures. Therefore, the preparation of budgets is an important prerequisite of *establishing cost rates* for costing purposes

- Any business must be aware to what extent its future income is likely to cover its future costs. The drafting of a budget will assist the business in determining when and to what extent price adjustments to its product range are likely to be necessary. *Pricing* is therefore facilitated.

- As co-ordination of all budgets must be achieved at the budget preparation stage, if each manager achieves budgeted performance he/she will have made his/her contribution to the overall business moving in the direction which was planned at the budgeting stage and accepted by the board of directors. A sense of *direction* is given to the organization.

- The setting of a budget for each budget centre allows decisions to be made at budget centre level provided they are within the prescribed budget. This avoids every decision being made at the top of the organization, but at the same time provides some constraint on the decisions being made at budget centre level. *Decentralization* is facilitated.

- In any organization the goals or aims of functional heads may not be the same as those of the organization as a whole. For example, the sales manager may wish to achieve maximum sales volume, irrespective of the costs involved, whereas the organization as a whole may only wish for additional sales at an acceptable cost. Preparation of budgets helps to resolve these differences by making personal goals subordinate to organizational ones, except where they coincide. *Goal congruency* is encouraged.

15   DISADVANTAGES OF BUDGETING

In spite of the many advantages of operating a system of budgetary control, there are a number of problems associated with its introduction and operation:

- Some managers will understandably try to ensure that a budget is approved for their particular function of the business which will be very easy for them to achieve in practice. If they are responsible for an expenditure budget, for example, they will try to obtain approval for as high a budget allowance as possible. Conversely, if they are responsible for a revenue budget they will try to ensure that their income budgets are approved at as low a level as possible. This is known as *budgetary slack*, and the budget committee must do all it can to detect and discourage such approaches to budget setting.

- There is a tendency in many organizations to create a budget by taking the current year's expected actual expenditure and adding a notional percentage for, say, expected increased price levels in the budget period. This approach, called *incremental budgeting*, should be discouraged as it is unlikely to create a budget which is relevant to the particular conditions likely to be experienced in the budget period. Furthermore, items of non-recurring expenditure or income unique to the current year will tend to be included in the budget for the succeeding year, and no effort is made to consider items peculiar to the budget period.

- Some chief executives fail to adopt a participative approach to preparing budgets by not involving their line managers in the budgeting process. The managers then feel that targets are set which are not achievable, and a *lack of motivation* to achieve the budgeted performance results.

- Some managers feel that the budget allowance for the budget period represents the total which must be spent. This results in their *spending up to the budget allowance* even though they could comfortably achieve savings. This action particularly applies to overhead and capital expenditure budgets, and tends to be pursued by the manager for two reasons.

    i)   Because an incremental approach to budgeting is often adopted, high current expenditure means that a high budget allowance is easily obtained in subsequent years.

    ii) There is a fear that any failure to take advantage of approved high expenditure levels will be accompanied by a reluctance on the part of top management to allow underspending to be carried forward to a subsequent budget period.

- Although a variance may arise under a particular budget heading, *the variance may not have been caused by the manager for that budget centre*. For example, an overspending on direct material costs due to excess wastage which appears under the production budget may not be controllable by the production manager as it may be due to the purchasing manager buying inferior quality material.

- The establishment of a single *fixed budget* for a budget period does not satisfactorily provide a yardstick for control where a different level of production or sales is achieved from that predicted in formulating the budget. Some of the costs will change, therefore, not due to underspending or overspending arising from good or poor cost control, but due to differences which arise by virtue of the fact that the actual activity level differs from that budgeted.

- Control is usually exercised by comparing actual expenditure and income periodically against the budget for the period, and taking action if the variance is adverse to an unacceptable degree. This is essentially *feedback control*. There are circumstances, however, where an adverse variance arises due to seasonal factors and a variance in one part of the year does not mean that by the end of the year an adverse variance will persist. *Feed-forward* control overcomes this problem by incorporating a predictive mechanism into the budgeting process so that the year's outturn is predicted at each reporting point during the year and management can determine whether corrective action is needed.

- There is a growing point of view among some large organizations that the setting of budgets is an unnecessarily restrictive approach which acts as a strait-jacket on the organization. Budgets tend to stifle quick organizational responses often regarded as necessary in a fast-changing business environment. There is a tendency in such organizations to apply direction and control by the introduction of systems other than budgets.

> *You should now be able to attempt tasks 5.2 and questions 5.4 and 5.5 at the end of this chapter.*

16 | SUMMARY

Budgetary control is the process of control whereby financial and quantitative budgets are produced for a budget period, and actual expenditure and income are compared with the budget allowance throughout that period.

Any difference arising between the budgeted performance and the actual performance is known as a *variance*. Variances can be *favourable*, where actual performance is better than that budgeted (income is greater and/or expenditure is less), or they can be *adverse* (actual expenditure is higher than budgeted and/or actual income is lower).

Control is exercised by ensuring that budgets are produced for each manager in charge of a definable area of the business (*function managers*). They are required to take action to eliminate any variances where they are adverse to an unacceptable degree.

While budgetary control is a very useful device for achieving motivation, responsibility, co-ordination, control and effective decision making within an organization, it also suffers from a number of problems which must be guarded against when operating such a system.

> *You should now be able to attempt the objective test at the end of this chapter.*

STUDENT ACTIVITIES (* denotes questions with answers at the end of the book)

Task 5.1
You are working in a local company and the production manager has agreed that there is no need for him to co-ordinate his budget with other managers. Send him a memo giving examples of where problems can arise if there is no co-ordination of budgets.

Task 5.2
You are required to write an article for a business journal. The title is: 'why budgetary control does not work'. Your theme should be the problems of budgetary control and how they can be resolved.

Task 5.3
Draw up a personal cash flow budget for the next six months. You should plan your cash income and expenditure, together with a balance at the end of each month. Monitor your actual income and expenditure against the budgeted

figures. Develop the cash flow budget into a rolling budget by adding another month's budget as each month passes so that at any time you have a plan for the succeeding six months. Does the process get easier or more difficult?

Question 5.4

The planned or budgeted direct labour hours for *Victoria Fabrications Ltd* is made up of the following working practices in each of the three departments machining, fabrication and finishing.

Machining

Fifteen operators are classified as direct labour. During the year (of 52 weeks), one week is taken up with bank holidays and the company employees are entitled to three weeks' holiday per annum. On average, the operators are sick for one week each year.

A 40-hour basic week is worked, with overtime which is expected to average at four hours per week per operator. 'Natural breaks' average 2.5 hours per week per operator, waiting time 3.5 hours, and other lost time amounts to an hour.

Fabrication

The conditions of employment are largely the same in the fabrication department as those in the machine department. However, only five operators are employed and virtually no overtime is worked.

Finishing

The conditions of employment are largely the same in the finishing department as those in the machine department. However, only five operators are employed and an average of two hours overtime is worked per employee.

Required

Calculate the budgeted annual productive or chargeable hours for each of the departments of the factory.

Question 5.5

Sonron plc produces two types of electric drill, the basic and the super. The budgeted production data for the year 20X1 for each product is as follows, each drill passing through the production departments of manufacturing, assembly, and finishing:

Production time

		Hours per unit	
		Basic	Super
Manufacturing	– machine hours	0.2	0.2
Assembly	– labour hours	0.1	0.15
Finishing	– labour hours	0.1	0.1

Direct materials

	Costs per unit	
	Basic	Super
Motors	1 @ £3	1 @ £4
Parts	20 @ £0.25	25 @ £0.30
Cases	1 @ £2	1 @ £2.50

Sales and finished goods stocks

	Units	
	Basic	Super
Sales	132,000	72,000
Opening stocks	20,000	14,000
Desired closing stocks	8,000	2,000
Selling prices	£30	£40

Direct labour hourly rates

	£ per hour
Manufacturing	12.00
Assembly	8.00
Finishing	7.00

It is the company's production planning policy for one operator in the manufacturing department to supervise two machines.

Other stocks

	Basic			Super		
	Motors	Parts	Cases	Motors	Parts	Cases
Opening stocks	750	15,000	1,000	350	5,000	400
Desired closing stocks	2,000	10,000	1,000	500	4,000	1,000

Production overheads

	£ per annum
Indirect wages	124,000
Wages on cost (holiday pay, etc)	120,400
Supervision	33,360
Machine maintenance wages	28,000
Supplies	5,200
Power	8,400
Tooling	26,600
Insurance – Buildings	3,200
– Machinery	5,040
Depreciation – Machinery	21,000
Rent and rates	24,800
	400,000

Assume all production overheads accrue evenly throughout the year irrespective of production levels. Sales and production levels vary quarterly, but are constant per month during each quarter. The spread of production and sales is as follows:

	Sales		Production	
Quarter	% of annual sales		% of annual production	
	Basic	Super	Basic	Super
1	25	15	30	20
2	25	30	25	30
3	35	30	35	35
4	15	25	10	15

Required

Using spreadsheet software of your choice, prepare monthly budgets for the year commencing January 20X1 suitable for presentation to the budget committee of Sonron plc. Your budgets should include:

i)   Production quantities budget

ii) Sales quantities and sales revenue budgets

iii) Finished goods closing stock budget

iv) Direct materials cost budget

v)   Direct materials purchases budget

vi) Direct labour cost budget

Question 5.6*

Pan-European Tours Ltd operate weekly tours of the Rhine Valley. During the year, they operate 20 of these tours, using 50-seater coaches, on which the load factor is 80 per cent over the whole season.

In 20X1 they operated these tours with a profit of £67,000, made up as follows:

	£	£
Tour price: £300 per person		240,000
Costs:		
Hire of coach: £480 per week	9,600	
Fuel: 1,200 miles per tour at 10 mpg at £2 per gallon	4,800	
Driver: £300 per week	6,000	
Courier: £150 per week	3,000	
Ferries:	4,000	
Hotels: six nights including meals at £25 per person per night	120,000	
Excursions to bierkellers: two excursions per person per tour	9,600	
Head office administration:		
Share of HO costs to these twenty Rhine valley tours	16,000	173,000
		£67,000

For next season, 20X2, the following changes in costs are expected:

Coach hire:	increase by 5 per cent
Fuel:	increase of 10p per gallon
Driver:	wage increase of £20 per week
Courier:	wage increase of £10 per week
Ferries:	increase of 10 per cent
Hotels:	increase of 4 per cent
Excursions:	increase of £1 per excursion
HO charge:	increase of 5 per cent
Selling price:	reduced to £250 per person to maintain demand.

No change is expected in the number of tours or the average load factor.

Required

i) Produce the budget for 20X2 for the Rhine Valley tours.

ii) Calculate the increase in the load factor necessary to maintain the same profit as in 20X1.

Question 5.7

E. *Exmouth* operates a system of flexible budgetary control. He has investigated each cost item and wishes to classify it as either fixed (F), variable (V), or semi-variable (SV) from the following costs incurred at two levels of activity, 50,000 units and 80,000 units respectively:

Budget for the year 20X1

Activity level		50%	80%	Classification
Production units		50,000	80,000	
		£	£	
Direct costs	Labour	210,000	336,000	
	Expenses	20,000	32,000	
Overheads	Business rates	20,000	20,000	
	Depreciation	14,000	16,400	
	Supervision*	25,000*	50,000	
	Insurances	4,000	4,000	
	Indirect wages	21,000	29,400	
	Maintenance	42,000	60,000	
	Cleaning	10,000	10,000	
	Canteen	30,000	42,000	
	Consumables	5,000	8,000	
	Power	5,000	7,400	
	Administration	35,000	35,000	

*Represents one supervisor. An additional supervisor at the same rate required when activity level reaches 60 per cent.

Question 5.8

Using the data for E. *Exmouth* in the previous question, and the same approaches as those used in the chapter, determine the budget allowance for 60,000 units of output.

OBJECTIVE TEST* *(tick the appropriate box)*

i) When fixed budgets are used, the variance is calculated by determining the difference between:

a) the budget allowance and the original budget ☐

b) the actual expenditure and the budget allowance ☐

c) the actual expenditure and the original budget ☑

d) none of these ☐

ii) When flexible budgets are used, the variance is calculated by determining the difference between:

a) the budget allowance and the original budget ☐

b) the actual expenditure and the budget allowance ☒

c) the actual expenditure and the original budget ☐

d) none of these ☐

iii) The major drawback with fixed budgets is that:

a) they are drawn up for a single level of activity only ☒

b) they cannot show the differences between budgeted and actual cost ☐

c) they can never be used for cost control purposes ☐

d) they are drawn up for the short term only ☐

iv) Flexible budgets can only be used where:

a) the actual level of activity is uncertain ☐

b) production and sales are equal ☐

c) costs are classified according to cost behaviour ☒

d) a fixed budget is impossible to construct ☐

v) Budgets are used for:

a) motivation ☐

b) planning ☐

c) control ☐

d) all of these ☒

PART III

COSTING AND PRICING

CHAPTER 6

Cost allocation and apportionment

1 OBJECTIVES

At the end of this chapter you should be able to:

- understand the principles of cost allocation and apportionment;
- understand how cost allocation and apportionment enables total product costing to take place;
- define terms such as cost unit, cost centre, and cost object;
- appreciate some of the drawbacks which accompany any system of cost allocation and apportionment.

2 INTRODUCTION

Where a range of different products is produced in a single factory, a cost and management accounting system is required in order to provide answers to a number of important questions, such as:

- What is the cost of operating each section or department of the business?
- How can individual managers in the organization be made responsible for particular costs?
- What is the cost of producing each of the products manufactured?
- What prices should be charged for each product in order to give an adequate profit margin, both for the particular product and overall?
- How can costs be estimated so that each of the above questions can be considered in advance?

Cost allocation and apportionment are the first steps in answering these questions. The ultimate aim of the costing system may be to build up a cost of production of each of the products produced.

3 COST UNITS AND COST OBJECTS

A *cost unit* is any item, product, sub-assembly, part or service produced by the organization for which it is desired to provide a cost per unit.

Cost units are often the final products which are manufactured by the organization.

Example

Industry	Cost unit
Vehicle manufacture	Vehicle
Aerospace	Aircraft
Shipbuilding	Vessel
General engineering	Job

The cost unit is not necessarily restricted to the final product of the organization, however. If the final cost unit is either big or complex, the costing system may be organized so that the costing of intermediate parts or sub-assemblies takes place. In these cases, each part costed is treated as a cost unit. For example, in manufacturing a motor vehicle, a final cost unit, the engine, the gearbox, the body and the electrical parts may be treated as separate cost units if manufactured by the same organization.

Where small units of output are produced, it is usual to combine the output into batches so that the cost unit does not have a cost which is so small as to be virtually immeasurable.

Example

Industry	Cost unit
Pen manufacture	1,000 pens
Brick making	Batch
Newsprint production	Tonne
Paper bag manufacture	1,000 bags

A *cost unit* may also be described as a *cost object*. A *cost object* is any product, service, sub-assembly, department or area of the business, such as a production or service cost centre or a function, for which the management wishes to determine and collect a separate cost.

> *You should now be able to attempt question 6.4 at the end of this chapter.*

4	COST CLASSIFICATION BY PRODUCT COST

When we looked at cost classification it was demonstrated that where costs are classified according to *product* or *cost unit*, the cost of production is made up as follows:

		£
Direct costs:	Materials	X
	Wages	X
	Expenses	X
Prime cost:		X
Indirect costs or overheads:		
	Production	X
Production cost:		X

In building up a total cost there is also the addition of other overheads which are administration, selling, distribution and, in some cases, research. The process of allocation and apportionment is, however, primarily concerned with production costs and therefore is more often applied to production overheads rather than any of the other overhead categories.

5 | COST CENTRES

As well as collecting costs by *cost unit*, or *cost object*, a manufacturer may also wish to build up the cost of particular sections or departments of the business. These sections or departments are known as *cost centres*. A *cost centre* is any part of the business for which costs are collected. It may be a single factory, a department or section, a single machine or group of machines, an individual or a group of individuals.

In a business producing model cars, for example, the production processes may be organized into moulding, machining, and assembly departments. The management may wish to know the cost of running each of these for the purpose of making managers responsible for their own costs (*cost control*) and to identify expensive processes where savings might be made. There are two types of cost centre: *production cost centres* and *service cost centres*.

Production cost centres are those cost centres in which part of the production process is carried out.

Example

Product	Production cost centre
Model cars	Moulding, machining, assembly
Furniture – wooden	Preparation, shaping, assembly, finishing
– metal	Moulding, welding, assembly, finishing
Yachts	Hull, spars, fitting out, finishing
Books	Typesetting, printing, binding, cutting

You should now be able to attempt task 6.1 and question 6.5 at the end of this chapter.

Service cost centres are those cost centres which are incidental to the production processes, although necessary for them to take place. For example, a canteen, stores, boiler-house, maintenance department. Notice that the service cost centres are incidental to production in the sense that the products or cost units are not produced or handled by them. However, service cost centres are often just as important and necessary to the carrying out of production as the production cost centres themselves.

Any costs which are incurred or charged to service cost centres must be transferred subsequently to production cost centres to be incorporated in the cost of the product produced.

6 | COST ALLOCATION

Cost allocation is carried out where a cost can easily be identified with, and charged to, a particular *cost unit* or *cost centre*. Therefore it is not necessary to analyse the cost on an arbitrary basis in order to reflect the use of that cost item by the cost unit or cost centre.

Direct costs – In costing the cost unit, direct costs are usually *allocated* to the cost unit because they can easily be identified with it. In any costing system, costs are established by analysing documentation which the business either receives from outside or generates internally. The documents which enable the business to allocate the costs to cost units are as follows:

Cost	*Documentation*
Direct wages	Time sheets, clock cards, computer time records, job cards, work tickets
Direct materials	Invoices received, material requisitions, stores issue notes, stores transfer notes, stores returns notes, direct charge vouchers, goods received notes
Direct expenses	Invoices received, direct charge vouchers, time sheets, work tickets

Production overheads – In charging production overheads to cost units it is not possible to use the same analysis as that used for direct costs. For example, where a general purpose machine is producing a range of different products it is not possible to determine directly how much rent, business rates or insurances should be borne by product A as opposed to product B. This is because, in general, production overhead costs, unlike product direct costs, are not incurred by product. Production overheads, therefore, cannot be *allocated* to products, but must go through a more roundabout and complex system to charge them to the cost units or cost objects.

7 | ALLOCATION OF PRODUCTION OVERHEADS

Although it is not usually possible to *allocate* production overheads to products or *cost units*, it is often possible to *allocate* some of these costs to *cost centres*.

This may be done where the costs are directly attributable to a cost centre. For example, where a maintenance facility exists for the sole use of the machine shop, then this cost could be described as a *cost centre direct cost*. This is because its cost is incurred on behalf of, and therefore can be traced to, the machine shop. Therefore it is *allocated* to the machine shop even though maintenance is classified as an overhead. Similarly any depreciation of machine shop plant and machinery can be *allocated* to the machine shop cost centre as a cost centre direct cost. This is because such depreciation is easily traceable to each individual piece of equipment in the machine shop.

Some overhead costs, however, cannot be treated as cost centre direct costs as they are shared by a number of cost centres. These costs are *cost centre indirect costs*, and they require *cost apportionment* to enable them to be charged to cost centres.

8 | APPORTIONMENT OF PRODUCTION OVERHEADS

Cost apportionment is the charging of proportions of each indirect or overhead cost item to *cost centres* using an appropriate *basis of apportionment* so as to reflect the relative use of that cost item by each cost centre.

Example

Overhead cost item	Basis of apportionment to cost centres
Business rates	Area or volume occupied
Rent	Area or volume occupied
Insurance of machinery	Capital values of machinery
Insurance of buildings	Area or volume occupied
Supervision	Number of personnel employed
Depreciation of buildings	Area or volume occupied
Indirect wages	Number of personnel employed
Power	Machine hours, horsepower, or horsepower/hours
Cleaning	Area occupied
Light and heat	Area or volume occupied
Canteen	Number of personnel

Notice that with a number of overhead costs there is a choice of the basis of apportionment. In each case the most appropriate one should be chosen, and the most appropriate basis of apportionment should have the following characteristics.

- It should be related in some way to the manner in which the cost is incurred by each of the cost centres benefiting from its use.

- It should reflect the use by the cost centre of the resources represented by the overhead cost.

- It should be a basis which is relatively easily obtainable from the records of the organization.

- It should apportion the costs which are shared by the cost centres in a way which could be described as fair, reasonable or equitable. Notice that because the methods of apportionment are arbitrary, and alternative methods can be used for the same cost, then they cannot necessarily be described as 'accurate' or 'correct'.

Example

Lord's Sports Equipment operates a small business manufacturing cricket bats and tennis racquets. There are three production cost centres, namely machining, assembly and finishing departments. The overheads budget for next year is set out below, together with the cost centre details, and *Lord's* asks you to determine the annual cost of running each production cost centre.

Annual overheads budget

	£
Rent	20,000
Business rates	40,000
Consumables	10,000
Power	4,750
Cleaning	6,000
Light and heat	2,120
Maintenance	10,200
Depreciation – Machinery	8,000
– Buildings	15,900
Indirect wages	19,600
Canteen	23,800
Insurance – Machinery	4,250
– Buildings	5,300
Supervision	42,000
Total	211,920

Cost centre details

Basis	Machining	Assembly	Finishing	Total
Area (square metres)	5,000	2,000	3,000	10,000
Volume (cubic metres)	25,000	10,000	18,000	53,000
Capital values (£'000)	70,000	10,000	5,000	85,000
Number of employees	10	20	5	35
Machinery (hp/hours)	8,750	350	400	9,500
Maintenance (£)	9,500	500	200	10,200
Depreciation of machinery (£)	6,500	1,000	500	8,000
Consumables (£)	8,000	1,000	1,000	10,000

Solution

The total overhead cost of each cost centre can be obtained by constructing an overhead cost analysis statement, sometimes also referred to as an overhead cost distribution summary. This statement allocates costs to each cost centre if they are cost centre direct costs. If they are cost centre indirect costs then they are apportioned or shared between the cost centres using a suitable basis of apportionment.

Lord's Sports Equipment
Overhead cost analysis statement

| Item | £ | Basis | Cost centres | | |
			Machining £	Assembly £	Finishing £
Rent	20,000	Area	10,000	4,000	6,000
Rates	40,000	Area	20,000	8,000	12,000
Consumables	10,000	Actual	8,000	1,000	1,000
Power	4,750	Hp/hours	4,375	175	200
Cleaning	6,000	Area	3,000	1,200	1,800
Light and heat	2,120	Volume	1,000	400	720
Maintenance	10,200	Actual	9,500	500	200
Depreciation – Machinery	8,000	Actual	6,500	1,000	500
– Building	15,900	Volume	7,500	3,000	5,400
Indirect wages	19,600	Number of employees	5,600	11,200	2,800
Canteen	23,800	Number of employees	6,800	13,600	3,400
Insurance – Machinery	4,250	Capital values	3,500	500	250
– Building	5,300	volume	2,500	1,000	1,800
Supervision	42,000	personnel	12,000	24,000	6,000
Total	211,920		100,275	69,575	42,070

The items which have been marked 'actual' have been *allocated* to cost centres as the overhead is directly attributable to those cost centres without apportionment being necessary. All other items have been charged proportionately to cost centres using a suitable *basis of apportionment*. For example, rent has been apportioned using floor area occupied as a basis, as follows:

Example

$$\text{Total cost to be apportioned} \times \frac{\text{Total cost centre's share of the basis}}{\text{Total apportionment basis}}$$

$$\text{Machining} = £20,000 \times \frac{5,000 \text{ square metres}}{10,000 \text{ square metres}} = £10,000$$

$$\text{Assembly} = £20,000 \times \frac{2,000 \text{ square metres}}{10,000 \text{ square metres}} = £4,000$$

$$\text{Finishing} = £20,000 \times \frac{3,000 \text{ square metres}}{10,000 \text{ square metres}} = £6,000$$

Alternative appropriate bases of apportionment may be used which will give different results from those obtained above. For example, building volume may be just as appropriate for the apportionment of rent, business rates and cleaning, whereas building area could have been used for light and heat, building depreciation and building insurance. It is important to find and use a basis of apportionment most appropriate for the cost being apportioned.

> You should now be able to attempt tasks 6.2 and 6.3 and questions 6.6 and 6.7 at the end of this chapter.

9 | RECIPROCAL COSTS

In section 6.5 we explained that some cost centres are *service cost centres* and that the total costs which make up the cost of service cost centres must be recharged to the production cost centres. The reason for this is because the ultimate aim of the system is to ensure that the production overheads are charged to the *cost units* or the products produced. As these cost units pass through production cost centres and do not pass through the service cost centres, to ensure that the cost of service cost centres is included in the cost of the product they must be recharged to production cost centres.

In some circumstances, however, a complication arises where a service cost centre carries out work for another service cost centre, which also carries out work for the first. For example, the maintenance cost centre may carry out maintenance work on the equipment used by the canteen, which may also provide canteen services to personnel employed by maintenance. This reciprocal arrangement needs to be taken into consideration when dealing with the apportionment of costs.

The major methods of dealing with these reciprocal costs are the *repeated distribution* or *continuous allotment method* and the approach using *simultaneous equations*.

Example

A company has three production cost centres and two service cost centres. The following are the total production overhead costs which have been charged to those cost centres:

		£
Production cost centre	A	32,300
	B	42,400
	C	68,900
Service cost centre	1	15,200
	2	18,800

The total costs of the service cost centres are to be apportioned as follows:

Cost centres	A	B	C	1	2
Service cost centre 1	30%	40%	20%	–	10%
Service cost centre 2	50%	20%	10%	20%	–

Solutions

- *Repeated distribution method*

This method repeatedly apportions each total service cost centre cost using specified percentages until the figures are too small to continue.

	A	B	C	1	2
	£	£	£	£	£
Total costs	32,300	42,400	68,900	15,200	18,800
Apportion 1	4,560 (30%)	6,080 (40%)	3,040 (20%)	(15,200)	1,520 (10%)
	36,860	48,480	71,940	–	20,320
Apportion 2	10,160 (50%)	4,064 (20%)	2,032 (10%)	4,064 (20%)	(20,320)
	47,020	52,544	73,972	4,064	–
Apportion 1	1,219	1,626	813	(4,064)	406
	48,239	54,170	74,785	–	406
Apportion 2	203	81	41	81	(406)
	48,442	54,251	74,826	81	–
Apportion 1	24	33	16	(81)	8
	48,466	54,284	74,842	–	8
Apportion 2	4	2	–	2	(8)
	48,470	54,286	74,842	2	–
Apportion 1	1	1	–	(2)	
Final Totals	48,471	54,287	74,842	–	

- *Using simultaneous equations*

This method obtains the total amounts chargeable to the service cost centres 1 and 2 respectively, and the percentages chargeable to the production cost centres are applied to these totals.

Let service cost centre 1 $= x$

Let service cost centre 2 $= y$

Equations are:

$$x = £15,200 + 0.2y \ldots\ldots\ldots(1)$$
$$y = £18,800 + 0.1x \ldots\ldots\ldots(2)$$

Rearrange equations:

$$x - 0.2y = £15,200 \ldots\ldots\ldots(3)$$
$$-0.1x + y = £18,800 \ldots\ldots\ldots(4)$$

Multiply (3) by -0.1: $-0.1x + 0.02y = £-1,520$

Subtract (4) $\quad -0.1x + \quad y = £18,800$

This eliminates the 'x' term $\quad -0.98y = £-20,320$

Divide both sides by -0.98 $\quad y = £20,735$ (rounded)

Substitute in (1) $\quad x = £15,200 + 0.2 (£20,735)$

$$x = £19,347$$

Now apply the percentages for production cost centres A, B and C to the values of x and y calculated by simultaneous equations:

	A £	B £	C £
Production cost centres	32,300	42,400	68,900
Service cost centres:			
Cost centre 1(x)	5,804 (30%)	7,739 (40%)	3,869 (20%)
Cost centre 2(y)	10,368 (50%)	4,147 (20%)	2,074 (10%)
Final totals	48,472	54,286	74,843

The small differences in the final totals chargeable to the production cost centres arising from the two methods is primarily due to rounding.

> *You should now be able to attempt question 6.9 at the end of this chapter.*

---

10 | SUMMARY

The techniques of *allocation* and *apportionment* are important steps in charging the production overhead costs to departments or *cost centres* of the business. This is done:

- to determine the cost of operating each cost centre;
- to determine how much production overhead should be borne by each product or cost unit worked on by each production cost centre. (This aspect will be covered in Chapter 7.)

Product direct costs of wages, material and (occasionally) expenses can be *allocated* to *cost units* as they can be traced relatively easily to products by the analysis of documentation such as invoices, stores issue notes and time sheets. *Indirect product costs* or *production overheads* cannot be charged directly to cost units as they are generally not incurred on a product basis.

However, some production overheads can also be allocated to cost centres as cost centre direct costs where they can be related to cost centres as costs solely incurred by them. Otherwise, where overhead costs are shared by cost centres, they need to be *apportioned*. This is achieved by using a basis of apportionment which reflects the use by the cost centres of the resources represented by the overhead cost.

Alternative appropriate bases of apportionment may be used, which will necessarily give a different total overhead cost for each cost centre when compared with the result achieved by the use of other bases.

> *You should now be able to attempt the objective test at the end of this chapter.*

STUDENT ACTIVITIES (* *denotes questions with answers at the end of the book*)

Task 6.1
Draw up a list of the cost centres that you consider are appropriate for the organization where you work or study.

Task 6.2
The manager of the company where you work has always allocated the factory rent on the basis of the number of employees occupying the various departments. Write him a memo explaining the limitations of this basis and propose alternatives.

Task 6.3
Your manager considers that the apportionment and allocation of costs are essentially the same thing. Write a memo to him explaining the difference between the two ways of handling overhead costs, giving the reasons why costs are treated in these ways.

Question 6.4
Suggest suitable cost units for the following industries:

i)   Shirt manufacturer

ii)   Dairy

iii)   Oil refinery

iv)   Box manufacturer

v)   Pencil manufacturer

vi)   Housebuilder

vii)   Bridgebuilder

viii) Television manufacturer

ix)   Zinc smelter

x)   Paint producer

Question 6.5
Refer to the previous question. Suggest possible production cost centres which might exist in the industries for which you have already identified the cost units. Assume that some of the production for the housebuilder and the bridgebuilder is in prefabricated sections manufactured in a factory.

Question 6.6
Redraft the overhead cost analysis statement shown in section 8 of the chapter using building volume as a basis of apportionment for rent, rates and cleaning,

and building area as a basis of apportionment for light and heat, building depreciation and building insurance. Round all figures to the nearest pound.

What difference does it make to the total costs of each cost centre?

In what way are the differences important to the managers in charge of each cost centre?

Are the totals of each of the costs which have caused the differences to arise controllable by the cost centre managers?

If the answer to the previous question is 'yes', explain how.

If the answer to the previous question is 'no', who is capable of controlling these costs?

Question 6.7*

Durban Production Ltd's factory has three cost centres, machining, fabrication and finishing, and the company's budgets for next year include the following total production overheads:

	£
Cleaning	10,000
Rent and business rates	40,000
Building insurance	1,000
Indirect labour	12,000
Machinery depreciation	11,000
Supervision	50,000
Material handling	22,000
Power	50,500
Canteen	50,000
	246,500

The three production cost centres have the following characteristics:

	Machining	Fabrication	Finishing
Machine horsepower	100	5	–
Machine hours	5,000	1,000	–
Number of personnel	15	5	5
Area (square metres)	1,600	1,000	1,400
Value of materials (£)	1,000,000	50,000	50,000
Indirect labour hours	3,000	1,500	1,500
Capital values of machinery (£)	100,000	5,000	5,000

Required

Draw up the overheads budget for each cost centre for the year.

Question 6.8

Multiproducts Ltd produces three products, basic, extra and deluxe. The profit and loss account for the year is as follows:

Multiproducts Ltd
Profit and loss account for the year ending 31 December 20X2

	£	£
Sales		400,000
Production cost of sales		275,000
Gross profit		125,000
Selling and distribution:		
Advertising	20,000	
Salesmen's costs	5,275	
Sales office expenses	3,150	
Delivery	15,750	
Packing	3,150	
Storage	1,575	
Administration	10,000	
Credit control	1,050	
		59,950
Net profit		65,050

The following bases are used for the apportionment of revenue and costs between products:

	Basic	Extra	Deluxe
Sales (£)	50,000	150,000	200,000
Production cost (% of sales value)	70%	60%	75%
Advertising (proportion per product)	25%	25%	50%
Salesmen's costs	as a percentage of sales value		
Sales office expenses	as a percentage of sales value		
Credit control (orders received)	100	120	200
Delivery, packaging, storage (packages delivered)	5,000	6,000	10,000
Administration	as a percentage of sales value		

Required

Prepare a statement to show the net profit made by each product based on the apportionments shown.

Question 6.9

Clevedale Manufacturing Ltd has set up both production and service cost centres. Its production overheads charged to those cost centres for the year are as follows:

	£000s
Production cost centres:	
Machine	500
Assembly	300
Finishing	160
Service cost centres:	
Stores	100
Maintenance	140

The company has decided that the service cost centre costs should be charged as follows:

	Stores (%)	Maintenance (%)
Production cost centres:		
Machine	35	45
Assembly	30	30
Finishing	20	15
Service cost centres:		
Stores	–	10
Maintenance	15	–

Required

Apportion the costs to the production cost centres using:

(a) the repeated distribution method;

(b) simultaneous equations.

OBJECTIVE TEST* *(tick the appropriate box)*

i) A cost centre may be:

    a) a product ☐

    b) a sub-assembly ☐

    c) a service ☐

    d) none of these ☐

ii) Costs must be allocated to a cost centre or cost unit if:

    a) they are indirect costs ☐

    b) they are direct costs ☐

    c) they are production overheads ☐

    d) they are other overheads ☐

iii) Costs must be apportioned to a cost centre if:

    a) they are indirect costs ☐

    b) they are direct costs ☐

    c) they are shared costs ☐

    d) they cannot be allocated ☐

iv) The reasons for charging costs to cost centres are:

    a) to determine the costs of operating a cost centre ☐

    b) to enable overheads to be charged to products ☐

    c) neither of these   ☐

    d) both of these   ☐

v) A cost unit may be:

    a) a department   ☐

    b) a factory   ☐

    c) neither of these   ☐

    d) both of these   ☐

CHAPTER 7

Absorption costing

1 OBJECTIVES

At the end of this chapter you should be able to:

- understand what is meant by overhead cost absorption;
- understand how total production costs are charged to products;
- use alternative absorption methods;
- appreciate the advantages and disadvantages of each method;
- understand simple production overhead variance analysis.

2 INTRODUCTION

In the previous chapter we saw how direct costs (prime costs) are allocated to products, cost units or cost objects. However, this is not possible with production overheads because overheads are not generally incurred per product. For example, it is not possible to calculate how much factory rent should be charged to a product in quite the same way as direct materials can be, so we charge production overheads to the product in a more roundabout way.

As already explained, the first stage in this process is to either *allocate* or *apportion* the overheads to cost centres. You should make sure that you thoroughly understand the contents of the previous chapter before proceeding. In this chapter we are going to look at how the overhead costs are now transferred from the production cost centres to the products or cost units which are made in those cost centres. The method which is used to carry out this process is known as *overhead cost absorption* or *absorption costing*.

3 COST ABSORPTION

Cost absorption is a costing technique in which the production overheads, having been charged to production cost centres by the techniques of allocation or apportionment, are transferred to (*absorbed* by) the cost units, cost objects or products produced by those cost centres.

In order to charge the total costs of the production cost centre to the cost units, we need to calculate a rate for each cost centre known as the *overhead cost absorption rate* (or *overhead cost recovery rate*). These rates are always calculated before the accounting period starts and therefore are usually based on budgeted figures. The general formula for the calculation of an overhead cost absorption rate is:

$$\frac{\text{Total budgeted production cost centre overheads}}{\text{Total budgeted production}}$$

Although it is usual to calculate cost absorption rates in advance for a year, and therefore both budgeted costs and production will be for that period, shorter period rates are used in some organizations.

The *total budgeted production cost centre overheads* can be obtained by budgeting these overheads in total for the period, and then applying the techniques of *allocation* and *apportionment* described in the previous chapter to get budgeted totals for each production cost centre.

In absorption costing there are a number of ways of measuring production. This is because a single measure would not be appropriate to all the cost centres in a factory, because not only do the production methods vary but also the types of products being produced. For example, a common way of measuring production is to express it in numbers of units manufactured. This is acceptable if a cost centre is always producing a single standard product, but if a production cost centre for half the time makes, say, 100 window frames, and the other half 55 door frames, we cannot say that the production has been 155 units. This is because window frames and door frames are so different in terms of size, time taken to produce and value, that they cannot reasonably be added together.

Another common way of measuring production is in direct labour hours worked. The use of this measure is certainly acceptable where a cost centre's production is carried out primarily by direct labour. This we would call a labour intensive cost centre. However, some cost centres are machine intensive and to measure production in direct labour hours would be less appropriate than using machine hours.

There are a number of ways in which production can be measured in order to calculate an overhead cost absorption rate. A different way of measuring production may be used (although not necessarily) for each production cost centre in the factory. If the total overhead costs are charged to cost centres by allocation and apportionment, then a separate rate for each cost centre will almost certainly be calculated.

In some circumstances, however, a single rate may be calculated for the factory as a whole. This is known as a *blanket rate*, but is generally regarded as less 'accurate' than individual cost centre rates. This is because the individual rates are meant to transfer the costs of each cost centre to the products which use its resources. With the use of blanket rates, costs of some areas of the business are borne by a product which may not use those resources in its production.

4   RATE PER UNIT OF PRODUCTION

In some cost centres the production may be expressed as the number of units of production. This is an appropriate means of measuring output if all the items produced by the cost centre are similar in terms of size, time spent being worked on by the cost centre and other characteristics.

Example

In *Barry Furniture Company* the assembly department assembles one type of standard chair. Next year's budgeted production overhead for the department is £162,500, and the total number of chairs budgeted to be produced is 100 per day over a year of 220 working days.

Required

Calculate the overhead absorption cost rate per chair necessary to absorb into the output the budgeted cost centre production overheads of the assembly department for the year.

Solution

Overhead absorption cost rate per chair

$$= \frac{\text{Total budgeted cost centre production overheads}}{\text{Total budgeted units}}$$

$$= \frac{£162,500}{100 \text{ chairs} \times 220 \text{ working days}}$$

$$= £7.39 \text{ (rounded)}$$

This means that each chair produced by the assembly department must have £7.39 added to it in order to ensure that each unit bears a fair share of assembly department overheads.

5 | RATE PER DIRECT LABOUR HOUR

In the previous example the use of a rate per unit would not be possible if the assembly department produced both chairs and tables. A single unit of production cannot be applied as a measure to both tables and chairs because of their obviously different characteristics. For this reason, a method of measuring production must be found which can be applied to both chairs and tables, and at the same time reflect the method of production used in the assembly department.

Because the assembly department carries out a labour intensive activity, the use of *direct labour hours* is both a useful and appropriate method of measuring output.

Example

Barry Furniture Company has decided to extend their product range and the assembly department produces both chairs and tables. The budgeted production overhead for the department is still £162,500, but the budgeted production is expected to be 10,000 chairs and 10,000 tables, each taking 3 and 4.5 direct labour hours respectively.

Required

i) Calculate the overhead cost absorption rate per direct labour hour necessary to absorb the budgeted cost centre overheads of the assembly department into the output.

ii) Calculate the amount of assembly department production overheads which will be borne or absorbed by a chair and a table if the budgeted times are actually achieved.

Solution

i) Rate per direct labour hour

$$= \frac{\text{Total budgeted cost centre production overheads}}{\text{Total budgeted direct labour hours}}$$

$$= \frac{£162,500}{(10,000 \times 3) + (10,000 \times 4.5)}$$

$$= \frac{£162,500}{75,000 \text{ direct labour hours}}$$

$$= £2.17 \text{ per direct labour hour (rounded)}$$

ii) This means that each chair produced by the assembly department must have 3 hours × £2.17 = £6.51 added to it to ensure that each unit bears an appropriate share of assembly department overheads. A table would require 4.5 hours × £2.17 = £9.77 added to it for the same reason.

This approach charges more overhead to tables than to chairs, as the former tend to take longer to assemble. This illustrates the fairness of using the rate per direct labour hour in this case. The longer a product is worked on in a department, the greater should be the share of overhead borne by that product.

The overhead charged to a chair using this method is £6.51, whereas using the rate per unit of production in the example in the previous section it was £7.39. This shows that the system of cost absorption is not intended to be an accurate system, but rather one that ensures that all the production overhead is accounted for in the costing of the product in a fair or equitable way. Thus, the use of different absorption techniques may cause different levels of costs to be borne by the cost unit.

6 | RATE PER MACHINE HOUR

In the previous example a rate per direct labour hour was advocated for the assembly department where a range of dissimilar products are produced and the method of production is labour intensive. Where a range of different products is produced or worked on in a cost centre, but the method of production is machine intensive, a more appropriate method of measuring production is in machine hours, and a production overhead cost absorption rate per machine hour is calculated.

> *You should now be able to attempt question 7.4 at the end of this chapter*

7 | PERCENTAGE ON DIRECT LABOUR COST

If the rate per direct labour hour method is used for overhead absorption it is necessary to maintain a record of the direct labour hours spent on each job, product or cost unit. This is necessary in order to determine the share of overhead it should bear. As the direct costs are normally allocated to cost units (see the previous chapter) and direct costs include direct labour cost, an alternative absorption method is to use a *percentage on direct labour cost*. In this case, the production is being measured in terms of the direct labour cost incurred.

Example

Barry Furniture Company is considering using a percentage on direct labour cost for the absorption of production overhead cost in the assembly department as an alternative to using the rate per direct labour hour shown in the example in the previous section. The wages rates payable to the operators are £10 per hour when producing chairs and £12 per hour when producing tables.

Required

i) Calculate an overhead absorption rate for the assembly department using the percentage on direct labour cost method of overhead absorption.

ii) Calculate the amount of assembly department production overheads which would be borne or absorbed by a chair and a table if the budgeted times are actually achieved.

Solution

i) The budgeted production overhead for the assembly department is £162,500. The budgeted direct labour costs are:

	£
Chairs 30,000 hours × £10 per hour =	300,000
Tables 45,000 hours × £12 per hour =	540,000
	840,000

The overhead absorption rate:

$$= \frac{\text{Total budgeted cost centre production overheads} \times 100}{\text{Total budgeted direct labour cost}}$$

$$= \frac{£162,500 \times 100}{£840,000}$$

$$= 19.35\% \text{ (rounded)}$$

This means that whatever direct labour is charged to a product, 19.35% of direct labour cost will be added to the product cost in order to ensure that the product bears a share of the production overheads.

ii) Each product would bear production overhead of:

Chair: 3 hours × £10 × 19.35%   = £5.81

Table: 4.5 hours × £12 × 19.35%   = £10.45

The value of overhead charged to chairs and tables is based on the direct labour cost of each product. If the same labour hour rate is paid for the production of both products, then the overhead borne by each product would be identical to that shown in the solution in the previous section where a rate per direct labour hour was used. Prove this by recalculating the absorption rates and the solution above, assuming that a labour rate of £10 per hour is paid for the production of both tables and chairs. Note that a small difference may arise due to rounding.

> You should now be able to attempt question 7.5 at the end of this chapter.

8 | PERCENTAGE ON DIRECT MATERIAL COST

As the prime costs are allocated to the cost units, it follows that direct material costs are also allocated as part of the prime costs. It is possible to use a *percentage on direct material cost* as a basis for absorbing production overhead costs into the product or cost unit.

The rate per direct labour hour, the rate per machine hour and the percentage on direct labour cost all charge overheads to production on the basis of time taken. This ensures that those products which take a longer time to produce are charged with a greater share of overhead cost. This may be regarded as a fair and equitable basis of overhead absorption as production overheads also tend to be incurred on a time basis. However, the use of the percentage on direct material cost basis does not relate overheads charged to time taken, and this may be regarded as a major drawback in the use of this method. It may be used, however, where material costs are a substantial element of total production cost.

> You should now be able to attempt question 7.6 at the end of this chapter.

9 PERCENTAGE ON PRIME COST

Percentage on prime cost can also be used as a basis for absorbing production overheads, but may be criticized, as can the percentage on direct material cost method, since it is not entirely time based.

> You should now be able to attempt task 7.3 and question 7.7 at the end of this chapter.

10 RATE PER STANDARD HOUR

If a system of work measurement exists within an organization, then *standard hours* may be used to measure output. A standard hour is a measure of work produced based on time and is a very useful concept because it enables us to add dissimilar items together. For example, if we have determined, by using work measurement techniques that a desk is equivalent to 10 standard hours work and a cupboard is equivalent to 7 standard hours work, then we can express output in standard hours for both products. Thus, if we have produced 100 desks and 25 cupboards during a period this can be measured as equivalent to 1,175 standard hours work:

Desks	100 × 10 standard hours =	1,000 standard hours
Cupboards	25 × 7 standard hours =	175 standard hours
	Total standard hours =	1,175

It follows therefore that an overhead absorption rate can also be calculated using standard hours as a method of measuring production, using the formula:

$$\frac{\text{Total budgeted cost centre production overheads}}{\text{Total budgeted standard hours of production}}$$

If the cost centre overheads are budgeted at £185,200 for the year and the budgeted production is 23,150 standard hours, then the overhead rate per standard hour is:

$$\frac{£185,200}{23,150 \text{ standard hours}} = £8 \text{ per standard hour}$$

A desk would therefore be charged with 10 standard hours × £8 = £80 for production overhead and a cupboard with 7 standard hours × £8 = £56 for production overhead.

Another benefit which arises if a rate per standard hour is used is that an efficiency percentage can be calculated in each cost centre.

11 | COST ABSORBED

Having calculated the overhead cost absorption rate, the overhead cost charged to production, known as the *cost absorbed* or *cost recovered*, is determined for each cost centre by using the formula:

Actual cost centre production × Cost centre overhead cost absorption rate

where the actual production is expressed in the same terms as the absorption rate is calculated. Thus, if an absorption rate is expressed as a rate per unit, then actual production is also expressed in units; if the rate is expressed as a percentage on direct labour cost, then production must also be expressed in labour cost terms.

Example

Beach Ltd's machine department overhead cost was budgeted at £264,000 for the year and the budgeted machine hours at 105,600. By the end of the year the actual production totalled 110,260 machine hours.

Required

Calculate the total overhead cost absorbed by the production for the year.

Solution

Absorption rate:

$$= \frac{£264,000}{105,600 \text{ machine hours}}$$

$$= £2.50 \text{ per machine hour}$$

Cost absorbed for the year:

$$= 110,260 \text{ machine hours} \times £2.50$$
$$= £275,650$$

Beach Ltd absorbed more cost than was budgeted for the department, £275,650 compared to £264,000. This difference of £11,650 represents a gain which arose because the production expressed in machine hours was greater than budgeted. The extra 4,660 machine hours worked at the absorption rate of £2.50 per hour created the gain of £11,650. This gain is known as a *cost over-absorption* or *cost over-recovery* and represents an addition to the profits of the business.

Example

Ogmore Ltd's finishing department's production is measured in units and was budgeted to produce 120,000 units in the year just ended. The budgeted production overhead was £762,000 and actual production fell short of that budgeted by 18,000 units.

113

Required

Calculate Ogmore Ltd's overhead absorbed by the output of the finishing department for the year.

Solution

Finishing department overhead absorption rate:

$$= \frac{£762,000}{120,000 \text{ units}}$$

$$= £6.35 \text{ per unit}$$

Finishing department overhead cost absorbed:

$$= (120,000 - 18,000) \times £6.35$$
$$= £647,700$$

Ogmore Ltd's cost absorbed falls short of that budgeted by £114,300 (£762,000 – £647,700). This is made up of the 18,000 fewer units produced at £6.35 per unit (£114,300). This is known as an *under-absorption* or *under-recovery* of overhead cost and represents a reduction in the profits of the business.

> You should now be able to attempt questions 7.8 and 7.9 at the end of this chapter.

12 | STOCK VALUATION

Absorption costing is often used in manufacturing organizations to value at the end of an accounting period both the work in progress up to the stage of production reached and finished goods for inclusion in manufacturing accounts and profit and loss accounts.

You may recall that in the UK, Statement of Standard Accounting Practice (SSAP) 9 requires stock to be valued at the lower of cost or net realizable value. In valuing stocks of work in progress and finished goods, cost is normally regarded as total production cost. Total production cost is made up of the product direct costs of materials, labour and expenses plus the production overheads.

We covered the alternative methods of pricing materials from store to production in Chapter 2, and the first-in-first-out (FIFO), last-in-first-out (LIFO) and average cost (AVCO) methods were discussed in detail. These approaches may also be applied to the unit costs of valuing work in progress and finished goods using the overhead absorption system.

You can see that the overhead cost absorption system described in this chapter enables production overhead to be charged to products so that stock valuations at total production cost may be calculated at the end of an accounting period for inclusion in the organization's accounts.

13 │ SIMPLE OVERHEAD VARIANCE ANALYSIS

We have seen how a department's budgeted overhead cost is not necessarily the same as that absorbed, the difference arising because a different level of actual production is achieved compared with that budgeted. For instance, in the example of *Beach Ltd* (section 7.11 above) the overhead budgeted was £264,000 and that absorbed was £275,650, resulting in a gain of £11,650. Because this *difference* or *variance* is due to the actual production in machine hours exceeding the budgeted production in machine hours, it could be described as an *activity* or *volume variance*.

There is yet another difference which could arise in Beach Ltd's machine department. Assume that at the end of the year the *actual expenditure* on production overheads was £270,000, which was £6,000 more than planned or budgeted.

We now have three items for the machine department or cost centre:

- Production overhead *absorbed*: £275,650 (actual production × budgeted absorption rate)

- Production overhead *budgeted*: £264,000 (budgeted production × budgeted absorption rate)

- Production overhead *incurred*: £270,000 (actual overhead paid and accrued)

The difference between the overhead absorbed and overhead budgeted we have described already as an activity or *volume variance* of £11,650, being a gain or *favourable variance*. The difference between the overhead budgeted and overhead incurred arises because there is an overspending of £6,000, therefore this is described as an *unfavourable* or *adverse expenditure variance*.

We now have a *total variance* made up of the difference between the production overhead cost absorbed of £275,650 and the production overhead cost incurred of £270,000, namely £5,650 favourable. This can be analysed into a favourable activity or volume variance of £11,650 and an adverse expenditure variance of £6,000. This is shown in the following table.

Production overhead absorbed: £275,650		
	Volume variance:	£11,650 (F)
Production overhead budgeted: £264,000		
	Expenditure variance:	£5,000 (A)
Production overhead incurred: £270,000		
Total variance: (£275,650 – £270,000)		£5,650 (F)

These overhead variances are important to management because they show the financial results of different performance. If production is different from that budgeted this causes the activity or volume variance, and the expenditure variance occurs if actual expenditure is different from that planned.

> *You should now be able to attempt tasks 7.1 and 7.2 and questions 7.10 and 7.14 at the end of this chapter.*

14 | SUMMARY

The process of *cost absorption* is the transfer of the department or cost centre production overheads to the product or cost unit by using cost absorption or recovery rates. The rates used are based on budgeted or predetermined figures and are calculated using the general formula:

$$\frac{\text{Total budgeted cost centre production overheads}}{\text{Total budgeted production}}$$

Alternative time-based methods are:

- rate per direct labour hour;
- rate per machine hour;
- percentage on direct labour cost;
- rate per standard hour.

Other methods are:

- rate per unit;
- percentage on direct material cost;
- percentage on prime cost.

A single rate is calculated for each *cost centre*, but different methods may be used for each cost centre of the business depending on the characteristics of that cost centre; for example, whether it is machine or labour intensive. The cost centre costs are then absorbed into *cost units* by the general formula:

Actual cost centre production × Cost absorption rate

The actual production must be expressed in the same terms as the absorption rate is calculated:

- number of direct labour hours worked;
- number of machine hours operated;
- direct labour cost incurred;
- number of units produced;
- direct material cost incurred;
- prime cost incurred;
- number of standard hours produced.

By comparing the departmental overhead absorbed with that budgeted, it is possible to establish a *volume* or *activity variance*. By comparing the departmental overhead budgeted with that actually incurred, it is possible to establish an *expenditure variance*. By comparing the departmental overhead absorbed with that incurred, it is possible to establish a *total variance*.

The main difficulties experienced by students are:

- Confusing cost allocation, cost apportionment and cost absorption. Remember, costs are allocated if they can be directly charged to a cost unit or a cost centre. Direct costs are usually allocated to cost units; production overheads are allocated to cost centres if they can be solely identified with it. Otherwise shared costs are apportioned between cost centres using a basis of apportionment. Total cost centre production overheads are then absorbed using one of the alternatives for each cost centre.

- Forgetting that the overhead cost absorption rates are based on budgeted figures and calculated in advance.

- Forgetting that actual costs absorbed are based on actual production × overhead cost absorption rates.

- Failing to express production in the correct way, e.g. in direct labour hours worked if a direct labour hour rate is used, in units if a rate per unit is used.

- Forgetting that a total variance is the difference between overhead absorbed and overhead incurred, and *not* the difference between the overhead budgeted and the actual overhead incurred.

> *You should now be able to attempt the objective text at the end of this chapter.*

STUDENT ACTIVITIES (* *denotes questions with answers at the end of the book*)

Task 7.1
Draft a plan of the cost collection procedures necessary to determine the manufacturing cost of any product of your choice. The plan should include:

- a list of the costs incurred in the manufacture of the product;
- an appropriate classification of those costs;
- a list of the prime documents from which those costs are collected;
- details of how the costs are to be charged to the product, particularly where the product is one of a product range;
- consideration of alternative methods of treating some costs, where appropriate.

Task 7.2
A friend has opened a mountain bike repair shop. He is competent to undertake all types of repair work from mending a puncture to a complete overhaul. He has calculated that his total overheads will be £8,000 per annum and he intends to charge them to each job on the basis of the number of repairs he estimates he will do in a year. Write him a letter explaining the problems with his proposal and suggest an alternative.

Task 7.3
Your manager is confused by the many alternative methods of overhead cost absorption available. She feels that there should be only one definitive unit cost of

a product and is concerned that the use of different absorption techniques results in the calculation of different unit costs. Write a memo to her explaining how this situation can arise and whether it should be regarded as a problem.

Question 7.4

Barry Furniture Company machining department is machine intensive and produces dining chairs, tables and rocking chairs. The budgeted production overheads for the department next year are £192,500 and the number of machine hours are budgeted at 55,000.

Required

i) Calculate the absorption rate to be applied per machine hour to charge production overheads to the output.

ii) If a dining chair normally takes two hours to machine, a dining table five hours and a rocking chair six hours, calculate the production overhead cost to be charged to each unit of product for the machine department.

Question 7.5

Barry Furniture Company finishing department is labour intensive, and a percentage on direct labour cost is to be used to absorb the finishing department production overheads to cost units. The budgeted finishing department overheads are £219,350 for next year and the budgeted departmental direct labour costs are £107,000 for the same period.

Required

i) Calculate the production overhead cost absorption rate for the year for the finishing department.

ii) The finishing department handles the dining chairs and tables and rocking chairs. The normal direct labour cost incurred in the department by each product is as follows:

	Direct labour cost per unit £
Dining chair	6
Dining table	14
Rocking chair	20

Calculate the production overhead cost to be charged to each product using a percentage on direct labour cost as a method of cost absorption.

Hint: This method differs from the others previously considered so far because a percentage rate is used. In these cases the calculation is:

$$\frac{\text{Total budgeted cost centre production overheads} \times 100}{\text{Total budgeted direct labour costs}}$$

Question 7.6

Barry Furniture Company is considering using a production overhead cost absorption rate for the finishing department using a percentage on direct material

cost as a basis. The budgeted production overheads for the department are
£219,350 and the budgeted total direct material costs are £109,675.

Required

i) Calculate the finishing department overhead cost absorption rate based on a
percentage on direct material cost.

ii) The normal direct material costs for each of the three products is as
follows:

	Direct material cost per unit £
Dining chair	4
Dining table	26
Rocking chair	10

Calculate the production overhead cost to be charged to each unit of product
using a percentage on direct material cost absorption rate.

Question 7.7

Using the information for *Barry Furniture Company* in Questions 7.5 and 7.6
above, calculate the production overhead cost rate for the finishing department
based on a percentage on prime cost rate for absorbing overheads and determine
the overhead to be absorbed by each product. There are no direct expenses. Work
to the nearest pound.

Question 7.8

Nelson Machinery Ltd's annual budget contains the following information:

Direct labour:

Machine Shop	6,000 hours @ £10 per hour
Paint Shop	9,000 hours @ £8 per hour

Production overheads:

Indirect labour	£5,000
Salaries	£10,000
Depreciation	£15,000
Maintenance	£11,000
Rent, rates, etc.	£21,000

Cost centre information:

	Machine shop	Paint shop
Plant valuation	£45,000	£30,000
Maintenance	£7,000	£4,000
Floor area	7,000 sq m	3,500 sq m
Number of employees	6	9

Required

i) Calculate an overhead absorption rate for each cost centre based on a rate per direct labour hour.

ii) From the following information, calculate the total production cost of jobs 42 and 99:

	Job 42	Job 99
Direct materials	£76	£124
Sub-contract work	£115	–
Direct wages:		
Machine shop	9 hours	11 hours
Paint shop	–	7 hours

Question 7.9

The assembly department at *Tenby Ltd* has budgeted overheads for the year at £210,000 and has chosen a percentage on direct labour cost as a method of overhead absorption, budgeting direct labour at £84,000 for the period. The assembly department's actual direct labour cost incurred was £75,000.

Required

i) Calculate the overhead absorbed for the year.

ii) Calculate the amount of over-recovery or under-recovery.

Question 7.10

If the finishing department at *Ogmore Ltd*'s actual overhead expenditure was £792,000 (see section 7.11), calculate the volume, expenditure and total variances for the year.

Question 7.11

If *Tenby Ltd*'s assembly department had incurred actual overhead expenditure of £185,000 (see Question 7.9), calculate the volume, expenditure and total variances for the year.

Question 7.12

Machine Parts Ltd has two production cost centres (machine and assembly) and one service cost centre (maintenance). The company calculates absorption rates monthly, based on the budgeted results for that month. Maintenance costs are apportioned to production cost centres in proportion to the total costs which are incurred by those cost centres. The actual results for January were as follows:

	Machine £	Assembly £	Maintenance £
Overheads incurred:			
Indirect materials	550	450	230
Indirect labour	1,280	975	840
Rent and rates	240	180	80
Supervision	800	560	200
Depreciation of machinery	700	100	150
Light and heat	100	80	30
Other expenses	20	25	40

	Machine	Assembly
Operating time:		
Machine hours	300 hours	
Direct labour hours		4,800 hours
Budgeted results:		
Overheads	£4,200	£2,800
Machine hours	280 hours	
Direct labour hours		4,200 hours

Required

i) Calculate the overhead absorption rate for January.

ii) Prepare a statement to show how the total overhead for the month is borne by each of the cost centres.

iii) Calculate the to be over-recovery or under-recovery of overhead for the month for each production department.

Question 7.13*

Princetown Products Ltd has calculated the overhead rates for the current year ending next 31 December 20X1 for two of its departments A and B from the following budgets:

	Department A £	Department B £
Indirect materials	9,000	15,000
Indirect labour	50,000	4,000
Supervisors' salaries	15,000	3,000
Canteen costs	5,000	1,000
Depreciation		
Factory buildings	4,000	12,000
Factory equipment	3,000	33,000
Repairs and maintenance	2,000	10,000
Power and light	1,000	3,000
Maintenance	1,000	4,000
Total overheads	90,000	85,000

Budgets for direct labour costs, direct labour hours and machine hours for the current year are as follows:

	Department A	Department B
Direct labour costs	£150,000	£23,375
Direct labour hours	15,000 hours	2,125 hours
Machine hours	3,000 hours	42,500 hours

During January the firm completed three orders which used the facilities of Departments A and B only. Details of the relevant data and costs are as follows:

	Job 1	Job 2	Job 3
Direct material costs	£550	£740	£950
Direct labour costs:			
Department A	£1,104	£2,040	£5,060
Department B	£270	£304	£638
Direct labour hours:			
Department A	120 hours	200 hours	300 hours
Department B	24 hours	26 hours	55 hours
Machine hours:			
Department A	25 hours	45 hours	55 hours
Department B	400 hours	500 hours	1,000 hours

Required

i)   Calculate the possible overhead recovery rates for the two departments, using the following bases:

  a)   direct labour costs

  b)   direct labour hours

  c)   machine hours

ii) Examine the data carefully and recommend which of the three methods of overhead recovery in (i) above should be used by each department. Give reasons for your choice.

iii) Calculate the total production costs of each of the three jobs using your chosen method of overhead cost absorption.

Question 7.14

Marine Motors Ltd manufactures two models of engine. The company has two production departments, a machine shop and an assembly department, as well as a canteen which serves all the employees. The budgeted sales and costs for the next year are as follows:

	Albatross	Buzzard
Selling price per unit	£600	£700
Sales/production volume	2,000 units	2,500 units
Material costs per unit	£80	£50
Direct labour		
Machine shop		
(£10 per hour)	50 hours/unit	60 hours/unit
Assembly department		
(£8 per hour)	40 hours/unit	40 hours/unit
Machine hours		
Machine shop	30 hours/unit	80 hours/unit
Assembly department	10 hours/unit	–

	Machine shop	Assembly dept	Canteen	Total
Production overhead				
Variable	£260,000	£90,000	–	£350,000
Fixed	£420,000	£300,000	£160,000	£880,000
Total	£680,000	£390,000	£160,000	£1,230,000
Number of employees	150	90	10	
Floor area (sq m)	40,000	10,000	10,000	

Required

i) Advise the company on the method of overhead absorption which should be used for each department. Give reasons for your choice.

ii) Calculate an appropriate overhead absorption rate for each production department.

iii) Calculate the total budgeted cost per unit of each model of engine.

iv) Assuming that the company operates a full absorption costing system, calculate the effect on budgeted profit for next year if the actual unit costs are as predicted, except that sales and production of the Albatross engine are 300 units more than budget. (You may need to refer to the behaviour of fixed and variable costs when production levels change given in Chapter 3.)

OBJECTIVE TEST* *(tick the appropriate box)*

i) The total cost absorbed is obtained from the formula:

   a) actual production × actual absorption rate ☐

   b) budgeted production × actual absorption rate ☐

   c) actual production × budgeted absorption rate ☒

   d) budgeted production × budgeted absorption rate ☐

ii) Production can be measured as:

   a) direct labour costs ☐

   b) direct material costs ☐

   c) prime costs ☐

   d) none of these ☐

   e) all of these ☒

iii) The best overhead absorption cost rates are based on:

   a) actual cost ☐

    b)   actual production ☐

    c)   time ☒

    d)   none of these ☐

iv) The volume variance is the difference between:

    a)   total cost recovered and total cost incurred ☐

    b)   total cost recovered and total cost budgeted ☒

    c)   total cost budgeted and total cost incurred ☐

    d)   none of these ☐

v) The total overhead variance is the difference between:

    a)   total cost recovered and total cost incurred ☒

    b)   total cost recovered and total cost budgeted ☐

    c)   total cost budgeted and total cost incurred ☐

    d)   none of these ☐

vi) The expenditure variance is the difference between:

    a)   total cost recovered and total cost incurred ☐

    b)   total cost recovered and total cost budgeted ☐

    c)   total cost budgeted and total cost incurred ☒

    d)   none of these ☐

ASSIGNMENT

Brisbane Briefcases Ltd

Context

You are the assistant to the chief accountant of *Brisbane Briefcases Ltd* who has gone home ill with suspected flu. The managing director bursts into your office with the news that he has arranged a meeting with Sydney Suitcases Ltd tomorrow with a view to discussing the possibility of setting up a jointly owned plant to produce a new range of leather briefcases. He already has some projected data previously supplied by the chief accountant, but asks you to present the data in a more easily understandable form for tomorrow's meeting.

Four types of briefcases are planned and the planned monthly data are as follows:

Type	Selling price £ per unit	Production units	Sales units
Deluxe	100	400	200
Excel	75	400	100
Swish	50	300	200
Flash	50	200	100

Direct costs per unit:

Type		Direct Wages Costs		
	Materials £	Cutting £	Making £	Finishing £
Deluxe	11.00	3.00	4.50	6.00
Excel	9.50	2.00	3.00	4.00
Swish	8.00	1.00	1.50	2.00
Flash	8.00	1.00	1.50	2.00

The total figures per month:

	£	£
Material purchases		14,400
Production overheads:		
Allocated: Cutting	1,000	
Making	2,250	
Finishing	1,000	
		4,250
Apportioned:		5,625
Administration overheads		8,480
Selling and distribution overheads		9,334

125

It is company practice

- to value finished goods stock at full production cost (prime cost plus production overheads);
- to apportion production overheads on the basis of departmental direct wages;
- to charge other overheads to products using the basis of the full production cost of goods sold;
- to ignore work in progress.

Student activities

Rearrange the data for the managing director's meeting showing:

i)   Material cost of production, per product

ii)   Direct wages, per product and per department

iii) Departmental overhead absorption rates

iv)   Total production costs, per product

v)   Overhead absorption, per product

vi)   Value of closing stock of raw materials

vii) Value of closing stock of finished goods, by product

viii) Sales, by product

ix)   Production cost of goods sold, by product

x)   Profit and loss account, analysed by product

Format

Tables of data, with calculations and comments where considered necessary.

Objectives

The student should show an appreciation and understanding of:

- cost classification
- cost allocation
- cost apportionment
- cost absorption
- budgeting
- stock valuations

References

Chapters 2 to 7.

CHAPTER 8

Marginal costing

1 OBJECTIVES

At the end of this chapter you should be able to:

- explain what is meant by marginal costing;
- appreciate the difference between marginal costing and absorption costing;
- understand what is meant by fixed and variable costs;
- understand the uses of marginal costing in decision making;
- appreciate the strengths and weaknesses of marginal costing;
- understand the profit measurement implications of using marginal costing.

2 INTRODUCTION

We saw in Chapter 7 how *absorption costing* was used to build up the cost of a product or service. Direct costs are directly charged to cost units because they are directly identifiable with them, and production overheads are charged to the product by absorption techniques. Other overheads, such as administration, selling and distribution overheads, are often added to the product costs as a percentage of total production cost.

In general, absorption costing does not take into account cost behaviour considerations; it charges both variable and fixed overheads to the product. In Chapter 3 we considered how costs can be analysed into variable and fixed costs. *Marginal costing*, also known as variable or direct costing, is the costing system which builds up product costs taking into consideration cost behaviour. Review Chapter 3 before continuing further.

3 COST BEHAVIOUR

In simple terms, costs may be classified as variable or fixed in nature. *Variable costs* are those costs which, in total, increase or decrease in sympathy with production or activity levels. As production changes, so the variable costs will also tend to change in proportion to those production levels. *Marginal costs* are those variable costs expressed as a rate per unit of production. This analysis, therefore, usually expresses marginal cost as a constant rate per unit. Examples are direct materials, consumable materials, power and direct labour cost.

Notice that direct labour cost is treated here as a variable cost, which assumes that labour cost is capable of being adjusted according to activity levels. Clearly this is only true if labour is rewarded on a piecework basis, that is, payment is made per unit produced. This is rarely the case in a modern legislative environment, where labour contracts give security of employment, making difficult the termination of employment contracts in the short term. However, attempts are made in practice to record labour as a variable cost by charging only productive time as direct labour. Any idle or non-productive time is treated as an overhead cost.

In examination questions treat all product direct costs, including direct labour, as variable in nature unless there are indications to the contrary. Variable costs may make up some of the production overheads (power and consumable materials), and other overheads such as administration, selling and distribution may also include elements of variable costs. Be prepared for some variable selling and distribution overheads to vary according to sales volume rather than production levels.

Fixed costs are those costs which remain unchanged, in total, irrespective of changes in production or activity.

4 | MARGINAL COSTING

In marginal costing, only the variable costs are charged to products or cost units. The total cost and profit *per unit* are not calculated, but by deducting the marginal cost from the selling price, we arrive at the unit contribution for each product. Thus, marginal costing is different from total absorption costing which charges all production costs, both variable and fixed, to the products or cost units. In marginal costing, profit is finally calculated by deducting the fixed overheads *in total* for the period from the *total* contribution for the period.

A statement which shows variable and fixed costs separately, with a calculation of the contribution is known as a *marginal* or *variable costing statement*.

Example

Marginal or variable costing statement

	Per × Production	=	Total
	unit 5,000 units		
	£		£
Sales price	40 Sales revenue		200,000
Less Marginal costs:			
Direct materials	6		30,000
Direct labour	5		25,000
Direct expenses	2		10,000
Variable production overheads	5		25,000

Variable selling overheads	3		15,000
Total marginal cost	21	Total variable costs	105,000
Unit contribution	19	Total contribution	95,000
		Fixed overheads:	
		Production	20,000
		Administration	15,000
		Selling	10,000
		Distribution	10,000
		Total fixed overheads	55,000
		Total profit	40,000

Notice in the above marginal cost statement that:

- The fixed overheads are not expressed as a rate per unit. This is because the fixed cost per unit will change according to the number of units produced; the greater the number of units produced, the lower the fixed cost per unit.

- The total fixed production overheads are treated as lump sums chargeable against the contribution. This is because under a marginal costing system the fixed overheads are not charged to the product, but rather treated as a period cost.

- The other overheads, administration, selling and distribution, are also analysed into variable and fixed elements. The variable cost element can be expressed as a marginal cost per unit, whereas the fixed cost element is treated as a lump sum period cost, similar to fixed production overheads.

- The variable production overheads are often charged to the product by absorption-like techniques. It is important in these circumstances that the bases for absorbing the variable production overheads are themselves variable in nature, and therefore the use of a rate per direct labour hour or a percentage on direct labour cost are common bases for variable overhead cost absorption.

- The way marginal costing may be used for *decision making* can be seen from the statement. The impact on profits of a change in production/sales can be determined by the change in the total contribution. An increase in production would increase profits in the short term by an amount equal to the product of the contribution per unit and the increased number of units produced.

5 | PROFIT MEASUREMENT

Apart from the use of marginal costing for *decision making*, its other major use is for the determination of profit or *profit measurement*. Just as absorption costing is used to value work in progress and stocks of finished goods at total production cost up to the stage of production reached, so marginal costing is used to value these items at marginal cost. The difference in the stock valuations will be that absorption costing includes an element of fixed production overheads, whereas marginal costing valuations are based on marginal or variable costs only.

The valuation of stocks is important in determining the amount of profit or loss for a particular accounting period. It follows, therefore, that methods of stock valuation which give different valuations will also result in different profit levels. The two accounting systems are shown diagrammatically in sections 8.6 and 8.7 below.

6 ABSORPTION COSTING EFFECTS

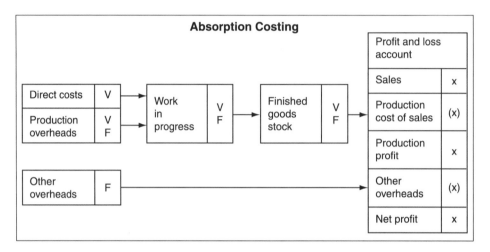

The diagram shows that the direct costs, sometimes known as the prime costs, are regarded as variable in nature, and these, together with both variable and fixed production overheads, are charged into work in progress by absorption costing techniques. As work in progress is completed, the accumulated costs are transferred to finished goods stock, which is therefore valued on the basis of direct costs plus all production overheads. Finally, when the finished goods are sold, the cost value of the goods sold are taken from stock and charged against sales in the profit and loss account to obtain the production or gross profit.

The other overheads are the administration, selling and distribution overheads which, unlike the production overheads, are not inventoried, but charged as a period cost against profits in the profit and loss account to give the net profit. Although the other overheads are described in the diagram as fixed, it is possible that some of the selling and distribution overheads may vary according to sales volume, but this does not materially alter their treatment in an absorption costing environment.

7 MARGINAL COSTING EFFECTS

The diagram below shows that only variable direct costs and variable production overheads are inventoried, so that when the goods sold are taken from finished goods stock they are charged against sales in the profit and loss account at marginal or variable cost. This enables the contribution to be shown in the profit and loss account as the difference between the sales and the variable cost of sales.

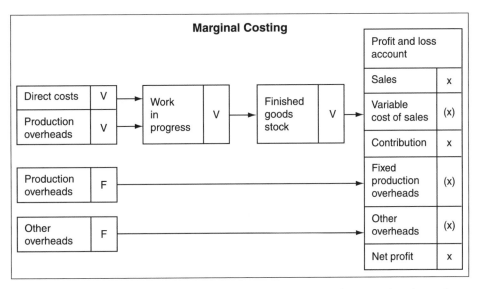

The fixed production overheads, together with the other overheads such as administration, selling and distribution, are charged to the profit and loss account as period costs. None of these fixed costs are inventoried or used in the valuation of either work in progress or finished goods.

You should now be able to attempt tasks 8.1 and 8.3 at the end of this chapter.

8   CALCULATION OF DIFFERENT PROFITS

An organization will, in practice, use only one of the two systems. However, the choice of system may be influenced by the way profits are affected in the short term by each of the systems. Over the longer term, however, the impact upon profits is to smooth out the differences between the two systems.

Example

Kingswood Products Ltd is a small company which makes and sells a single product, and the following data refer to three accounting periods. The company operates an absorption costing system, and the chief executive asks for a summary of each period's profit and loss account under *absorption costing* rules. He further wishes to see what the profits would be if *marginal costing* rules are used.

	Period 1 Units	Period 2 Units	Period 3 Units
Production	600	500	700
Sales	500	500	750

Planned or budgeted costs for each period were as follows, and these were actually incurred:

	£
Selling price per unit	60
Marginal cost per unit	45
Fixed overheads for each period	5,200

Budgeted levels of activity 650 units

Solution

(i) *Absorption costing*

	Period 1			Period 2			Period 3		
	Units	Rate	£	Units	Rate	£	Units	Rate	£
Sales	500	60	30,000	500	60	30,000	750	60	45,000
Cost of sales:									
Opening stock	–	–	–	100	53	5,300	100	53	5,300
Variable costs	600	45	27,000	500	45	22,500	700	45	31,500
Fixed costs*	600	8	4,800	500	8	4,000	700	8	5,600
	600	53	31,800	600	53	31,800	800	53	42,400
less Closing stock	100	53	5,300	100	53	5,300	50	53	2,650
Cost of sales	500	53	26,500	500	53	21,200	750	53	39,750
Apparent profit	500	7	3,500	500	7	3,500	750	7	5,250
Over/(under) recovery of fixed costs**	(50	8	400)	(150	8	1,200)	50	8	400
Absorption profit	500		3,100	500		2,300	750		5,650

*The fixed overheads charged in the profit and loss account under an absorption costing system is based on the production × fixed overhead absorption rate. The fixed overhead absorption rate is based on budgeted fixed overheads divided by the budgeted production, in this case £5,200/650 units = £8 per unit.
**Where the actual level of activity achieved is different from the budgeted level of activity, an over- or under-recovery or absorption of costs will arise equal to the difference between the actual and budgeted levels of activity, multiplied by the fixed overhead absorption rate, £8 per unit in this case. This arises because the actual production volume is either inadequate to recover fixed costs (an under-recovery), or alternatively are greater than the level of production needed to recover those costs (an over-recovery).

(ii) *Marginal costing*

	Period 1			Period 2			Period 3		
	Units	Rate	£	Units	Rate	£	Units	Rate	£
Sales	500	60	30,000	500	60	30,000	750	60	45,000
Cost of sales:									
Opening stock	–	–	–	100	45	4,500	100	45	4,500
Variable costs	600	45	27,000	500	45	22,500	700	45	31,500
	600	45	27,000	600	45	27,000	800	45	36,000
less Closing stock	100	45	4,500	100	45	4,500	50	45	2,250
Cost of sales	500	45	22,500	500	45	22,500	750	45	33,750
Contribution	500	15	7,500	500	15	7,500	750	15	11,250
Fixed costs			5,200			5,200			5,200
Marginal profit	500		2,300	500		2,300	750		6,050

Differences in profits:

	Period 1	Period 2	Period 3
Absorption profits	3,100	2,300	5,650
Marginal profits	2,300	2,300	6,050
Differences	800	–	(400)

The differences in profits are due to the different methods of stock valuation. The stock is valued under absorption costing rules to include an element of fixed overheads, whereas under marginal costing the stock is valued at marginal cost. Under absorption costing an element of fixed overheads incurred during the period is carried forward to the next period in the closing stock, therefore the differences in profit are made up of the change in stock levels (the difference between the opening and closing stocks) over the period at the fixed overhead absorption rate, in this case £8. Thus:

Period 1	Period 2	Period 3
£	£	£
+100 units @ £8 = 800	no change	−50 units @ £8 = (400)

Conclusions

Some general conclusions can be drawn from the solution to the question.

- When stocks increase over the period (see period 1), i.e. when production volumes exceed sales, profits under absorption costing rules will tend to be greater than those under marginal costing rules because under the former some of the fixed overheads are carried forward to the next period in the increased stock.

- When stocks do not change over a period (see period 2), i.e. production and sales volumes are equal, profits under both methods are the same.

- When stocks reduce over a period (see period 3), i.e. sales exceed production, profits under absorption costing rules will tend to be lower than those under marginal costing rules. This is because under the former some fixed overheads are brought forward from the previous period to be borne by the period where sales exceed production.

- The fixed overheads included in the stock valuations under absorption costing rules are based on budgeted rates and, provided the differences between actual and budgeted are not excessive, are not necessarily affected by actual costs incurred.

> *You should now be able to attempt questions 8.4, 8.5 and 8.6 at the end of the chapter.*

| 9 | ARGUMENTS FOR THE USE OF MARGINAL COSTING |

- A strong argument against the incorporation of fixed overheads into product costs is that fixed overheads incurred are unrelated to production levels and their inclusion in product costs is on an arbitrary basis. Fixed overheads can only apply to one level of activity when expressed as a rate per unit of product. This is because the rate per unit for fixed overheads will fall as production rises and increase as production falls.

- Where many products are produced, the general fixed overheads which each product will bear are based on arbitrary apportionments of those costs. This strengthens the argument for calculating the respective *contributions* from each of the products and treating the fixed overheads as a lump sum charge against the sum of those contributions.

- The use of marginal costing for stock valuation purposes means that profits are related more to levels of sales volume rather than production. In an extreme case where no sales are made, the loss for the period would be equal to the fixed overheads incurred because none of the fixed overheads are inventoried, but charged against sales. It also ensures a conservative approach to profitability in not carrying forward fixed overheads in stocks which might not be saleable in the future.

- Marginal costing is useful in facilitating decision making. The unit contributions from each product will represent the differential profit or loss which would arise from changes in sales activity in the short term. Similarly, the contribution shown by a particular business segment would represent the impact on profits if that segment were eliminated. Even organizations which do not use a marginal costing system for cost ascertainment must use *ad hoc* marginal costing data in decision making.

Example

Kingsfield Productions PLC is a company which operates on a single site but has organized itself into business segments. The general fixed overheads are apportioned across the segments, but because *Kingsfield* analyses its costs according to cost behaviour, it is able to provide a marginal costing segmental analysis (see below). The management is considering closing down segment D, but asks your advice.

Kingsfield Productions PLC
Summarized Income Statements

	A	B	C	D
	£'000	£'000	£'000	£'000
Sales	300	700	400	600
Variable costs	150	400	200	400
Contribution	150	300	200	200
Fixed overheads	100	200	150	250
Profit/(loss)	50	100	50	(50)

Solution

Because the fixed overheads are general fixed overheads and are apportioned across segments they will be unaffected by the elimination of any single segment. The apportionments are on arbitrary bases with a view to making each segment bear an equitable share of the fixed overheads.

The elimination of segment D would reduce overall profits by its present contribution, namely £200,000. Current overall profits are £150,000, and on the elimination of segment D the loss would be £50,000. This is because D's variable costs would be avoidable, but the fixed overheads currently borne by segment D would need to be borne by the remaining segments, as follows (totals only):

	Eliminate Segment D £'000	Retain Segment D £'000
Sales	1,400	2,000
Variable costs	750	1,150
Contribution	650	850
Fixed overheads	700	700
Profit/(Loss)	(50)	150

Other things being equal, segment D should be retained.

> *You should now be able to attempt question 8.7 at the end of this chapter.*

10 ARGUMENTS FOR THE USE OF ABSORPTION COSTING

- Fixed overheads are as much part of total cost as variable costs and represent the cost of resources which are essential to carry out the production activity. There is every reason, therefore, for fixed overheads to be included as part of product cost.

- Although the apportionment of fixed overheads may be argued to be arbitrary, it is essential that they are included in product cost so that ultimately all costs are included when establishing prices and measuring profitability.

- The inclusion of fixed production overheads in stock valuations means that where sales are low then they would not be required to bear the fixed overheads for the period, as under marginal costing. Absorption costing causes fixed costs to be inventoried and carried forward to a period when the sales are actually made.

- SSAP 9, the accounting standard which determines the method to adopt for stock valuation in published accounts, favours the absorption approach.

Whilst stock valuation for management accounting purposes could adopt a system not approved by accounting standards, it would make sense to adopt a consistent approach for both management and financial accounting.

> *You should now be able to attempt task 8.2 and the objective test at the end of this chapter.*

STUDENT ACTIVITIES (* *denotes questions with answers at the end of the book*)

Task 8.1
Your chief executive has attended an accounting course where he was told that different accounting systems cause different levels of profit to be revealed. He doesn't understand how this can come about, and he asks you to write a paper to the board of directors explaining how different profits arise from the respective use of absorption costing and marginal costing techniques. Give examples to illustrate your reasoning.

Task 8.2
There are strong arguments both in favour of and against the use of marginal costing systems within a manufacturing organization. List those arguments, and explain each one. On balance, do you favour the use of marginal costing, or some alternative system? Give reasons for your preference.

Task 8.3
Construct two diagrams which illustrate the respective systems of marginal and absorption costing, and draw up notes which explain the diagram you have constructed.

Question 8.4
Kingsbridge PLC makes and sells a single product. The following budgets apply to the four quarters of the year:

	Quarter 1 Units	Quarter 2 Units	Quarter 3 Units	Quarter 4 Units
Production	200	230	200	220
Sales	160	220	240	200

The costs and revenue for the year are budgeted at:

	£
Marginal cost per unit	45
Selling price per unit	85
Total fixed costs	18,700

Required

a) Prepare abridged profit statements for each quarter based on

    i)   absorption costing

    ii) marginal costing.

b) Reconcile the profits shown by each method for each quarter.

Question 8.5

The following data were taken from the books of *Greens Ltd*, which makes and sells a single product:

	£ per unit
Selling price	75
Direct material	20
Direct labour	5
Variable overhead	10

Fixed production overheads are budgeted at £500,000 per annum, and budgeted production levels are 25,000 per annum.

The following pattern of sales and production are anticipated for the first two quarters of the year:

	Quarter 1 Units	Quarter 2 Units
Sales	5,000	5,500
Production	6,500	5,000

There was no opening stock at the beginning of the year.

Required

a) Prepare profit statements for each of the two quarters under

    i)   marginal costing rules

    ii) absorption costing rules.

b) Reconcile the two profits for each quarter shown in (a) above.

Question 8.6*

Cleeve Products Ltd produce and sell a single product, for which the budgeted details per unit are as follows:

	£
Selling price	43.50
Variable costs per unit:	
Direct labour	6.00
Direct materials	6.50

Total fixed overheads are £96,000 per annum and variable overheads are 200 per cent of direct labour. Annual budgeted production is 24,000 units.

In the month of January, when actual production was 2,200 units, it exceeded sales by 300 units.

Required

Calculate the profit for the month of January using both absorption and marginal costing techniques.

Question 8.7

Budgets for next year for *National Products Ltd* show the following:

	Product A	Product B	Product C
Sales (units)	200,000	340,000	210,000
	£	£	£
Unit selling price	15	16	7
Unit variable costs	7	16	5
Directly attributable			
Fixed costs	180,000	345,000	260,000

General fixed overheads are apportioned between products according to sales values and amount to £2,973,000.

National is considering the elimination of product C because of its poor performance.

Required

a) Calculate the budgeted profit for each product, A, B and C.

b) Recalculate the budgeted profit on the assumption that C is discontinued if sales of A and B are unaffected.

c) Advise *National* whether the elimination of C is justified.

d) Calculate the percentage increase in the sales volume of B required to compensate for the effect on profit of a 10 per cent reduction in its selling price. State any assumptions made.

OBJECTIVE TEST* (tick the appropriate box)

i) Marginal costing is mainly used for:

    a) profit measurement ☐

    b) decision making ☐

    c) neither of these ☐

    d) both of these ☐

ii) Marginal costing is preferable to absorption costing because:

    a) its use is recommended by SSAP 9 ☐

  b) it includes fixed production overheads in product costs ☐

  c) it is better for decision making ☐

  d) it includes administration, selling and distribution overheads
      in the product costs ☐

iii) Profits under marginal costing are related to:

  a) production levels ☐

  b) sales levels ☐

  c) both ☐

  d) neither ☐

iv) The total contribution is equal to sales revenue minus:

  e) fixed production costs ☐

  f) all fixed costs ☐

  g) variable costs ☐

  h) direct costs ☐

  v) Profits under absorption costing are greater than under marginal
      costing when:

  a) sales exceed production ☐

  b) production exceeds sales ☐

  c) production equals sales ☐

  d) all of these ☐

  e) none of these ☐

CHAPTER 9

Activity-based costing

1 OBJECTIVES

At the end of this chapter you should be able to:

- understand the reasons for the current developments in management accounting;
- understand just-in-time management;
- understand activity-based costing;
- understand throughput accounting;
- understand backflush accounting.

2 INTRODUCTION

We have explained in earlier chapters that absorption costing is concerned with the collection of costs by product, cost object or cost unit and described how production overhead costs are absorbed by those products by the establishment of overhead absorption rates. If you do not remember the way an absorption costing system operates, you should revise Chapters 6 and 7.

The absorption rates which are commonly used in manufacturing organizations include those which are based on direct labour. These rates are a rate per direct labour hour and a percentage on direct labour cost. The changes which have taken place in recent years in the manufacturing sector in many cases now preclude the use of direct labour as a basis for overhead cost absorption, and other methods of cost collection are now being developed.

3 MANUFACTURING DEVELOPMENTS

The changes which have recently taken place in manufacturing may be summarized as follows.

- *Greater mechanization* – The introduction of high technology methods of production has accelerated, and even higher levels of productivity have been achieved with the introduction of robot technology. This change has caused the overhead costs associated with the operation of machinery such as power, depreciation and maintenance to increase relative to the other costs of production.

- *Changes in the incidence of direct labour* – As that proportion of total product cost defined as production overhead has increased, so the proportion of direct labour cost has declined. Robots and advanced production techniques have replaced direct labour on the production line, and the reduction of labour cost as a proportion of total cost, in some cases to a level of less than 12 per cent, has made it increasingly more difficult to justify direct labour as a basis for absorbing overheads to products.

- *Changes to characteristics of direct labour* – In many organizations the distinction between manual and staff status has also become less well defined. Production personnel in many cases now enjoy the same benefits and conditions of employment as those formerly given only to staff employees. In many cases production personnel are no longer paid on an hourly basis but are remunerated by an annual salary. Under these circumstances direct labour costs are difficult to define, and furthermore no longer behave as a variable cost related to production levels.

- *Just-in-time developments* – There is an increasing tendency in manufacturing to produce using just-in-time (JIT) techniques. JIT is concerned with the organization of production in such a way as to minimize the levels of raw material and finished goods stocks and work in progress. If stocks are reduced, then where profitability levels need to be determined the valuation of such stocks becomes less important. You will remember from earlier chapters that valuations of opening and closing stocks are necessary in order to measure the profit made in an accounting period.

- *Value-added approach to production* – Managements are increasingly adopting a value-added approach to the operations which take place in converting raw materials into finished product. This means that managements are attempting to eliminate operations which add cost but do not add value to the product. For example, moving parts and materials within the organization, quality control checks, inspection and testing are all regarded as non-value added activities to be eliminated provided the final product quality is not impaired.

4 | DRAWBACKS OF ABSORPTION COSTING

Absorption costing techniques have long been used in manufacturing industry to establish product costs for both stock valuation purposes and for profit measurement. However it is recognized that traditional absorption costing techniques suffer from a number of drawbacks. The major drawbacks are described below.

- *The encouragement of production for finished stock* – Because overhead absorption rates are based on budgeted projections then, provided actual costs do not exceed budgeted levels, when actual production exceeds budgeted production levels an over-recovery of fixed production overheads results. An over-recovery of overheads is normally treated as an addition to profits, and thus profits may be increased where additional production is achieved even though it is not sold. It should be appreciated that this approach may only be effective in increasing profits in the short term as the increased closing stock of one period becomes the opening stock of the succeeding period. Nevertheless, there exists in absorption costing an inherent encouragement to produce for stock.

- *Valuation of stocks is essentially for financial accounting purposes* – Stock valuation is a necessary requirement for the production of the published financial accounts of an enterprise to ensure that the costs incurred in the creation of those stocks are charged against the sales only when those stocks are sold. You will recall that there are a number of alternatives applied to stock valuation, including first-in-first-out (FIFO), last-in-first-out (LIFO) and average cost (AVCO), applicable both to marginal and absorption costing. Each method will result in different measures of profit for a period, and it is argued that these alternative approaches to stock valuation have little impact on the true performance of an organization, but are mechanisms to enable financial accounts to be produced in conformity with certain rules. In general, however, absorption costing values stocks and work in progress at total production cost in conformity with Statement of Standard Accounting Practice No. 9.

- *Costs are not incurred solely on a direct labour basis* – Absorption costing often uses direct labour as a basis for absorbing production overhead costs by the product in spite of the fact that many of the overhead costs are fixed and not incurred on the same basis as, or are driven by, direct labour. It is recognized that other cost drivers exist, and that a multitude of activities throughout the organization may cause costs to be incurred. For example, it may not be appropriate to charge material handling costs to products based on the direct labour incurred. In producing those products such costs may be more likely to be driven by the number of issues to production based on batch size or, alternatively, the units of raw material used by each product produced.

- *Fixed costs tend to be independent of production levels* – Absorption costing often charges fixed costs to products based on production volumes, a basis which fails to recognize that fixed costs tend to be incurred independent of production levels. This approach fails to recognize the activities or cost drivers which cause such fixed costs to be incurred.

- *Changes in the incidence of costs* – Changes in manufacturing techniques have caused the incidence of fixed costs to increase, and absorption costing techniques have found it difficult to accommodate these higher fixed costs on a rational basis. Absorption costing continues to use direct labour-based approaches for overhead cost absorption even though there has been an increase in the proportions of fixed overheads incurred compared to direct labour cost.

- *Absorption costing and variance analysis* – The usual variance analysis associated with absorption costing and standard costing is often meaningless. For example, a favourable variance on maintenance overheads may not indicate a favourable situation when the saving has been brought about by lower maintenance activity. This may well cause greater machine downtime in the future, with all the consequences of lost production and lower profitability which this may cause. Similarly, favourable variances, or over-recoveries as described earlier, which might arise from over-activity, may be misleading if it would have been more beneficial not to have produced the additional production anyway because of lack of sales demand.

Example

Essen plc produces a range of three products, Alpha, Beta and Gamma, by means of a single process. It currently operates an absorption costing system, and the budgeted costs and production for the year to 31 December 20X1 were as follows:

	Alpha	Beta	Gamma
Production quantity (units)	4,000	3,000	1,600
Resources per unit:			
Direct materials (kilos)	4	6	3
Direct labour (minutes)	30	45	60

The budgeted direct labour rate of pay was £10 per hour, and the budgeted material cost was £2 per kilo. Production overheads in total were budgeted at £99,450 and were absorbed to products using a rate per direct labour hour.

Required

Prepare a statement for management showing the unit costs and total costs for each product for the year ended 31 December 20X1 using the absorption costing technique.

Solution

	Alpha	Beta	Gamma	Total
(a) Quantity (units)	4,000	3,000	1,600	–
(b) Direct labour (minutes)	30	45	60	–
(c) Direct labour hours (a × b)	2,000	2,250	1,600	5,850

Overhead rate per direct labour hour

$$= \text{Total budgeted overheads} \div \text{Total budgeted DL hours}$$
$$= £99,450 \div 5,850 \text{ hours}$$
$$= £17 \text{ per DL hour.}$$

Unit costs

	Alpha £	Beta £	Gamma £
Direct costs:			
Direct labour ($£10 \times \frac{30}{60}$)	5.00	($£10 \times \frac{45}{60}$) 7.50	($£10 \times 1$) 10.00
Direct materials ($£2 \times 4$)	8.00	($£2 \times 6$) 12.00	($£2 \times 3$) 6.00
Production overhead:			
($£17 \times \frac{30}{60}$)	8.50		
($£17 \times \frac{45}{60}$)		12.75	

	Alpha £	Beta £	Gamma £
$(£17 \times \frac{60}{60})$			17.00
Total unit costs	21.50	32.25	33.00
Number of units	4,000	3,000	1,600
Total costs	£86,000	£96,750	£52,800

5 ACTIVITY-BASED COSTING

Activity-based costing, ABC as it is more generally known, is a costing method which recognizes that costs are incurred by the activities which take place within the organization, and for each activity a cost driver may be identified. Those costs which are incurred or driven by the same cost drivers are grouped together into cost pools and the cost drivers are then used as a basis for charging the costs of each activity to the product.

A *cost pool* is a collection of costs which may be charged to products by the use of a common cost driver. A *cost driver* is any activity or series of activities which take place within an organization which cause costs to be incurred. Cost drivers are not restricted to departments or sections, as more than one activity may be identified within a department. Examples of cost pools and cost drivers are:

Cost pool	*Cost driver*
Power	Number of machine operations, machine hours
Material handling	Quantity or weight of material handled
Material receipt	Number of batches of material received
Production planning	Number of jobs planned
Sales administration	Number of customer orders received
Set-up costs	Number of jobs run
Buying	Number of orders placed

Example

Refer to the previous example of absorption costing. *Essen plc* is now considering adopting a system of activity-based costing, and before it develops the complete system the directors are keen to determine the impact which such a system would have on the existing product costs set out in the previous example. Use the existing budgets for the year ended 31 December 20X1 together with the additional information set out below.

The budgeted overheads were analysed into

	£
Material handling	29,100
Storage costs	31,200
Electricity	39,150

The cost drivers were defined as:

Material handling	Weight of materials handled
Storage costs	Number of batches of material
Electricity	Number of machine operations

Data on the cost drivers were:

	Alpha	Beta	Gamma
For complete production:			
Batches of material	10	5	15
Per unit of production:			
Number of machine operations	6	3	2

Required

Prepare a statement for the management to show the product costs for the year ended 31 December 20X1 using the principles of activity-based costing. Compare your result with the previous example which used absorption costing as a basis.

Solution

	Alpha	Beta	Gamma	Total
Quantity	4,000	3,000	1,600	–
Weight per unit (kilos)	4	6	3	–
Total weight (kilos)	16,000	18,000	4,800	38,800
Machine operations per unit	6	3	2	–
Total operations	24,000	9,000	3,200	36,200
Total batches of material	10	5	15	30

Material handling – rate per kilo = £29,000 ÷ 38,800 kilos = £0.75 per kilo
Electricity – rate per machine operation = £39,150 ÷ 36,200 operations = £1.082 per machine operation
Storage – rate per batch = £31,200 ÷ 30 batches = £1,040 per batch

Unit costs

	Alpha £	Beta £	Gamma £
Direct costs:			
Direct labour $(£10 \times \frac{30}{60})$	5.00	$(£10 \times \frac{45}{60})$ 7.50	$(£10 \times 1)$ 10.00
Direct materials $(£2 \times 4)$	8.00	$(£2 \times 6)$ 12.00	$(£2 \times 3)$ 6.00
Production overheads:			
Materials handling $(£0.75 \times 4)$	3.00	$(£0.75 \times 6)$ 4.50	$(£0.75 \times 3)$ 2.25
Electricity $(£1.082 \times 6)$	6.49	$(£1.082 \times 3)$ 3.25	$(£1.082 \times 2)$ 2.16
Storage			
$(£10 \times \frac{£1,040}{4,000})$	2.60		
$(£5 \times \frac{£1,040}{3,000})$		1.73	
$(£15 \times \frac{£1,040}{1,600})$			9.75
Total unit costs	25.09	28.98	30.16
Number of units	4,000	3,000	1,600
Total costs	£100,360	£86,940	£48,256

The difference in the total costs under the absorption and ABC approaches is due solely to the difference in the overhead borne by each of the products. The ABC system recognizes the greater proportion of the activities engaged in producing Alpha, and ensures that Alpha should also bear commensurately more overhead as a consequence.

> *You should now be able to attempt task 9.1 and question 9.3 at the end of this chapter.*

6 ADVANTAGES AND DISADVANTAGES OF ACTIVITY-BASED COSTING

The main advantages of activity-based costing are as follows.

- *A more equitable method of charging costs to products* – The products which use the activities which cause the costs to be incurred bear those costs associated with those activities in a more equitable manner. This overcomes the drawback in absorption costing where general overheads are spread over the product range using methods largely unrelated to the way costs are generated or driven.

- *Takes into consideration product complexity* – The costs charged to products relate to the production circumstances in which those products are produced. Under ABC, short runs and complex products might attract consequently higher levels of unit cost compared to long runs and simple products. This aspect would have considerable impact, therefore, in the measurement of relative product profitability compared to the absorption costing approach.

- *Costs are more closely related to activity levels* – Those costs which under absorption and marginal costing approaches are traditionally regarded as fixed in total may be treated as variable in the longer term under ABC. As a consequence ABC encourages the measurement of efficiency levels of administrative functions. For example if the cost driver for the Planning and Progress Section is regarded as the number of jobs planned, then reductions in the number of jobs could be expected to be accompanied by a commensurate reduction in the cost of that activity in the longer term.

- *Encourages a more realistic approach to stock policy* – ABC does not encourage the build up of finished goods stock in the same way as absorption costing tends to do as described earlier. In activity-based costing the over-recoveries which encourage stock build-up in absorption costing do not arise to the same extent because a greater proportion of the costs are treated as variable rather than fixed.

- *Improves cost control* – ABC reflects more closely what is happening in the production environment and identifies those elements which should be subject to managerial control. It recognizes that cost management can best be achieved through the management of those activities which cause costs to be incurred.

The *disadvantages* of activity-based costing are as follows.

- *More detailed analysis required* – A more detailed analysis of cost pools and cost drivers than necessary for absorption costing is usually required for an effective ABC system, with the consequent increase in the cost of administration of the accounting system.

- *Some simplification required* – The identification of cost pools and cost drivers is not always a straightforward exercise and it is sometimes necessary to rationalize the number of cost pools and cost drivers in the interests of reducing the complexity and cost of ABC. This may be regarded as a compromise to the ABC system.

- *Does not always conform to SSAP 9* – The ABC system encourages all costs, including selling and distribution costs, to be charged to work in progress and finished goods as product costs. This cuts across the normal basis for valuing stocks for financial accounting purposes. SSAP 9 requires stocks and work in progress to be valued at total production cost up to the stage of production reached, which would normally exclude selling and distribution costs.

- *A more complex system of absorption costing* – ABC is regarded by some as not so very different from absorption costing in that absorption rates as rates for each cost driver are still required, and furthermore a greater number of individual cost rates are required to be computed under ABC in order to recover the costs for each cost pool.

> You should now be able to attend task 9.2 and questions 9.4 and 9.5 at the end of this chapter.

7 | SUMMARY

There have been substantial changes to manufacturing systems in recent years which have been brought about by improvements in production technology and developments in management philosophies. These changes have concentrated on just-in-time and value added manufacturing systems which in turn have had an impact on the accounting systems in use within manufacturing organizations.

It is recognized that absorption costing systems suffer from a number of serious drawbacks, particularly when applied to modern manufacturing systems. The development of the activity-based costing approaches in both the manufacturing and service sectors have gone some way to overcoming the drawbacks associated with absorption costing.

> You should now be able to attempt the objective test at the end of this chapter.

Task 9.1
Draw up a list of activities which take place in the departments or sections where you work or study. Determine the most appropriate cost drivers for each activity, and the ways in which each cost driver should be measured.

Task 9.2
The company where you work has always used a system of absorption costing in establishing product costs. You feel, however, that the company would benefit from the introduction of activity-based costing (ABC) in determining product costs. Write a report to the managing director of the company setting out why ABC should be adopted, including:

i)   the drawbacks of the current absorption costing system;

ii) the benefits which might arise from the introduction of ABC;

iii) the measures which are required to be taken in order to establish a successful ABC system.

Question 9.3
Junior Ltd has produced the following monthly overhead budget:

	£
Machine running costs	51,000
Production planning	42,000
Job set-up costs	27,000
Quality control	24,600
Material receipts	32,400
Packaging	18,000
	195,000

Planned production for the month is as follows:

	Product 1	Product 2	Product 3
Production/sales (units)	6,000	8,000	4,000
Direct labour hours per unit	1 hour	1.5 hours	1 hour
Machine hours per unit	0.5 hours	1 hour	1.5 hours
Selling price per unit	£31	£41	£35
Variable costs per unit:			
Material	£8	£12	£10
Labour	£10	£15	£10

From an analysis of purchasing, stores and sales office records the following further information is available:

Per month	Product 1	Product 2	Product 3
Number of customer orders	6	20	10
Number of production runs	6	16	8
Number of component receipts	18	80	64
Number of components per unit	3	5	8

Junior Ltd currently uses absorption costing and it is concerned about the variation in gross profit per unit from the two separate absorption bases which could be used. The company is now considering the alternatives of a contribution approach which, it feels, may be more useful as it has to make product market/price decisions, or an activity-based costing approach.

Required

i) Calculate the profit per unit and the total profit, using the two possible absorption rates.

ii) Prepare a contribution statement for the budgeted demand.

iii) Prepare a statement showing the profit per unit and the total profit where the overheads are treated using an activity-based costing approach.

Question 9.4*

Hightec plc manufactures and sells two products. The following statement of profitability by product was produced for the year ended 31 March 20X6:

	£'000				
	Product A	*%*	*Product B*	*%*	*Total*
Sales	1,760	100	1,040	100	2,800
Variable production costs	440		290		730
Fixed production costs	920		490		1,410
Total costs	1,360		780		2,140
Gross profit	400	22.7	260	25.0	660
Other costs:					
General administration					140
Marketing and distribution					250
Research and development					110
					500
Net profit					160

The costs and revenues per unit for each of the products is as follows based on planned volumes which were actually achieved:

	Product A				Product B	
Planned volumes (units)	20,000				10,000	
	£				£	
Selling price		88				104
Direct materials	10			12		
Direct labour:						
Department 1 (1 hr)	6		(0.5 hr)	9		
Department 2 (0.5 hr)	2		(0.75 hr)	3		
Variable overhead:						
Department 1 (1 DLH)	2		(1.5 DLH)	3		
Department 2 (1 MH)	2		(1 MH)	7		
Fixed overhead:						
Department 1 (1 DLH)	6		(1.5 DLH)	9		
Department 2 (1 MH)	40	68	(1 MH)	40		78
Gross profit		20				26

In an attempt to more closely relate overhead expenditure to particular products, a cost investigation was undertaken. Hightec plc's budgeted and actual fixed production overheads were analysed to provide the bases upon which the overhead absorption rates were calculated.

	£'000	
Cost pool	Department 1	Department 2
Staff	60	400
Productive (power, depreciation, maintenance)	80	700
Materials procurement	30	60
Information technology	40	40
	210	1,200

Each cost pool was found to have one major cost driver whose impact and analysis was found to be as follows:

Cost pool	Cost driver	Department 1			Department 2		
		Total	Product		Total	Product	
			A	B		A	B
Staff	Numbers	5	2	3	40	15	25
Productive	Productive assets						
	(£ million)	0.5	0.2	0.3	2.0	1.2	0.8
Materials	Orders						
procurement	placed	1,200	300	900	800	400	400
Information	Computing	1,250	350	900	2,500	1,250	1,250
technology	hours						

A similar investigation into other overheads revealed the following analysis:

	£'000			
	Attributable	Product A	Product B	Total
General Administration	equally	70	70	140
Marketing	variable	40	60	100
Distribution	variable	50	100	150
Research and development	fixed	40	70	110

Required

Prepare product profitability statements using activity-based costing approaches to cost allotment.

Question 9.5

BAC plc produces printed circuit boards for computers. The business began with a large contract for a standard board for a home computer which was produced in large volumes. After two years a new customer asked for a new non-standard board which became known as the Special. The Special used some components of the Standard board and some unique to that product, but the labour time taken was the same, 2 hours per unit, and additional design and tooling costs were incurred.

As the expansion of the home computer business tailed off, BAC plc was able to fill the capacity with the production of Special boards for which a slightly higher price was obtained and although the Special was produced in smaller batches, its production levels in total were approaching those of the Standard. Data from last year's accounts (Figure 1 below) showed that 15,000 Standards and 10,000 Specials were produced.

The Marketing Department reports further pressure on the price of the Standard, and demand for the Special continues to increase, and as the net profit as a percentage of sales is already lower for Standards there is pressure to go for more Specials and fewer Standards.

There is concern, however, over what is being revealed about product profitability by the existing absorption accounting system. As a result it was decided to examine the four production cost centres and produce a list of activities, cost drivers and costs. These are shown in Figure 3, and the production overhead analysis is shown in Figure 2. It has also been established that marketing, research and development and administration overheads were all fixed, and that of the production overhead, software and support group, depreciation group and general group were also fixed for the activity levels achieved. Other production overhead is considered to vary with direct labour, the cost of which is £12 per hour.

Required

Produce an alternative income statement for 20 × 6 based on activity-based costing approaches.

Figure 1

Income Statement by product – 20X6

	Standard £	Special £	Total £
Sales	2,700,000	2,000,000	2,700,000
Direct costs:			
Materials	1,110,000	790,000	1,900,000
Labour	180,000	120,000	300,000
Production overhead	600,000	400,000	1,000,000
Total production costs	1,890,000	1,310,000	3,200,000
Gross profit	810,000	690,000	1,500,000

* Marketing, R&D and
    Administration   344,681   255,319   600,000
Net profit   465,319   434,681   900,000

    Net profit as percentage of sales   17.23%   21.73%   19.15%

(* apportioned on the bases of sales value.)

Figure 2

Production Overhead Analysis – Budget 20X6

	Production	Engineering	Material Control	Inspection
	£	£	£	£
Indirect labour group	180,000	120,000	120,000	80,000
Indirect material group	15,000	10,000	—	—
Energy group	43,000	1,000	1,000	5,000
Software and support group	30,000	40,000	180,000	—
Depreciation group	70,000	5,000	15,000	5,000
General group	25,000	20,000	20,000	15,000
	363,000	196,000	336,000	105,000
	637,000	(196,000)	(336,000)	(105,000)
	1,000,000	–	–	—

Figure 3

Investigation into support service activities – findings

Support service	Cost driver/activity	£	Units of activity occurrence per 50-week year		
			Standard	Special	Total
Production	Set-up	125,000	250	1,000	1,250
	Production orders	238,000	60	100	160
		363,000			
Engineering Department	New and redesigns (CAD)	120,000	7	23	30
	Production delays	76,000	5	40	45
		196,000			
Material Control	Placing and receiving supply orders	168,000	48	132	180
	Issuing materials	168,000	200	250	450
		336,000			
Inspection	No. of units inspected	105,000	3,000	20,000	23,000
Marketing,	Marketing	80,000	(50:50)		
R&D and	No. of promotions	64,000	14	66	80
Administation	No. of R&D projects	120,000	6	9	15
General	General R&D	120,000	(50:50)		
	Customer Liaison	80,000	40	360	400
	Other Administration	136,000	(50:50)		

OBJECTIVE TEST* *(tick the appropriate box)*

i) Absorption costing techniques suffer from:

   a) too much complexity ☐

   b) an inability to enable product unit costs to be computed ☐

   c) an inherent encouragement to produce for stock ☒

   d) a lack of the use of cost rates ☐

ii) Modern approaches to manufacturing have a tendency to:

   a) use just-in-time techniques ☒

   b) encourage production for stock ☐

   c) maximize work in progress ☐

   d) increase the proportion of direct labour cost ☐

iii) The basic assumption behind ABC is that costs are generated by:

   a) products ☐

   b) activities ☒

   c) personnel ☐

   d) production ☐

iv) The characteristics of ABC are said to be that it:

   a) takes into consideration production complexity ☒

   b) ignores production complexity ☐

   c) gives the same product costs as absorption costing ☐

   d) encourages production for stock ☐

CHAPTER 10

Process costing

/劝 的才化

At the end of this chapter you should be able to:

- understand the basics of process costing;
- understand the concept and treatment of normal losses;
- understand the concept and treatment of abnormal losses;
- understand the concept and treatment of abnormal gains;
- understand the treatment of common costs between joint products;
- understand the treatment of by-products.

2   INTRODUCTION

Process costing is the costing method which is found in an environment where production passes from one process to another until it is finally placed into stock from where it is sold. An example is the chemical industry. The characteristics of process costing are that costs are accumulated over the whole production process, and average unit costs of production are computed at each stage. Special rules are applied in process costing to the valuation of *work in progress, normal* and *abnormal losses*. It is also usual to distinguish between the main product of the system, joint products and by-products.

3   AVERAGE COST

At its simplest, where one product is produced, the costs of each process are determined and divided by the output of the process to obtain the average unit cost. In these cases the output of the process may be measured in units, e.g. kilograms or any other suitable measure appropriate to the output.

Example

Blay Processing Ltd produces the chemical Blaychem from a single process. The following costs were incurred during the month of March 20X6.

	£
Direct labour	8,460
Direct materials	30,990

Production overheads were absorbed at a rate of £275 per process hour. 30,000 kg of Blaychem were produced in the month, and the process took 42 hours. There were no process losses during the period.

Required

Calculate the average production cost per kg of Blaychem for the period.

Solution

Input	kg	£	Output	kg	£
Direct labour		8,460	Output	30,000	51,000
Direct materials	30,000	30,990			
Overheads (42 × £275)		11,550			
	30,000	51,000		30,000	51,000

$$\text{Average cost per kg} = \frac{\text{Net process costs}}{\text{Output in kg}} = \frac{£51,000}{30,000 \text{ kg}} = £1.7 \text{ per kg}$$

---

4 | NORMAL LOSSES

Losses which arise as part of the process may be *normal losses* or *abnormal losses*. Normal losses are represented by a level of loss which is regarded as acceptable, perhaps based on a historical record of losses experienced in the past. As it is axiomatic in costing that the cost of normal losses is part of the normal cost of production, then it is usual not to value the normal losses so that the cost per unit of good output is inflated so as to bear the cost of the normal loss.

Example

Continuing to use the same example, a review of past records suggests that 10 per cent of the input of chemicals into the process by weight represents a level of normal loss.

Required

Recalculate the average production cost per kg of Blaychem.

Solution

Input	kg	£	Output	kg	£
Direct labour		8,460	Output	27,000	51,000
Direct materials	30,000	30,990	Normal loss (30,000 × 10%)	3,000	–
Overheads		11,550			
	30,000	51,000		30,000	51,000

$$\text{Average cost per kg} = \frac{\text{Net process costs}}{\text{Output in kg}} = \frac{£51,000}{27,000 \text{ kg}} = £1.89 \text{ per kg}$$

This example shows that the average cost per kg has increased compared to the previous example due to the inclusion of the normal loss at nil value.

In some circumstances where the waste, loss or scrap has a small realizable value, the procedure may be to credit the process with the income from the sale of the scrap material so that the average unit cost of the good output is reduced by the income from the sale of the normal loss.

Example

Continuing to use the same example, assume that the normal waste has a saleable value of £0.25 per kg and it is accounting policy to credit the process account with the proceeds.

Required

Recalculate the average production cost per kg of Blaychem.

Solution

Input	kg	£	Output	kg	£
Direct labour		8,460	Output	27,000	50,250
Direct materials	30,000	30,990	Normal loss (3,000×£0.25)	3,000	750
Overheads		11,550			
	30,000	51,000		30,000	51,000

$$\text{Average cost per kg} = \frac{\text{Net process costs}}{\text{Output in kg}} = \frac{£50,250}{27,000 \text{ kg}} = £1.86 \text{ per kg}$$

In this example the average cost per kg has reduced compared to the previous example due to the income from the sale of waste which has reduced the overall process cost.

5   ABNORMAL LOSSES

An *abnormal loss* is any level of loss in excess of the normal loss. Because the abnormal loss should not form part of the normal cost of production it is usual to value the abnormal loss, credit the resultant value to the process account, and charge it to an abnormal loss account. The abnormal loss is usually valued on the same basis as the good output.

Example

Continuing with the same example, assume that the good output totals 26,000 kg.

Required

Calculate the abnormal loss and the revised average production cost per kg of Blaychem.

Solution

Input	kg	Rate £/kg	£	Output	kg	Rate £/kg	£
Direct labour			8,460	Output	26,000	1.86*	48,389
Direct materials	30,000		30,990	Normal loss	3,000	0.25	750
Overheads			11,550	Abnormal loss	1,000	1.86*	1,861
	30,000		51,000		30,000		51,000

$$\text{Average cost per kg} = \frac{\text{Net process costs}}{\text{Expected output}} = \frac{£51,000 - 750}{27,000 \text{ kg}} = £1.86^* \text{ per kg}$$

(* to 2 decimal places)

In this example the abnormal loss is valued on the same basis as the good output.

6 | ABNORMAL GAINS

An *abnormal gain* arises where the actual loss incurred is less than the level set for the normal loss. The same considerations apply to the abnormal gain as are applied to the abnormal loss, i.e. the abnormal gain is valued on the same basis as the good output and its value transferred from the process account to an abnormal gain account.

Example

Continuing to use the same example, assume that the good output totals 28,000 kg.

Required

Calculate the abnormal gain, and the revised average production cost per kg of Blaychem.

Solution

Abnormal gain = Normal loss – Actual loss = 3,000 kg – 2,000 kg = 1,000 kg

Input	kg	Rate £/kg	£	Output	kg	Rate £/kg	£
Direct labour			8,460	Output	28,000	1.86*	52,111
Direct materials	30,000		30,990	Normal loss	3,000	0.25	750
Overheads			11,550	Abnormal loss	(1,000)	1.86*	(1,861)
	30,000		51,000		30,000		51,000

$$\text{Average cost per kg} = \frac{\text{Net process costs}}{\text{Expected output}} = \frac{£51,000 - £750}{27,000 \text{ kg}} = £1.86^* \text{ per kg}$$

(* to 2 decimal places)

In this example the abnormal gain is valued on the same basis as the good output and the effect of the abnormal gain being deducted from the credit or output side gives the same result as adding the same amounts to the debit or input side. Either treatment is acceptable.

> You should now be able to attempt task 10.1 at the end of this chapter.

7 | WORK IN PROGRESS

Unfinished work which remains in a process at the end of an accounting period is known as *work in progress* (WIP) or *work in process*. Such work is valued on a *first-in-first-out* (FIFO) or *average cost* (AVCO) basis on transfer to the next process or finished stock. If you are not sure what these terms mean, you need to revise Chapter 2.

Example

Clifton Chemicals Ltd operates Process X in which, for the month of June 20X6, the opening work in progress of 500 units was valued at £1,500. This valuation was the same both for FIFO and AVCO bases. During the month, 1,000 units of materials were added to the process, and labour and overheads of £5,000 incurred; 1,100 units of output were passed to Process Y, and 400 units of closing work in progress remained in Process X.

Required

Value the closing work-in-progress as at 30 June 20X6 using the FIFO and the AVCO bases of valuation, and write up the process accounts.

Solution

FIFO

Input	Units	Rate £/kg	£	Output	Units	Rate £/kg	£
Opening WIP	500	3.00	1,500				
Direct materials	1,000	1.00	1,000	FG output	1,100		5,100
Direct labour				Closing WIP	400)	6.00	2,400
and overheads			5,000				
	1,500		7,500		1,500		7,500

$$\text{Closing WIP} = 400 \times \frac{£6,000}{1,000} = £2,400$$

$$\text{FG (finished goods) output} = 7,500 - 2,400 = £5,100$$

AVCO

Input	Units	Rate £/kg	£	Output	Units	Rate £/kg	£
Opening WIP	500	3.00	1,500				
Direct materials	1,000	1.00	1,000	FG output	1,100	5.00	5,500
Direct labour and				Closing WIP	400)	5.00	2,000
overheads			5,000				
	1,500		7,500		1,500		7,500

$$\text{Closing WIP} = 400 \times \frac{£7,500}{1,500} = £2,000$$

$$\text{FG (finished goods) output} = 1,100 \times \frac{7,500}{1,500} = £5,500$$

8 | EFFECTIVE UNITS

A further complication in the valuation of work in progress in process costing is that elements of the work in progress may be at different stages of completion. For example, where the work in progress at the end of the period is made up of elements of material, labour and overheads, all the material may have been input to the process, but the labour and overhead may be only, say, half complete. To accommodate these circumstances, the concept of *effective* or *equivalent units* is used to convert the work in progress to equivalent completed units. For example, 1,000 units of work in progress 50 per cent complete as to labour would represent the equivalent of 500 effective completed units for that element of cost.

Example

Pensford Processors Ltd use a system of effective units to value work in progress, which is valued at average cost (AVCO). For the month of May 20X6 the opening work in progress amounted to 400 units, 100 per cent complete as to material and 60 per cent complete as to labour and overhead, valued at £1,600 and £1,920 respectively. The closing work in progress at the end of the month was 600 units, 100 per cent and 50 per cent complete as to material and labour respectively. During the month, 3,000 units of material were input to the process at a cost of £15,400, and the labour and overhead cost was £30,630.

Required

Value the closing work in progress and write up the process account for the month of May 20X6

Solution
AVCO

| Inputs | Quantity | | Materials | | | | Labour and Overheads | | | Total |
		%	Effective units	Rate £/kg	£	%	Effective units	Rate £/kg	£	£
Costs	3,000	100	3,000		15,400				30,630	46,030
Opening WIP	400	100	400	4.00	1,600	60	240	8.00	1,920	3,520
	3,400		3,400		17,000		3,100		32,550	49,550
FG output	2,800	100	2,800		14,000		2,800		29,400	44,400
Closing WIP	600	100	600		3,000	50	300		3,150	5,150
	3,400		3,400		17,000		3,100		32,550	49,550

Although the number of effective units is different for materials (3,400) and labour (3,100), they refer to the same units of production, but to different degrees of completion. The closing work in progress is valued as follows:

$$\text{Materials} \quad \frac{£17,000}{3,400} \times 600 = £3,000$$

$$\text{Labour and Overheads} \quad \frac{£32,550}{3,100} \times 300 = £3,150$$

> You should now be able to attempt questions 10.4 and 10.5 at the end of this chapter.

---

9 | JOINT PRODUCT COSTING

The output of some processes may be made up of only one main product, but in other cases the output may be made up of two or more products. If the products are regarded to be of equal economic significance then the products are described as joint products. Where joint products arise, the cost of each product may be determined by apportioning the *joint, common* or *pre-separation process costs* incurred in producing the products in proportion to the number of units, weight or volume, of each product produced.

Example

SWK Chemicals Ltd produce 11,265 kg and 9,535 kg of joint products Alpha and Beta respectively from process X. Pre-separation costs of labour, materials and overhead are £135,200 which are to be borne in relation to weight produced.

Required

Determine the amounts of common or pre-separation costs to be borne by each product.

Solution

	kg		£
Alpha	11,265	× £6.50*	73,222.50
Beta	9,535		61,977.50
	20,800		135,200.00

$$*\frac{£135,200}{20,800} = £6.50 \text{ per kg}$$

Other common methods of apportioning joint or pre-separation costs between joint products are those of using standard values or the sales value at the point of separation. The sales value at the point of separation is the sales income from the sale of each joint product less the costs of each independent process subsequent to separation.

Example

Hughes Processing Ltd produce joint products Gamma and Delta from Process S1. 3,400 units of Gamma were immediately sold for £10.50 per kg, whereas 2,600 kg of Delta were further processed in Process S2 at a cost of £23,000 before being sold for £18 per kg. There were no process losses in Process S2. The common pre-separation costs total £38,200.

Required

Apportion the pre-separation costs of Process S1 between the products based on the sales value at split-off point, and show each product's recorded profits.

Solution

	£	%
Gamma (3,400 kg × £10.50)	35,700	60
Delta (2,600 kg × £18.00)	46,800	
Less Cost of process S2	23,000	
	23,800	40
Total sales value at split-off point	59,500	100

	Sales	Process costs S1	Process costs S2	Profit
	£	£	£	£
Gamma	35,700	(22,920) 60%	–	12,780
Delta	46,800	(15,280) 40%	(23,000)	8,520
	82,500	(38,200)	(23,000)	(21,300)

You should now to be able to attempt task 10.2 at the end of this chapter.

<table>
<tr><td>**10**</td><td>**BY-PRODUCT COSTING**</td></tr>
</table>

Where the output of a process is made up of two or more products, and they are of unequal economic significance, then the products of lesser economic significance are known as *by-products*. By-products are products of saleable value produced at the same time as the main product. Scrap or waste which has a saleable value may sometimes be regarded as a by-product, and in practice it may be difficult to differentiate between scrap and by-products. A distinguishing factor may be that by-products are often the subject of further processing or require marketing when sold.

Joint or *pre-separation costs* are not usually apportioned between *main products* and *by-products*. Rather the income which arises from the sale of the by-products may be credited to the process, so reducing the costs which should be borne by the main product. Alternative approaches are either to credit a notional value to the process so that the cost of the main product is reduced, or credit the income from the sale of the by-products to other income, so that all the costs of the process are borne by the main product.

Example

Kingswood Chemicals PLC produce 7,250 kg of a main product X from one of its chemical processes, together with 350 kg of by-product Y and 270 kg of by-product Z. The total costs of the process are £146,375, and the by-products are sold for £2.00 and £2.50 per kg respectively. The management wish to consider the effect on unit costs of product X of two alternative methods of treating by-product income.

Required

Show the effect on the cost of main product X of each of two possible methods of treatment of by-product income.

Solution

i) Credit sales income from sales of by-products to the process:

	£
Total cost of process	146,375
Sales of by-product Y (350 kg @ £2.00)	700
Sales of by-product Z (270 kg @ £2.50)	675
Amount credited to process	1,375
Net cost of process	145,000

$$\text{Cost per kg} = \frac{£145,000}{7,250 \text{ kg}} = £20.00 \text{ per kg}$$

ii) Credit sales to other income (does not affect process account):

$$£$$

Total cost of process   146,375

$$\text{Cost per kg} = \frac{£146,375}{7,250\text{kg}} = £20.19 \text{ per kg}$$

> *You should now be able to attempt task 10.3, question 10.6 and the objective test at the end of this chapter.*

STUDENT ACTIVITIES (* *denotes questions with answers at the end of the book*)

Task 10.1

Assume that you work for a chemical company which uses a system of process costing. Your Finance Manager is considering how best to treat within the costing system the various types of losses experienced by the processes. Draft a memo to your manager setting out the definitions of normal and abnormal losses and gains, and explain how they might be established and valued in the process accounts. Give numerical examples.

Task 10.2

Draft a memo to your Finance Manager to explain the alternative bases which may be used to apportion common or joint product costs between products which are produced by a process. Explain why this procedure might be considered necessary, and answer the criticism that different methods give different product costs and therefore the whole approach is a subjective one. Give numerical examples.

Task 10.3

Explain the ways in which effective or equivalent units may be used to value work in progress in a process costing system. Add a note to explain how the alternatives of first-in-first-out (FIFO) and average cost (AVCO) may be incorporated into the respective valuation process. Give numerical examples.

Question 10.4

In *Putney Processing Ltd* product X passes through three processes to completion. The costs of production are as follows:

	Process 1	Process 2	Process 3	Total
	£	£	£	£
Direct material	2,000	3,020	3,462	8,462
Direct labour	3,000	4,000	5,000	12,000
Direct expenses	500	226	–	726
Production overhead	6,000			

One thousand units at £5 each were issued to Process 1. Other information available is as follows.

	Output units	Normal loss %	Realizable value of scrap per unit £
Process 1	920	10	3
Process 2	870	5	5
Process 3	800	10	6

There was no stock of materials or work in progress in any process at the beginning or end of the period. The output of each process passes direct to the next process and finally to finished stock. Production overhead is apportioned to each process on the basis of 50 per cent of the cost of direct labour.

Required

Write up the respective process accounts, showing the treatment of normal losses and abnormal gains and losses.

Question 10.5
Keystone Chemicals Ltd operates a single process, and the information relating to the process for the month of June 20X1, when 15,000 units were produced and put into store, was as follows,

	£
Opening WIP	nil
Costs incurred for the month:	
Materials	25,000
Labour	10,000
Overheads	10,000
Closing WIP = 10,000 units	
Degree of completion:	
Materials	100%
Labour	50%
Overheads	50%

Required
Value the work in progress and prepare the process account for June 20X1.

Question 10.6*
Standard Processing Ltd produces a standard product called a Stampro by a single process. Details of the actual costs and production are as follows.

April

	£
Opening WIP (10,000 Stampros)	
Materials (100% complete)	6,400
Conversion (80% complete)	9,880

	£
Costs incurred during the month:	
Materials	48,600
Labour	17,820
Fixed overheads	65,000
Stampros	
Completed output	
Closing WIP	12,000
Materials (100% complete)	
Conversion (one sixth complete)	

May

	£
Costs incurred during the month:	
Materials (20,000 kg)	46,000
Labour 12,000 (hours)	25,000
Fixed overheads	63,000

Completed output = 90,000 units
Opening and closing WIP levels were constant.

Required

Prepare the process accounts for the months of April and May using work in progress valuations based on:

i)   the average cost (AVCO) method;

ii) the first in first out (FIFO) method.

OBJECTIVE TEST* *(tick the appropriate box)*

i)   Process costing is a form of:

    a)   Absorption costing ☐

    b)   Activity-based costing ☐

    c)   Average costing ☐

    d)   Marginal costing ☐

ii) Abnormal losses are:

    a)   normal loss less abnormal loss ☐

    b)   actual loss less normal loss ☐

    c)   actual loss plus abnormal gain ☐

    d)   abnormal gain less normal loss ☐

iii) Pre-separation costs are:

   a) common costs which are required to be shared between joint products ☐

   b) common costs which require to be shared between main and by-product ☐

   c) costs which are incurred by a product after separation point ☐

   d) process costs incurred before abnormal losses are valued ☐

iv) Pre-separation costs may be shared between products:

   a) based on the units of output produced ☐

   b) based on the sales value at split-off point ☐

   c) neither of these ☐

   d) both of these ☐

v) Sales value at split-off point may be calculated by:

   a) sales income from each product ☐

   b) notional sales value of each product from the joint process ☐

   c) sales income from each product less the cost of independent processes ☐

   d) sales income from each product plus the cost of independent processes ☐

CHAPTER 11

Other costing methods

1 | OBJECTIVES

At the end of this chapter you should be able to:

- understand the link between costing techniques and costing methods;
- understand job and batch costing;
- understand contract costing;
- understand service costing;
- use the various costing methods.

2 | INTRODUCTION

In earlier chapters we explained how the costs of products are built up by charging *direct costs* to *cost units* and adding production overheads by using methods of *cost absorption*. We have also shown you how *activity-based costing* (ABC) builds up product costs by establishing cost pools and using associated *cost drivers* to charge those costs to products or *cost units*.

In this chapter we will examine how each of these techniques is applied to various *costing methods* in order to build up unit costs. The costing method is often determined by the method of production which the business uses. The organization may produce individual products or batches of products. Alternatively, it may be concerned with producing individual jobs or contracts and in other organizations *services* are provided to customers as the main activity. In the chemical industry, for example, the production is carried out by the work passing from process to process. In each of these circumstances the appropriate costing methods may be *product costing, batch costing, job costing, contract costing, service costing* and *process costing* and may use either absorption costing or ABC to achieve unit cost. The unit cost thus derived may then be used to establish selling price if appropriately based on cost. The common aspect of all the methods is that direct costs and overheads are charged to the *cost units* or *cost objects* produced.

All methods of charging costs to cost units are based on allotting the costs to various degrees. For example, in costing services provided, the direct material element may be very small both in quantity and value, whereas in costing a product the direct material element may be substantial. The costs to be allotted are shown below.

	Cost *unit*
Direct material	X
Direct labour	X
Direct expenses	$\underline{X}$
Prime cost	X
Overheads (as appropriate):	
Production	X
Administration	X
Selling	X
Distribution	X
Research	$\underline{X}$
Total cost	$\underline{\underline{X}}$

3 | PRODUCT COSTING

Product costing is the collection of the costs of an organization by *cost unit*, where the cost unit is a product produced by the organization. In product costing, the product direct costs are direct labour, direct materials and direct expenses, and these are charged to the product usually by the use of documentation flows.

- *Direct labour* cost is charged to the product by the completion of time cards, clock cards, time sheets or direct data entry to a computer so that the time spent on producing a product is recorded. The time is then multiplied by the rate of pay in order to obtain a labour cost by product.

- *Direct material* cost is recorded either from the invoices received, where material is purchased and used by the production department on purchase, or, where material is put into store before use, materials issue notes or materials requisitions record the materials used. In each case, the materials quantities are multiplied by the issue prices to give the direct materials costs chargeable to the product.

- *Direct expenses*, because they usually represent work carried out by a third party, are charged to the product based on the invoices received.

- *The overheads* may be charged to the product by charging the overheads to cost centres by allocation or apportionment, and then absorbing the costs into the product by establishing overhead cost recovery rates, using one of a number of alternative cost absorption bases. If you are unsure of this system, revise Chapters 6 to 9 for a more detailed explanation of this approach.

In some organizations a *marginal* or *variable costing* approach is applied in obtaining product or service costs. This is where the variable costs only are charged to the *cost units* or *cost objects* and the fixed costs are regarded as period costs and are charged as a lump sum for the accounting period against sales in the profit and loss account. If your not sure how this works, revise the contents of Chapter 8.

An activity-based costing approach may also be used for product costing.

Under the ABC system costs are grouped into *cost pools*, where each cost pool is associated with a *cost driver*. Rates for each cost driver are calculated, and used to charge the cost pools to the product. This is covered in Chapter 9.

4 | JOB COSTING

Job costing is applied in organizations where the cost of each individual product or service is required. This particularly applies to organizations which produce one-off products to a particular customer's specification, and where each job may be different. It is usual in these circumstances to set up a job number for each job and to charge the direct costs to the job number, together with a share of overheads using the normal methods of allocation, apportionment and absorption. This approach is sometimes known as *specific order costing* or *job order costing*.

The following is an example of a typical job cost statement:

JOB COST SCHEDULE

Description _____   Job No: 6273

Customer ref. _____   Quantity _____

	Hours	Rate £	Cost £	Totals £
Labour cost				
Grade A	14	7.00	98.00	
Grade B	8	6.50	52.00	
Grade C	6	5.80	34.80	
Total labour cost				184.80

	Units	Rate £	Cost £	
Materials				
Code 61423	5	40.00	200.00	
Code 46146	6	37.00	222.00	
Code 32892	4	8.00	32.00	
Code 89721	1	4.00	4.00	
Total materials cost				458.00

	Hours	Rate £	Cost £	
Production overheads				
Cost centre 1	14	20.00	280.00	
Cost centre 2	8	26.00	208.00	
Cost centre 3	6	46.00	276.00	
Total overhead cost				764.00
Total production cost				1,406.80
Other overheads				
17% on total production cost				239.16
Total cost				1,645.96

In this example 'Production overheads' are absorbed to jobs as a rate per direct labour hour. 'Other overheads', which may include administration, selling and distribution costs, are absorbed as a percentage on total production cost. However, in practice other absorption methods may be used.

It is possible for an organization to set up batches of repetitive production into distinct and discrete jobs, and then apply job costing approaches in order to determine the total cost of that *batch*. In some circumstances, therefore, job costing may have similar characteristics to *batch costing*.

5 | BATCH COSTING

In many manufacturing environments, production of similar individual units of output are sometimes combined into *batches*, given a job number, and the costs of the batch are determined using the job costing techniques set out above. Individual unit costs may then be obtained by dividing the total batch cost by the number of units in the batch, so that a form of *average costing* may be resorted to.

6 | CONTRACT COSTING

Contract costing is a costing system which is applied to large contracts such as civil engineering projects (bridges and buildings) and ship and oil rig construction. Although the costing of these projects may be regarded as another form of job costing (see above), these projects possess the particular characteristics that they are long term, in that they take longer than a financial year to completion, and that a large proportion of the costs are direct costs which can be traced directly to the contract being costed.

Organizations which carry out this kind of work do not wait to the end of each contract before they take profit on the contracts. Because the contracts often last longer than a financial year, profits are taken on the contracts at the end of each financial year by valuing closing work in progress and the sales value of the work completed to date, and a proportion of profit earned to date is taken to the profit and loss account.

It is beyond the scope of this volume to cover in detail the way the interim profits are determined, but in order to take a conservative view of profits earned prior to the completion of a contract the profits are measured according to a formula which may vary according to the policy adopted by the construction company. A typical formula used to lower the interim profit appropriately is as follows.

Profit to be taken to the profit and loss account to date

$$= \frac{2}{3} \times \frac{\text{Cash received}}{\text{Work certified}} \times \text{Apparent interim profit}$$

where the cash received represents progress payments received on the contract to date, and the work certified represents the sales value of the estimated work completed to date and is usually supplied by a surveyor, architect or naval architect as appropriate.

Example

Cheddar Construction plc has won a contract to construct a bridge. The project is expected to take two years and at the end of the company's financial year, part way through the bridge contract, the following expenditure was shown on this contract account for the year ended 31 March 20X1.

	£m
Labour	1.6
Materials	0.8
Other direct costs	1.3
Share of head office and other costs	0.6
	4.3

The sales value of the work completed to date as certified by the architect was £5.0 million and the progress payments received to date amounted to £3.6 million.

Required

Calculate the profit on the contract to date which the company could reasonably take to the profit and loss account for the year ended 31 March 20X1.

Solution

The apparent profit to date is the sales value of work done less the costs incurred to date. This is £5.0 million − £4.3 million = £0.7 million. Using the formula:

$$\frac{2}{3} \times \frac{\text{Cash received}}{\text{Work certified}} \times \text{Apparent interim profit}$$

therefore, the profit to be taken to the profit and loss account is:

$$\frac{2}{3} \times \frac{\text{£3.6 million}}{\text{£5.0 million}} \times \text{£0.7 million} = \text{£0.336 million}$$

7 SERVICE COSTING

Some businesses are non-manufacturing organizations which offer services rather than products. In such organizations each service must be costed so that it is charged with the direct labour cost incurred in providing the service, any other direct expenses and a share of the organization's overheads. Any appropriate apportionment and absorption techniques which we have covered in Chapters 6 and 7, or the ABC approach covered in Chapter 9, can be used. In some cases a marginal costing approach can be used, and this is covered in Chapter 8.

Example

Kennet Garages Ltd carry out a car valet service and routine engine servicing. A system of allocation, apportionment and absorption rates is used, and the valet service has an hourly rate of £12, designed to include the recovery of consumable materials, and the engine service costs are £25 per hour plus parts.

Required

Calculate the total cost of servicing a customer's vehicle where the valet time spent was 3 hours, and 6 hours were taken to service the engine. Engine parts cost £98.

Solution

	£
Valet costs (3 hours @ £12 per hour)	36
Service costs (6 hours @ £25 per hour)	150
Parts cost	98
Total service costs	284

Within manufacturing organizations, service cost centres exist where parts of the business, such as particular divisions or departments, provide services to the manufacturing or production cost centres. It is normal for such service cost centres to be costed as part of an allocation and apportionment system, so that direct costs are allocated and a share of the overheads are apportioned to the service cost centres, and the resultant total finally charged to the production cost centres on a suitable basis.

Example

Clevedale Manufacturing Ltd operates an absorption costing system which allocates and apportions costs to cost centres. The costs chargeable to service cost centres of the generating station and the maintenance department are re-apportioned to the production cost centres based on electricity units consumed and maintenance hours worked respectively. The level of interdependence between the services is low, therefore their costs are only chargeable to the production cost centres. Details are as follows.

	Allocated costs £	Apportioned costs £	kWh	Maintenance hours
Manufacturing	42,612	37,518	251,621	2,101
Assembly	45,416	26,956	184,162	1,265
Finishing	26,502	17,411	46,877	596
Generating	13,627	10,506		
Maintenance	20,549	11,147		

Required

Charge the service cost centres costs to the production cost centres.

Solution

	Production cost centres			Service cost centres	
	Manufacturing £	Assembly £	Finishing £	Generating £	Maintenance £
Allocated costs	42,612	45,416	26,502	13,627	20,549
Apportioned costs	37,518	26,956	17,411	10,506	11,147
Total costs	80,130	72,372	43,913	24,133	31,696
Generating costs	12,581	9,208	2,344	(24,133)	–
Maintenance costs	16,808	10,120	4,768	–	(31,696)
Total costs	109,519	91,700	51,025	–	–

The service costs are re-apportioned as follows:

$$\text{Generating costs} = \frac{\text{Total generating costs}}{\text{Total units consumed}} = \frac{£24,133}{482,660} = £0.05 \text{ per kWh}$$

$$\text{Maintenance costs} = \frac{\text{Total maintenance costs}}{\text{Total maintenance hours}} = \frac{£31,696}{3,962} = £8.00 \text{ per hour}$$

This is covered in more detail in Chapter 6.

> You should now be able to attempt task 11.1 at the end of this chapter.

---

8 SOME OTHER COSTING METHODS

In earlier chapters we examined the main costing techniques of *absorption costing*, *marginal costing* and *activity-based costing*, and in this chapter we have described the main methods used to determine the costs of a *cost unit*. Other costing methods you may come across include the following.

- *Average costing* is a method of obtaining unit costs by dividing the total production cost by the number of items produced. Average costing is used where there is a very high degree of product homogeneity and the total production cost may be obtained by using many of the alternative costing techniques such as batch costing, process costing and service costing. In some organizations all costs are expressed as a rate per unit produced in the costing statements supplied to the management. For example, in an electricity generation and distribution organization, costs are expressed as a rate per unit of electricity, a rate per kilowatt hour. The costing of electricity generation systems which operate on a continuous basis may be described as *operating costing* (see below).

- *Unit costing* is used where the costing system produces an individual cost per unit of product, job or service. Unit costing may be generated as a result of job costing, service costing, process costing or batch costing.

- *Operating costing* is a form of costing applied to the provision of services within an organization and to the costing of a continuous operating system of production such as the generation of electricity or the operation of a telephone system by BT.

- *Uniform costing* is the application of a common costing system by a number of different organizations by adopting common costing principles and practices. It is not really a single costing method, but is used, for example, in a particular industry such as the printing industry, where many of the companies which are members of an employers' forum use a common costing system.

> *You should now be able to attempt tasks 11.2 and 11.3 at the end of this chapter.*

9 | BACKFLUSH ACCOUNTING

Backflush accounting is another approach to costing which has grown as a result of the recent changes in the management philosophies and technologies associated with JIT (just-in-time).

Backflush accounting assumes that, with the minimization of stock levels, valuation of stocks is immaterial in establishing an organization's profitability, and the charging of overheads to products no longer requires the complex absorption and ABC techniques. Backflush accounting adopts a simpler approach by working backwards to allocate costs between stock and cost of sales to establish profitability.

Absorption costing constantly charges costs to production or work in progress over the production cycle whereas backflush accounting charges cost to production at a limited number of 'trigger points' during the production cycle. In the simplest system these trigger points would be when materials are issued to production and when the goods are completed, hence the term 'backflush accounting'. Standard costs are often used as the rates at which the charges are made to production.

10 | SUMMARY

The *costing techniques* of *absorption costing, marginal costing* and *activity-based costing* may be applied to a number of *costing methods* in order to determine the costs of a *cost unit* or *cost object*. The cost unit may be a product or a service, and if a product the method of production will tend to determine the costing method adopted.

Job costing is used in an environment where job production takes place, and *batch costing* where jobs or products are combined together to form a discrete batch of output. *Contract costing*, although a form of job costing, is applied in circumstances where the job is large and likely to last longer than a year before completion. Interim profits on a contract may be taken to the profit and loss account.

Process costing is used where production passes from process to process, as in the chemical industry. Process costing may experience *normal losses* and *abnormal losses and gains*, and there are rules for the treatment of joint products and by-products and the way in which *pre-separation* costs are borne by the output.

Finally, the use of *average costing, unit costing, operating costing* and *uniform costing* were considered, and *backflush accounting* is a recent development.

> You should now be able to attempt the objective test at the end of this chapter.

STUDENT ACTIVITIES (* *denotes questions with answers at the end of the book*)

Task 11.1
Select an organization which is essentially concerned with providing services to the general public, such as an insurance company or a bank. Decide what you consider to be the cost units of such an organization, and write up a report to its management setting out in detail how the costs of each service could be determined. Design the documents which would be required to collect the costs, and sketch the document flow diagrams which trace the routes of those documents through the organization.

Task 11.2
Select five manufactured products in everyday use and consider what operations would be applied to them in their manufacture. Consider whether the collection of the unit costs of production would be by the operation of a job costing, batch costing, process costing or other form of costing system.

Task 11.3
You have been engaged by an employers' association to advise them on the adoption of a uniform costing system for their members. In setting up the uniform costing system you decide to write a costing manual to cover the main aspects of the system. Draft a list of the major topics which would be covered in the manual, together with sub-headings of the decisions which would need to be taken in respect of each of the major topics.

OBJECTIVE TEST* *(tick the appropriate box)*

i) Another name for job costing is:

   a) job order costing ☐

   b) specific order costing ☐

   c) batch costing ☐

   d) all of these ☐

   e) none of these ☐

ii) The main reason for the grouping of products into batches for costing purposes is that production is made up of:

   a) small units ☐

   b) large units ☐

   c) similar units ☐

   d) job production ☐

iii) Unit costs may be arrived at by using:

   a) process costing ☐

   b) job costing ☐

   c) batch costing ☐

   d) none of these ☐

   e) all of these ☐

iv) Uniform costing is applied across a number of:

   a) production cost centres ☐

   b) service cost centres ☐

   c) firms in an industry ☐

   d) departments ☐

v) Contract costing is different from other costing methods because:

   a) the cost unit is usually large ☐

   b) it is easy to identify the direct costs ☐

   c) profits are taken before the final product is completed ☐

   d) the cost unit bears a share of administration costs ☐

CHAPTER 12

Standard costing

1 OBJECTIVES

At the end of this chapter you should be able to:

- define what standard costs are;
- understand how standards are set;
- understand how standards are used;
- calculate cost variances;
- calculate sales variances;
- understand the causes of variances;
- construct a standard costing profit and loss account;
- understand alternative standard costing approaches.

2 STANDARD COSTING

Standard costing, like budgetary control, is a management reporting and control system where levels of expenditure and income are set in advance, and the differences between those levels and what is actually achieved, the variances, are reported to various levels of management for action.

Standard costing is linked to budgetary control in a manufacturing company because figures which make up budgets may also be used in standard costing and vice versa. The major difference between standard costing and budgetary control is that standard costing tends to be applied to individual products and processes whereas budgetary control is applied to departments, budget centres and the business as a whole.

Budgetary control can be applied to any kind of organization, from commerce and industry to charities and educational establishments. Standard costing, however, is more appropriate to organizations where a series of repetitive activities is carried out, but the existence of budgets is usually regarded as a prerequisite to the operation of a standard costing system.

As with budget setting, there are various levels to which standards may be set. A philosophy is required in setting standards in order to determine whether they should be set as a prediction of the performance to be achieved or whether some motivational aspect should be included so that 'tight' standards are set which may only be achieved with some effort.

Control is exercised by establishing and analysing variances according to cause, and taking remedial action if a particular variance is adverse to an unacceptable degree. Variances may either be favourable or adverse. Favourable variances are where actual expenditure is less than standard or actual income is greater than standard. Adverse or unfavourable variances are where actual expenditure is greater than standard or actual income is less than standard. Favourable variances represent an addition to profit and adverse variances reduce profits.

3   DIRECT COST VARIANCES

As we have seen, the product *direct costs* of a manufacturing organization are normally direct materials and direct wages. The reasons for over- or under-spending on either of these costs is based on the simple concept that:

Total cost of material or wages = Quantity used × Unit price

Differences between standard and actual total cost must be due to variations in either quantity used or unit price, or a combination of both.

4   DIRECT MATERIALS VARIANCES

Predetermined standards are set both for the level of *direct material* consumption for a given volume of production, and also for the price allowed per unit of direct material. The price standards are based on the price per unit expected to be paid or budgeted, for the level of purchases projected, over the period for which the standard is to be applied.

In general, any variations in price are regarded as the responsibility of the purchasing manager or buyer and any variations in the volume or quantity of materials consumed are regarded as the responsibility of the production manager. However, due to the interdependence of price and usage, responsibilities may be difficult to assign to specific functional heads. The calculation of the variances is as follows.

Direct materials price variances – This is calculated by the formula:

$$(SP - AP)AQ$$

where:

SP = standard price per unit of direct material

AP = actual price per unit of direct material

AQ = actual quantity of direct material consumed or purchased

The price variance may be calculated at the stage when the materials are purchased or when the materials are issued to production.

The formula may be expanded to:

$$(SP \times AQ) - (AP \times AQ)$$

where:

$AP \times AQ$ equals the actual cost of direct materials consumed or purchased as appropriate

Direct materials usage variance – This is calculated by the formula:

$$(SQ - AQ)SP$$

where:

SQ = standard quantity of direct material allowed for the actual level of production achieved

AQ = actual quantity of direct material consumed

SP = standard price per unit of direct material

5   DIRECT WAGES VARIANCES

The same principles apply to the calculation of direct wages variances as are applied to the direct material variances. Standards are established for the rate of pay to be paid for the production of particular products and the labour time taken for their production. The standard time taken is expressed in *standard hours*, which then becomes a measure of output. For example, if the standard direct labour hours allowed to produce a table is, say, 10 hours, then each time a table is produced 10 standard hours work will have been produced, irrespective of the actual time taken. By the comparison of standard hours allowed (or standard hours produced) and actual time taken, labour efficiency can be assessed. In practice, standard times are established by a combination of work, time and method study techniques.

Direct wages rate of pay variance – This is calculated by the formula:

$$(SR - AR)AH$$

where:

SR = standard rate per hour of direct labour

AR = actual rate per hour of direct labour

AH = actual number of direct labour hours worked

The formula may be expanded to:

$$(SR \times AH) - (AR \times AH)$$

where:

AR × AH equals the actual direct wages cost incurred

Direct wages efficiency variance – This is calculated by the formula:

$$(SH - AH)SR$$

where:

> SH = standard direct labour hours allowed for the actual level of output achieved
>
> AH = actual direct labour hours worked
>
> SR = standard rate per hour for direct labour

Total cost variances – In the cases of both direct materials and direct wages the total cost variance is obtained from the formula:

$$SC - AC$$

where:

> SC = the standard cost of the actual production, and
>
> AC = the actual cost of the actual production

Note that as direct materials and direct wages costs are both treated as variable costs, under the rules of flexible budgeting the standard cost allowances are based on the actual level of activity or production achieved rather than that budgeted.

Example

Motorway Signs Ltd budgets to produce 10,000 standard signs each quarter. It operates a system of standard costing for labour and materials, and its standard costs per sign are:

	£
Materials: 16 square metres @ £2 per square metre	32
Labour: 12 hours @ £8 per hour	96
Standard prime cost	128

For the first quarter of the year 7,500 standard signs were produced, and the actual costs incurred were:

		£
Materials:	125,000 square metres of material	252,000
Labour:	91,000 hours	682,500
Total actual prime cost		934,500

Required

Calculate the direct material and labour variances for the quarter, and reconcile standard and actual costs.

Solution

	£	£
Standard cost of the actual output:		
7,500 signs at £80 per sign		960,000

Direct material price variance:
$(SP \times AQ) - (AP \times AQ) = (£2 \times 125,000) - £252,000 = 2,000$ (A)

Direct material usage variance:
$(SQ - AQ)SP = [(7500 \times 16) - 125,000] £2 = 10,000$ (A)

Total direct material cost variance:
$SC - AC = (7,500 \times £32) \times £252,000 = \underline{12,000}$ (A)

Direct labour rate of pay variance:
$(SR \times AH) - (AR \times AH) = (£8 \times 91,000) - £682,500 = 45,500$ (F)

Direct labour efficiency variance:
$(SH - AH)SR = [(7,500 \times 12) - 91,000] £8 = 8,000$ (A)

Total direct labour cost variance:
$SC - AC = (7,500 \times £48) - £313,500 = \underline{37,500}$ (F)

Total prime cost variance:
$SC - AC = (7,500 \times £80) - £565,000 = \underline{25,500}$ (F)

Actual cost of the actual output		934,500

Notice that at no point in the answer is the budgeted level of production (10,000 units) used. The budget allowance for the variable items is always flexed to take into consideration the actual level of activity.

The technique of standard costing has been included in this chapter as applied to the product direct costs of material and labour. However, standard costing may also be applied to the overhead costs of a manufacturing enterprise.

> *You should now be able to attempt task 12.2 and questions 12.3 and 12.4 at the end of this chapter.*

6   OVERHEAD VARIANCES

As we have seen, the overheads of an organization are the product indirect costs, those which cannot be directly traced to the products or cost units. Although these overheads comprise production, administration, selling and distribution, the analysis of overhead variances is usually applied to production overheads. This is because detailed variance analysis is not usually applied to non-production overheads.

It is possible to analyse the budgeted and actual production overheads into cost behavioural characteristics and split them into variable and fixed overheads. This enables both variable and fixed overhead variances to be computed, and this approach has been adopted in this chapter. However, it is possible to calculate overhead variances without analysing costs into variable and fixed, but the degree of variance analysis will be restricted.

There is a strong linkage between absorption costing and overhead variance analysis. You will remember from Chapter 7 that absorption or recovery rates are calculated in advance of production by dividing budgeted production overheads by the budgeted production. This approach applies also to standard costing, where the rates are known as *standard rates* and being often expressed as a rate per unit or a rate per standard hour. Revise Chapter 7 before continuing with this section.

7 | VARIABLE OVERHEAD VARIANCES

The variances for variable overheads have similar characteristics to the variances calculated for the other variable costs such as direct materials and direct labour. The terminology used, however, is different.

The total variable overhead variance
The *total variable overhead variance* is obtained by the formula:

Actual production × variable overhead absorption rate (VOAR) – Actual variable overhead cost incurred

The first term, actual production × variable overhead absorption rate, is really the variable cost recovered or absorbed for the period, therefore another way of looking at this formula is to consider:

Variable overhead cost absorbed – Actual variable overhead cost incurred

Notice that this variance is *not* the difference between the budgeted and the actual variable overheads. Because variable overheads are variable costs, we have to apply the rules of *flexible budgets* and the actual cost incurred must be compared with a budget allowance, i.e. the budgeted variable overheads must be flexed for the level of activity actually achieved. This is what the variable overheads recovered actually represents.

In shorthand form the formula is:

$$SC - AC$$

Where:

      SC = standard variable overhead cost of the actual production

      AC = actual variable overhead cost incurred

The total variable overhead variance can be analysed into the *expenditure variance* and the *efficiency variance*.

The variable overhead expenditure variance
This isolates the amount of the total variable overhead variance which is due to over- or underspending. This may be the responsibility of a number of people in the management team, as the expenditure on variable overheads is unlikely to be the responsibility of one individual.

This is calculated by the formula:

$$(AH \times VOAR) - AC$$

where:

AH = actual hours worked

VOAR = variable overhead absorption rate (per standard hour)

AC = actual variable overhead cost incurred

The variable overhead efficiency variance

This isolates the amount of the total variable overhead variance which is due to efficiency losses or gains. Again, this may be the responsibility of a number of people in the management team, but as a measure of efficiency it is most likely to be under the control of the production function.

Under the direct wages variances described earlier, efficiency was defined as the measurement of output compared with input. The same concept applies here, and the formula is very similar to the one applied to direct wages with the exception that the rate used is, of course, not a labour rate but a standard rate for variable overheads. The formula is as follows:

$$(SH - AH) \times VOAR$$

where:

SH = standard hours allowed for the actual level of output achieved

AH = actual hours worked

VOAR = variable overhead absorption rate (per standard hour)

Example

Staple Machines Ltd budgeted its variable overheads for the period at £228,750 and planned to produce 1,525 units with a standard time allowed of 10 hours per unit. The actual hours worked for the period was 16,150 hours, during which time 1,485 units were produced. Its actual expenditure on variable overheads was £216,500.

Required

Calculate the total variable overhead variance for the period, and its analysis into expenditure and efficiency variances.

Solution

$$\text{Variable overhead absorption rate (VOAR)} = \frac{\text{budgeted variable overhead}}{\text{budgeted production}}$$

$$\text{Standard rate per unit} \quad \frac{£228,750}{1,525 \text{ units}} = £150 \text{ per unit}$$

$$\text{Rate per standard hour} \quad \frac{£228,750}{1,525 \times 10 \text{ hours}} = £15 \text{ per standard hour}$$

Total variable overhead variance:

> Variable overhead absorbed − Actual variable overhead incurred

Variable overhead absorbed:

Actual production × VORR = 1,485 units × £150 =	£222,750	
or 14,850 hours × £15 =	£222,750	
less Actual variable overheads incurred	£216,500	
Total variable overhead variance	6,250	Favourable

Variable overhead expenditure variance:

Actual hours worked × VORR = 16,150 hours × £15 =	£242,250	
Actual variable overheads incurred	£216,500	
Variable overhead expenditure variance	25,750	Favourable

Variable overhead efficiency variance:

Standard hours allowed =

	Hours
Standard hours allowed × actual production = 1,485 units × 10 hours =	14,850
Actual hours worked	16,150
	1,300

> 1,300 hours × standard rate per hour (£15) = £19,500 Adverse

Summary

Variable overhead expenditure variance	25,750 F
Variable overhead efficiency variance	19,500 A
Total variable overhead variance	6,250 F

Conclusion

The variable overheads were underspent compared with the budget allowance by £25,750, which increased profits. This was partly compensated by a loss due to lower efficiency where the operators took 16,150 hours to produce 14,850 standard hours work. This adverse efficiency variance reduced profits by £19,500 to give an overall net gain of £6,250.

8 FIXED OVERHEAD VARIANCES

Of all the cost variances, fixed overhead cost variances are the exception because they deal with fixed costs; all the other cost variances deal with variable elements of cost.

Total fixed overhead cost variance

The *total overhead cost variance* is obtained using the same formula as the one used for the total variable overhead cost variance, except, of course, the standard rate for fixed overheads is used as the fixed overhead absorption rate (FOAR). The shorthand formula is:

$$SC - AC$$

where:

SC = the fixed overheads absorbed (actual production × FOAR)

AC = the actual fixed overhead cost incurred

The total overhead cost variance may be analysed into the *expenditure variance* and the *volume variance*.

The fixed overhead expenditure variance

This isolates the amount of the total fixed overhead which is due to over- or underspending. As with variable overhead variances, this may be the responsibility of a number of people in the management team, as the expenditure on fixed overheads is unlikely to be the responsibility of one individual manager.

This is calculated by the formula:

Budgeted fixed overheads − Actual fixed overheads incurred

The fixed overhead volume variance

This isolates the amount of the total fixed overhead variance which is due to the shortfall or excess of the actual production achieved compared with the production budgeted. The fixed costs are absorbed or recovered based on the product of the actual production and the fixed overhead absorption rate. If the actual production is less than the budgeted level, then the budgeted fixed overheads will not be absorbed. If the actual production is higher than budgeted, then there will be an over-recovery of budgeted fixed overheads. As these variances are due to differences in production volume, they are therefore known *volume variances*.

The volume variance is calculated by the formula:

Fixed overheads absorbed − Budgeted fixed overheads

Example

Staple Machines Ltd budgeted its fixed overheads for the period at £144,875 and planned to produce 1,525 units with a standard time allowed of 10 hours per unit. The actual hours worked for the period was 16,150 hours, during which time 1,485 units were produced. Its actual expenditure on fixed overheads was £143,200.

Required

Calculate the total fixed overhead variance for the period, and its analysis into expenditure and volume variances.

Solution

$$\text{Fixed overhead absorption rate (FOAR)} = \frac{\text{budgeted fixed overhead}}{\text{budgeted production}}$$

Standard rate per unit $\dfrac{£144,875}{1,525 \text{ units}}$ $= £95$ per unit

Rate per standard hour $\dfrac{£144,875}{1,525 \times 10 \text{ hours}}$ $= £9.50$ per standard hour

Total fixed overhead variance:

Fixed overhead absorbed – Actual fixed overhead incurred

Fixed overhead recovered/absorbed:

Actual production × FOAR = 1,485 units × £95	= £141,075	
or 14,850 hours × £9.50	= £141,075	
less Actual fixed overheads incurred	£143,200	
Total fixed overhead variance	2,125 Adverse	

Fixed overhead expenditure variance:

Budgeted fixed overheads	= £144,875
Actual fixed overheads incurred	= £143,200
Fixed overhead expenditure variance	1,675 Favourable

Fixed overhead volume variance:

Fixed overheads absorbed:

Standard hours allowed/produced × actual production

$$= 1,485 \text{ units} \times 10 \text{ hours} = 14,850 \times £9.50 = £141,075$$

Budgeted fixed overheads	= £144,875
	3,800 Adverse

Summary

Fixed overhead expenditure variance	1,675 F
Fixed overhead volume variance	3,800 A
Total fixed overhead variance	2,125 A

Conclusion

The fixed overheads were overspent compared with the original budget by £2,125, which decreased profits. This was partly compensated by a gain due to the actual expenditure being £1,675 less than planned. The adverse volume variance was caused by production volume being less than budgeted by 40 units, which at an absorption rate of £95 per unit gives an adverse variance of £3,800.

9 | SALES MARGIN VARIANCES

It is also possible to set standards or budgets for income by product, and measure differences between what was planned and what was actually achieved. Sales income may be subjected to two basic variations. Because sales income is the product of the number of units sold and the price per unit, the two basic sales variances which could arise are a quantity or volume variance and a price variance.

The way the variances are valued is to use profit margins, hence the reason for the description as *margin variances*. We have seen that the cost variances are the responsibility of various managers, and the use of sales margin variances excludes those cost variances and restricts the sales variances to those that are controllable by the managers of the sales function. An example of the standard or budgeted sales margin per unit would be made up as follows:

	£
Standard selling price	<u>75</u>
Standard direct costs:	
Materials	10
Labour	12
Standard production overheads:	
Variable	15
Fixed	<u>12</u>*
Total standard cost	<u>49</u>
Standard or budgeted margin	<u>26</u>

*The standard fixed overheads per unit would normally be based on budgeted levels of production.

You can see from the above that the standard margin is the standard selling price less the total standard cost. Note that the *actual* margin is the *actual* selling price less the *standard* cost, not the *actual* selling price less the *actual* cost.

Total sales margin variance

The *total sales margin variance* is obtained by the formula:

(Actual sales volume × actual sales margin) −
(budgeted sales volume × standard sales margin)

Notice that the terms budget and standard tend to be interchangeable in this case as, for example, the standard sales volume is the same as the budgeted sales volume. Notice also that the sales margin variances show actual first in order to give the correct sign, + or −, for favourable or adverse variances. Because we are dealing with income variances here, we would expect the formula to be the other way round from cost variance formulae, which tend to show the standard first.

Sales margin price variance

This is the portion of the total sales margin variance which is due to the actual price charged for the product being different from the standard price planned. *The sales margin price variance* is calculated by the formula:

(Actual margin – standard margin) × actual sales volume
or (Actual selling price – standard selling price) × actual sales volume

Sales margin volume variance

This is the portion of the total sales margin variance which is due to the actual volume sold being different from the budgeted volume planned. *The sales margin volume variance* is calculated by the formula:

(Actual sales volume – Budgeted sales volume) × standard margin

Example

Midford Products Ltd budgets to sell 2,500 units of its main product, flogestan, in April at £45 per unit when the standard production cost of flogestan was £37 per unit. The company's actual sales for the month were 2,700 units, and the sales revenue amounted to £116,100.

Required

Calculate the total sales margin variance for the month of April, and analyse the total into the sales margin price and the sales margin volume variances.

Solution

Total sales margin variance:
(Actual sales volume × actual sales margin) – (budgeted sales volume × standard sales margin)

(2,700 units × £6) – (2,500 units × £8) = £3,800 Adverse

The sales margin price variance:

(Actual margin – standard margin) × actual sales volume
or (Actual selling price – standard selling price) × actual sales volume

(£6 – £8) × 2,700 units = £5,400 Adverse

The sales margin volume variance:

(Actual sales volume – Budgeted sales volume) × standard margin

(2,700 units – 2,500 units) × £8 = £1,600 Favourable

Summary

	£
Sales margin price variance	5,400 A
Sales margin volume variance	1,600 F
Total sales margin variance	3,800 A

Conclusion

The total adverse variance on selling activities has reduced profits by £3,800. There was a gain of £1,600 by selling more units than budgeted, but this was more than offset by the reduction in price which reduced profits by £5,400.

10 THE STANDARD COSTING PROFIT AND LOSS ACCOUNT

One of the objectives of a standard costing system is to enable a standard costing profit and loss account to be drawn up. A traditional profit and loss account for internal consumption would show the difference between the sales and the cost of sales to give the gross profit, from which the expenses would be deducted to give the net profit. The expenses would show actual wages, materials and overheads incurred.

In a standard costing profit and loss account the sales, wages, materials and overheads would be shown as the differences or variances between the budgets or standards and the actual performance. It is essentially an exception report, with the management only concerning themselves with the income and expenditure where the variances are adverse to an unacceptable degree, which should be a trigger for action to be taken. If elements of income and expenditure are within or close to standards or budgets, then only a small variance will result, meaning that no remedial action may be necessary.

A standard costing profit and loss also reconciles the profit which should have been made, the budgeted profit, with the actual profit achieved. This is done by listing the variances calculated through variance analysis to account for the differences.

When calculating the actual profit for constructing the standard costing profit and loss account, note that the stock is valued at *standard cost* not *actual cost*. This seems to contravene the SSAP 9 requirement that stock should be valued at the lower of cost or net realizable value, but is necessary in standard costing so that all the variances are disposed of during the accounting period and not carried forward in the stock valuation. In practice, if there is a substantial difference between standard and actual cost, for financial accounts the actual cost may be substituted.

Example

The standard cost card for a unit of product A610 is as follows:

	£
Direct materials	35
Direct labour	62
Production overheads	48
Total standard cost	145
Standard selling price	200
Standard margin	55

The budgeted production for the month of April was 1,000 units, but 1,200 units were actually produced and 800 sold. The actual results were:

	£
Actual sales income	168,000
Direct material costs	48,000
Direct labour costs	72,000
Production overheads	54,000

There were no opening stocks.

Required

Calculate the actual profit for the month of April.

Solution

	Units	Rate £	£	
Actual sales	800		168,000	
Costs incurred	1,200		174,000	
Less Closing stocks	400	145	58,000	@ standard unit cost
Cost of sales	800		116,000	
Actual profit	800		52,000	

11 | STANDARD MARGINAL OR VARIABLE COSTING

The examples above assume that a system of absorption costing is used where the fixed production overheads are charged to the product. If a marginal or variable costing system is in operation, then the margin used for the calculation of the sales margin variances would be the unit contribution. Similarly, the volume variance would not arise on fixed production overheads, the variance being restricted to an expenditure variance only.

12 | SUMMARY

Standard costs are used for the control of costs and revenue and the measurement of performance in the production of products and in the operation of processes. They are used in a similar way to the use of flexible budgets in that the variable items are flexed according to level of activity achieved.

Cost variances are calculated for direct materials and labour. The total cost variance can be analysed into a price variance and a usage variance for direct materials, which for direct wages become the rate of pay variance and the efficiency variance. It is also possible to calculate variances for production overheads, for which the latter are split between variable and fixed overheads.

The total variances for both overhead classifications are made up of the difference between the overhead cost absorbed and cost actually incurred. For variable overheads the total variance can be split into the expenditure variance and the efficiency variance, whereas the analysis of the total fixed overhead variance is split into the expenditure and the volume variances.

Sales margin variances, which are income variances, may also be calculated based on the budgeted and actual margins. Where an absorption costing system is used, the unit margin is the difference between the selling price and the total production cost, including fixed production cost. If marginal or variable costing is used then the unit margin is the unit contribution.

Ultimately, the variances are reported in a standard costing profit and loss account where the variances represent the reasons for the difference between the budgeted profit planned and the actual profit achieved.

> You should now be able to attempt questions 12.6 and 12.7 and the objective test at the end of this chapter.

STUDENT ACTIVITIES (* denotes questions with answers at the end of the book)

Task 12.1
Your friend is a highly paid marketing consultant and has been asked by a local company to investigate their financial controls. Her accounting knowledge is weak and she has told you that she does not know whether to recommend a standard costing system. Make a list of the questions you would require to be answered before you could advise her.

Task 12.2
Keep a record of the number and price of any one particular item you consume in a month. This could be a favourite chocolate bar or your usual drink. By multiplying the number by the cost per item you will arrive at the total cost. Imagine that the price has been increased by 25 per cent, but the number you consume decreases by 10 per cent per month. Calculate the direct materials price and usage variances.

Question 12.3
Perth Transport Company has set standards for the distribution of a client's products. The standard for a round trip is:

Driver's wages: £10 per hour

Time allowed: 9 hours

Fuel consumption: 74 litres

Fuel cost: 70 pence per litre

In the month of June the actual wage costs for making 21 round trips was £1,824, and the fuel consumed cost £1,404. In June, there had been a wage increase of 20 per cent per hour, and the price of fuel had been increased to 80 pence per litre.

Required

Calculate the fuel price and usage variances, and the wages rate of pay and efficiency variances for the month of June.

Question 12.4

Amsterdam Silver Products manufacture silver miniature coats-of-arms for which the standard prime cost is:

	£
Labour: 10 hours @ £20 per hour	200
Silver: 10 grams at £5 per gram	50
Total standard prime cost	250

The budgeted production is 1,000 units per month, but in the month of December, due to holidays, the production only reached 900 units and the actual costs were:

	£
Labour: 9,250 hours	171,125
Silver: 8,650 grams	41,520

Required

Calculate the possible variances, and give possible reasons for them.

Question 12.5*

Wooden Toys Ltd, who manufacture a range of toys, operate a standard costing system for the product direct costs. The standard costs of a toy house are as follows:

	£
Materials (9 square metres @ £2)	18
Wages (6 hours @ £10.50)	63
Prime cost per unit	81

The company budgeted to produce 1,200 units in the last quarter, but the actual production was 1,345 units, and the actual costs incurred amounted to:

	£
Materials (11,900 square metres)	25,320
Wages (8,200 hours)	92,250
	117,570

Required

Calculate the cost variances and draw up a statement reconciling the standard and actual costs of production for the quarter.

Question 12.6

Stapleton Electronics Ltd operates a standard costing system and has produced the following unit standard cost:

	£
Direct material (8 kilos)	32
Direct labour (4 hours)	40
Variable production overheads	8
Fixed production overheads	50
	130

The absorption method of product costing is used and both variable and fixed production overheads are absorbed on the basis of direct labour hours.

The standard unit selling price is £150 and budgeted sales and production have been set at 400 units per period.

The financial results for the previous period were as follows:

	£
Sales (380 units)	58,200
Production (410 units):	
Direct material purchases (4,000 kilos)	16,700
Direct labour cost (1,600 hours)	16,600
Variable production overhead	3,120
Fixed production overheads	13,400

There were no opening stocks but closing material stocks were 700 kilos and closing finished goods stock was 30 units. Both material stock and finished goods stock are valued at standard cost.

Required

i) To prepare for management control purposes, a detailed standard costing statement that highlights the reasons why actual profit differed from budgeted profit. Include as many individual sales and cost variances as possible.

ii) Explain how the above analysis would differ if *Stapletons* adopted the standard marginal costing method instead of the standard overhead absorption costing method. (Note, no calculations are required.)

Question 12.7

Frenchay Products Ltd uses marginal costing and budgets to make £59,500 profit for the month of October when its fixed factory overheads are expected to be £80,500. Its standard variable cost card is as follows:

Standard cost card	£ per unit
Direct materials (20 kilos @ £5)	100
Direct labour (6 hours @ £8)	48
Variable overheads – Production	96
– Selling	10
Total variable cost	254
Standard selling price	454

The actual results for October were as follows:

Sales (average price £470 per unit)	800 units
Production	900 units

	£
Direct material (17,600 kilos)	92,000
Direct labour (5,600 hours)	47,600
Variable overhead – Production	84,800
– Selling	8,500
Fixed production overhead	85,000

Required

i) Draw up an income statement on marginal costing lines to show the actual result for the period.

ii) *Frenchay Products* wish to change to a total absorption costing approach. Redraft the income statement based on absorption costing lines.

iii) In both cases show a reconciliation of the budgeted and actual profits with variance analysis.

OBJECTIVE TEST* *(tick the appropriate box)*

i) In standard costing the materials price variance is:

a) The standard price per unit less the actual price per unit multiplied by the actual units produced ☐

b) the standard price per unit less the actual price per unit multiplied by the actual units consumed ☐

c) The standard price per unit less the actual price per unit multiplied by the budgeted units purchased ☐

d) The standard price per unit less the actual price per unit multiplied by the actual units sold ☐

ii) In standard costing, the materials usage variance is:

a) the standard consumption less actual consumption ☐

b) the standard consumption for the actual production levels less actual consumption, both at actual cost ☐

c) the standard consumption for the budgeted production levels less the actual consumption, both at actual cost ☐

d) the standard consumption for the actual production levels less the actual consumption, both at standard cost ☐

iii) the wages efficiency variance is:

a) the standard hours produced less the actual hours taken, multiplied by the standard rate per hour ☐

b) the standard hours allowed less the actual hours taken, multiplied by the standard rate per hour ☐

c) both of these ☐

d) neither of these ☐

iv) the total variable overhead cost variance is:

a) the variable overhead absorbed less the variable overhead incurred ☐

b) the budgeted variable overheads less the variable overhead incurred ☐

c) the actual hours worked multiplied by the variable overhead rate, less the variable overhead incurred ☐

d) none of these ☐

v) the total fixed overhead cost variance is:

a) the budgeted fixed overheads less actual fixed overheads ☐

b) the fixed overheads recovered less the fixed overheads incurred ☐

c) the fixed overheads absorbed less the budgeted fixed overheads ☐

d) the actual fixed overheads incurred, less the actual hours multiplied by the fixed overhead absorption rate ☐

CHAPTER 13

Cost collection and recording

1 OBJECTIVES

At the end of this chapter you should be able to:

- understand the use of documentation in cost accounting;
- understand the alternatives in maintaining financial and cost ledgers;
- explain the use of control accounts;
- maintain an interlocking cost ledger;
- explain the relative strengths of interlocking and integrated accounts.

2 INTRODUCTION

In collecting cost and income data it is necessary to design a documentation flow whereby the forms generated are processed in order to obtain unit costs, income and profits of the business.

Cost collection and recording often uses double-entry bookkeeping methods, which have the advantage of ensuring that the costs which are actually incurred are all accounted for in the costing process. Such double-entry approaches are used to establish actual costs of jobs, batches or contracts where the cost of discrete products or groups of products are required. Although double-entry techniques can also be used in process costing, you will remember from Chapter 10 that process costing is essentially an average costing system, where the costs of each process are averaged over the output of each process.

There are three approaches to cost recording, all of which are concerned with linking the financial accounts and the cost accounts to various degrees. The three approaches are:

- completely separate cost and financial books of account, which are not linked in any way;
- interlocking accounts or books, where separate cost and financial books are maintained, but are linked to each other through a system of control or adjustment accounts;
- integrated accounts, where one set of books is maintained which provides information for both financial and management accounting purposes.

3 | DOCUMENTATION

Whatever method of accounting is adopted by an organization, it requires a documentation flow to enable the system to collect the transactions which make up the costs incurred and revenues generated. The precise document design and the terminology used may be peculiar to each organization, but there will be common characteristics applied to each document used to collect each element of cost.

Direct and indirect materials:
If the direct materials are put into store prior to being issued to production or *work in progress*, then documentation is needed to trace each item of material into stock. *Invoices, goods received notes* (GRNs) and *direct charge vouchers* (DCVs) may be used, each document recording the material description, commodity code, quantity, unit price and total cost. Prior to payment, approval will be given for quantity, quality and price by members of the team suitably qualified to sign for each aspect.

The issue of the materials from stock may be documented by *stores issue notes* or a *stock or stores requisition*, suitably authorized. Returns from production to stores will be covered by *stores returns notes* or *stores credit notes*. All stores documentation will be used to record the commodity code, the quantity, the unit cost and the total cost. It will also record a job or batch number to which the stocks are charged. Modern techniques such as *direct data entry* (DDE) are now often used where there is an on-line computer terminal situated in the stores to record issues and receipts.

Sometimes the items purchased are charged directly to production instead of going through a stock account, in which case the invoices or DCVs will charge the purchases directly to work in progress. Indirect materials will use the same documentation, but they will be charged to *production overheads* rather than directly to *work in progress*.

Direct and indirect wages:
Some production environments will lend themselves to recording labour times by direct data entry where on-line computer terminals may be situated in the workplace. Otherwise, documentation flows may arise from the use of *payroll analyses, time sheets* and *clock* or *job cards*. All documentation will record the time taken and will be multiplied by the appropriate rate of pay to give the wages cost either to be charged to work in progress by job, batch or contract number, or if indirect wages, charged to overheads.

Production overheads:
If production overheads are absorbed on either a labour time basis or a percentage on direct labour cost, then the times and costs obtained under direct and indirect wages above may be used as the basis for charging overheads to work in progress for each job, batch or contact. If machine hours, number of units or standard hours are used then a production record of those items must be completed.

Finished goods:
The number of completed finished goods will be recorded and transferred from work in progress to finished goods, usually at actual cost or, in a standard costing

system, at standard cost. The product of the quantity and the unit cost is charged into finished goods stock and, when sold, these values are charged as the *cost of sales* against the income from sales in the profit and loss account. This gives the gross profit.

Other overheads:
You will remember that these *administration, selling and distribution overheads* are not normally included in the valuation of work in progress or finished goods, but they are charged to the profit and loss account as period costs.

Unit costs:
Notice that all the documentation discussed above is designed to generate costs of each unit of production, hence the detail required on each form of the job, batch or contract code number to which the costs are chargeable. In practice total accounts, known as *control accounts*, are used, which enable the cost accounts to be maintained in summary form. Unit costs are maintained in detailed cost ledgers by job number, either manually or by computer.

4 | CONTROL ACCOUNTS

Control accounts are accounts which are maintained in total to reflect the detail which is shown elsewhere in the accounts. For example, the balance on the stock control account would represent the value of the total stock on hand at a particular point in time. This balance would be supported by the detailed balances, commodity by commodity, in the stock ledger. Similarly, the balance on the work in progress control would represent the total value of work in progress which would be supported in detail by analysis by individual job in the job ledger.
Other examples of control accounts are:

- wages control account
- production overheads control account
- finished goods control account
- creditors control account
- debtors control account

> *You should now be able to attempt task 13.2 at the end of this chapter.*

5 | SEPARATE FINANCIAL AND COST ACCOUNTING

This approach keeps two completely separate books of account for the financial and cost accounts, the books not being linked in any way. This method is rarely found in a modern accounting environment, mainly because it suffers from a number of major drawbacks which can be largely overcome by the two other alternatives. These drawbacks are:

- keeping two sets of books means that data would need to be input twice, once for the financial books and once for the cost books;

- separate accounting systems would require the respective profits which each reveals to be reconciled; this is because it is very unlikely that both systems would reveal identical profits for a given accounting period;

- some items of expenditure are unlikely to be recorded in both systems; for example, directors' fees and interest on loan capital are both regarded as financial items which may not feature in the product costs of the organization;

- similarly, there are items which may appear in the cost accounts which are not included in the financial books; an example may be notional costs, which are not necessarily incurred and therefore cannot be included in the financial books, but may be included in the cost accounts for comparison purposes.

> *You should now be able to attempt task 13.3 at the end of this chapter.*

6 | INTERLOCKING ACCOUNTS

This may be regarded as an intermediate stage between the system which uses two completely separate sets of books and the completely integrated system. This method maintains the cost and financial books separately, but each set of books is self-balancing by the introduction of a control or adjustment account providing a linkage between the cost and the financial books. A cost ledger control account is introduced into the cost books, through which the transfers between the cost books and the financial books are entered.

Examples of transfers from the financial books to the cost books are where the opposite entries to those in the cost books are in what is essentially a financial account. Entries in a creditors account, which appears in the financial books, would appear in the cost ledger control in the cost ledger. The same applies to entries in the cash book and the debtors control: they would all appear in the cost ledger control to make the cost ledger self-balancing.

Example

The following balances appear in the cost ledger of the *Dyrham Manufacturing Ltd* at the beginning of the accounting period:

	£	£
Stores control account	7,000	
Work in progress control account	6,000	
Finished goods control account	9,000	
Cost ledger control account		22,000
	22,000	22,000

The following transactions took place during the period:

	£
Purchases of raw materials	12,000
Direct wages paid	20,000
Administration costs incurred	5,000
Selling and distribution costs incurred	8,000
Raw materials issued	10,000
Production overhead incurred	10,000
Production overhead absorbed	9,000
Goods sold: At sales value	60,000
At cost	35,000
Transferred to finished goods	30,000

Required

Prepare the cost ledger accounts under a system of interlocking accounts.

Solution

The entries required to record these transactions in the cost ledger and the end of period trial balance are as follows:

Cost ledger of *Dyrham Manufacturing Ltd*

Stores control account

	£		£
Balance b/d	17,000	Work-in-progress control (e)	20,000
Cost ledger control (a)	22,000	Balance c/d	19,000
	39,000		39,000
Balance b/d	19,000		

Work-in-progress control account

Balance b/d	16,000	Finished goods control	40,000
Stores control	20,000	Balance c/d	45,000
Wages control	30,000		
Production overhead control	19,000		
	85,000		85,000
Balance b/d	45,000		

Finished goods control account

Balance b/d	19,000	Cost of sales	45,000
Work-in-progress control	40,000	Balance c/d	14,000
	59,000		59,000
Balance b/d	14,000		

Wages control account

Cost ledger control	30,000	Work-in-progress control	30,000

Administration overhead control account

Cost ledger control	15,000	Profit and Loss	15,000

Selling & distribution overhead control account

Cost ledger control	18,000	Profit and Loss	18,000

Production overhead control account

Cost ledger control	20,000	Work-in-progress control	19,000
(overhead cost incurred)		Costing profit and loss	1,000
		(under-absorbed overhead)	
	20,000		20,000

Cost ledger control account

Sales costing (profit and loss	95,000	Balance b/d	52,000
Balance c/d	78,000	Stores control (a)	22,000
		Wages control (b)	30,000
		Administration overhead control (c)	15,000
		Selling and distribution overhead control (d)	18,000
		Factory overhead control (f)	20,000
		Profit and Loss	16,000
	173,000		173,000
		Balance b/d	78,000

Cost of sales account

Finished goods control	45,000	Transfer to costing profit and loss	45,000

Costing profit and loss account

Cost of sales	45,000	Sales (cost ledger control)	95,000
Under-absorbed factory overhead	1,000		
Administration O/Head	15,000		
Selling and Distn. O/Head	18,000		
Net profit – transferred to cost ledger control	16,000		
	95,000		95,000

Closing trial balance

Stores control	19,000		
Work-in-progress	45,000		
Finished goods control	14,000		
Cost ledger control			78,000
	78,000		78,000

The financial books are also made self-balancing by the inclusion of a financial ledger control account through which the entries to and from the cost ledger are passed. It follows therefore, that the balance on the financial ledger control in the financial ledger should be equal and opposite to the balance on the cost ledger control in the cost ledger at any point in time. Thus a credit balance on the cost ledger control in the cost books should agree on a given date with the debit balance on the financial ledger control.

Interlocking accounts still suffer the drawback that the entries have to be entered twice, once in the financial accounts and once in the cost accounts. However, the books overall are self-balancing and the linkage between the two sets of books is ensured by the regular agreement of the respective cost ledger and financial ledger control accounts.

> *You should now be able to attempt questions 13.4 and 13.5 at the end of this chapter.*

7 | INTEGRATED ACCOUNTS

This method combines the cost and the financial accounts into a single set of books. This also uses the system of control accounts as used in the interlocking system, but the single set of books avoids the necessity for the respective cost and financial ledger control accounts. The major benefit from a fully integrated system is that the data need only be entered into the system once. It is a favoured system, particularly where computerized accounting approaches are concerned, and a number of computerized accounting packages use the fully integrated approach.

The flow chart for a fully integrated system is shown in the accompanying diagram (see p. 203).

Description of the flow chart

The flow chart shows that all the accounts are in one set of books. For example, in interlocking accounts the creditors control, the cash book and debtors control would all appear in the financial ledger. The entries in those accounts in the integrated ledger would appear in the cost ledger control account if interlocking accounts are used.

The work in progress control builds up the total costs of all the jobs in progress by collecting the direct wages (from wages control), the direct materials (from stock control), and the production overheads recovered or absorbed (from the production overheads control).

Completed work in progress becomes finished goods and is transferred from work in progress control to finished goods control. When these goods are sold the finished goods are moved from finished goods control to cost of sales, ultimately to be charged against sales in the profit and loss account.

The other overheads, these being the administration, selling and distribution overheads, are charged against profits as a period cost.

For the sake of simplicity, a standard costing system is not shown. However, any variances which arise throughout the system would be charged against profits in the profit and loss account if they are adverse variances, or credited if a favourable variance.

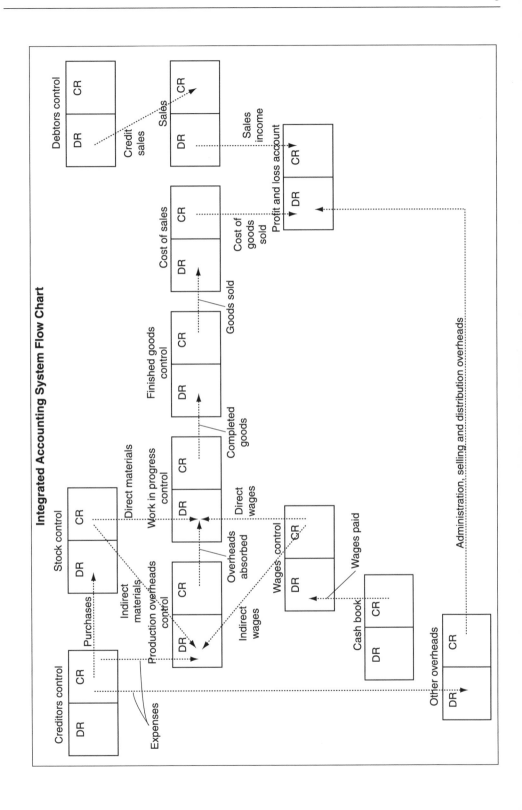

Integrated Accounting System Flow Chart

> You should now be able to attempt task 13.1, question 13.6 and the objective test at the end of this chapter.

STUDENT ACTIVITIES (* denotes questions with answers at the end of the book)

Task 13.1
Write a paper to your manager explaining the use and the relative strengths and weaknesses of the three alternative methods which may be used to record both cost and financial transactions in a manufacturing organization.

Task 13.2
Explain the benefits which arise from the use of control accounts when inter-locking or integrated accounts are used. Make a list of the control accounts which might be found in such accounting systems, and the entries which might be found in each of the control accounts you have listed.

Task 13.3
In the chapter, examples were given of items which appeared in the financial accounts, but would not be expected to be recorded in the cost accounts, and vice versa. Make a list of five further examples of each, and explain why each item should be in one set of books and not in the other.

Question 13.4
Wick Products PLC operates interlocking cost and financial ledgers and the cost ledger accounts had the following balances at the beginning of January 20X3:

	Dr £	Cr £
Cost ledger control account		81,000
Materials control account	31,000	
Work in progress control account	16,000	
Finished goods control account	34,000	
	81,000	81,000

The following entries occurred in the three months to 31 March 20X3:

	£
Materials purchases	160,000
Stock materials issued to production	169,000
Stock materials issued to maintenance	8,000
Total wages	90,000
Indirect labour costs included in wages above	6,000
Factory overhead expenses	48,000

Production overhead absorbed	54,000
WIP transferred to finished goods at cost	260,000
Factory cost of sales	265,000
Sales at selling price	296,000
Administration and selling overhead	43,000

Required

Record the entries in the appropriate accounts in the cost ledger for the above transactions, draw up a costing profit and loss account, and the trial balance at the end of the accounting period.

Question 13.5

Marshfield PLC manufactures a variety of products and the company operates interlinked cost and financial ledgers. The following information relates to the transactions in a three-month period ended 30 June 20X4:

i)   Opening balances consisted of:

Raw materials	£93,750
Work in progress	£62,500
Finished goods	£87,500

with the corresponding balance on the cost ledger control account.

ii)   Raw materials of £250,000 were purchased on credit

iii)   Issues of raw materials to production totalled £200,000

iv)   The total of indirect materials issued to production was £12,500

v)   Raw materials sent back to the suppliers as unsuitable were £2,500

vi)   Direct and indirect ages paid to employees by cheque were £320,000

vii)   £95,000 of those wages related to indirect production labour

viii)   Additional indirect production expenses of £32,500 were incurred in this period

ix)   Production overhead expenses charged to jobs by means of production overhead absorption rates totalled £145,000

x)   Non-manufacturing overhead incurred and paid was £43,750

xi)   The cost of jobs completed and transferred to the stock of finished goods was £500,000

xii)   The cost of goods delivered to customers from stock was £475,000

xiii)   Sales on credit were £625,000

Required

Open and complete the necessary accounts in the cost ledger, compile a costing profit and loss account for the period and construct a trial balance at the end of the period.

Question 13.6

The following transactions were made by *Warmlea PLC* in the month of March:

1. Raw materials of £227,500 were purchased on credit

2. Raw materials of £2,500 were returned to the supplier as unsuitable

3. Direct materials issued were £206,250

4. The total issues of indirect materials were £12,500

5. Gross wages of £231,250 were incurred during the period consisting of wages paid to employees £131,250, tax deductions payable to the Inland Revenue were £75,000 and National Insurance contributions due amounted to £25,000

6. All the amounts due in the previous transaction were settled by cash

7. The allocation of the gross wages were as follows:

    Direct wages   £181,250
    Indirect wages   £50,000

8. The employer's contribution for National Insurance deductions was £31,250

9. Indirect factory expenses of £51,250 were incurred during the period

10. Depreciation of production machinery was £37,500

11. Production overhead expenses absorbed by jobs amounted to £175,000

12. Non-manufacturing overhead incurred during the period was £50,000

13. Jobs completed and transferred to finished goods stock were valued at £375,000

14. The sales value of goods delivered to customers from stock was £500,000, and their cost value was £300,000

15. There were no opening balances on any of the control accounts

Required

i) Assuming that interlocking accounts are kept by *Warmlea PLC*, write up the cost ledger for the month of March.

ii) Assuming that integrated accounts are kept by *Warmlea PLC*, write up the integrated ledger for the month of March.

OBJECTIVE TEST* *(tick the appropriate box)*

i) Documentation required for accounting for materials includes:

a) direct charge vouchers ☐

b) stores issue notes ☐

     c)   stores requisitions ☐

     d)   none of these ☐

     e)   all of these ☐

ii)   Interlocking accounts use:

     a)   one set of books only ☐

     b)   two separate sets of books ☐

     c)   two separate sets of books, linked by control accounts ☐

     d)   none of these ☐

     e)   all of these ☐

iii) Control accounts are accounts which

     a)   control the assets which they represent ☐

     b)   are total accounts which are supported by detail elsewhere in the books ☐

     c)   are only used in interlocking accounts ☐

     d)   are only used in integrated accounts ☐

iv) Integrated accounts use

     a)   one set of books only ☐

     b)   two separate sets of books ☐

     c)   two separate sets of books, linked by control accounts ☐

     d)   none of these ☐

     e)   all of these ☐

v)   Cost and financial ledgers are made self-balancing by the use of

     a)   work in progress control accounts ☐

     b)   production overhead control accounts ☐

     c)   respective cost and financial ledger control accounts ☐

     d)   all of these ☐

     e)   none of these ☐

Westbank Foods Ltd

CONTEXT

Westbank Foods Ltd is a manufacturer and canner of foods and drinks. One of the company's lines is cartons of pure orange juice, which are packed into boxes and sold through wholesalers.

The company has a system of budgetary control and standard costing, and you as the assistant in the cost office, have been asked to explain the cost differences which arose during a particular day's production. The oranges are processed and packed by automatic machinery which needs only one operator at any time to set it up, feed it with oranges, and supervise the production. The budgeted production is 1,200 boxes per day, and the standard cost of one box is as follows:

		£
Oranges:	50 kg @ 6p per kg	3.00
Labour:	0.5 minute per box @ £4.80 per hour	0.04
Fixed overhead:	(based on direct labour hours)	
	0.5 minute @ £24 per hour	0.20
		3.24

The overhead charge of £24 per hour was calculated originally by dividing the budgeted overhead of £240 per day by 10 hours, which is the budgeted time for producing 1,200 boxes at $\frac{1}{2}$ minute per box.

On the day in question, only 1,000 boxes were produced, and the actual cost was as follows:

		£
Oranges:	45,000 kg @ 7p per kg	3,150
Labour:	10 hours @ £5.40 per hour	54
Fixed overhead:	(based on latest cost levels)	225
		3,429

Student activities

Write a memorandum to the general manager explaining the differences between planned and actual costs. Your memorandum should include calculations of the following variances:

Oranges:	price
	usage or consumption
Labour:	rate of pay
	efficiency
Overhead:	expenditure
	volume

Write a brief note on each variance of the possible reasons for the variance arising. You may make any relevant assumptions you wish about what troubles arose that day at the packing plant.

Format

A memorandum to the general manager, with tables of data with supporting calculations.

Objectives

The student should show an understanding and appreciation of:

- budgets
- standard costing
- flexible budgets
- variance analysis

References

Chapters 2 to 5 and (for overhead variances) 12.

PART IV

DECISION MAKING

CHAPTER 14

Cost-volume-profit analysis

1 | OBJECTIVES

At the end of this chapter you should be able to:

- explain what is meant by marginal or variable costing;
- define such terms as fixed and variable costs;
- understand what is meant by contribution;
- construct a marginal or variable costing statement;
- calculate a break-even point;
- construct a break-even chart or graph.

2 | INTRODUCTION

The first section of this chapter is concerned with the way in which costs behave in relation to levels of output or sales. It would be useful, therefore, to revise your understanding of this topic by reviewing Chapter 3.

The calculation of profit, particularly for one unit, can be misleading if there are changes in the level of activity. This is because some costs are *fixed* and *do not* change in total in relation to levels of activity; and some costs are *variable* and *do* change in total in relation to levels of activity.

Cost-volume-profit analysis (CVP) considers how changes in *costs* resulting from different *volumes* of production and sales affect the levels of *profits* which are made by a business.

3 | MARGINAL OR VARIABLE COSTING

In *marginal costing*, only the *variable costs* are charged to the cost units. The profit *per unit* and total cost *per unit* are not calculated. By deducting the variable costs from the sales, we arrive at a figure of *contribution*. Thus, marginal costing is different from *total absorption costing* which charges all production costs, both fixed and variable, to the products or cost units (see Chapters 6 and 7). In marginal costing, profit for a period is calculated by deducting the fixed costs for the period from the total contribution for the period.

A statement which shows variable and fixed costs separately with a calculation of contribution is known as a *marginal* or *variable costing statement*.

Example

Marginal or variable costing statement

	Per × unit	Production 2,000 units		=	Total
	£			£	£
Sales price	10	Sales revenue			20,000
Less Marginal costs:		*Less* Variable costs:			
Materials	4	Materials	8,000		
Labour	2	Labour	4,000		
Variable overheads	1	Variable overheads	2,000		
	7				14,000
Unit contribution	3	Total contribution			6,000

Notice that when variable costs are expressed as a rate per unit they are known as *marginal costs*, i.e. the additional cost incurred in producing the extra or marginal unit of production, hence the title marginal costing.

To provide management with useful information about CVP, it is often necessary to construct a marginal costing statement.

Example

Perth Pens Ltd manufactures 1,000 plastic penholders per month. The costs are 25p for the plastic, and 25p for wages in respect of each penholder manufactured. The monthly costs (overheads) of the factory are £1,000, which in this case are incurred whatever the level of activity. The penholders are sold for £2 each. What is the company's profit for the month, and the profit per penholder?

Solution

Profit statement for the month
Production: 1,000 penholders

	£	£
Sales (1,000 × £2)		2,000
Less Cost of sales:		
Direct materials (1,000 × £0.25)	250	
Direct labour (1,000 × £0.25)	250	
Factory overheads	1,000	
		1,500
Total profit		500

$$\text{Profit per penholder} = \frac{£500}{1,000} = 50p \text{ each}$$

On these figures, we might calculate that the profit for 500 penholders in one month should be 500 × 50p = £250. This would be wrong, however, and a profit and loss statement shows why.

Perth Pens Ltd
Profit and loss statement for the month
Production: 500 penholders

	£	£
Sales (500 × £2)		1,000
Less Cost of sales:		
Direct materials (500 × £0.25)	125	
Direct labour (500 × £0.25)	125	
Factory overheads	1,000	
		1,250
Total loss		(250)

If you calculate the costs per penholder at the different levels of activity, the reason for the loss is easy to appreciate:

Level of activity	*Total costs*	*Cost per penholder*
1,000 penholders	£1,500	£1.50
500 penholders	£1,250	£2.50

The average cost per penholder increases because the factory overheads of £1,000 must be paid no matter what the level of activity. Costs of this type are known as *fixed costs*.

4   FIXED AND VARIABLE COSTS

Fixed costs are those costs which, in total, stay the same regardless of changes in the level of activity (usually measured in terms of production or sales). The term *fixed* is directly related to *activity*. However, these fixed costs *may* change or fluctuate for other reasons. For example, the local authority may increase the business rates. This has nothing to do with activity levels, and the cost is therefore still regarded as *fixed*.

Variable costs are those costs which, in total, change in relation to changes in the level of activity. For example, if a worker is paid 25p for every penholder he makes, the total wages cost will increase as the worker makes more penholders.

Fixed costs, in total, stay the same as activity changes, but the fixed cost per unit changes as activity changes.

Example

	100 penholders	*500 penholders*	*1,000 penholders*
Total fixed costs	£1,000	£1,000	£1,000
Fixed costs per unit	£10	£2	£1

Variable costs, in total, increase or decrease in line with activity, but stay the same per unit.

Example

	100 penholders	500 penholders	1,000 penholders
Total variable costs	£50	£250	£500
Variable costs per unit	£0.50	£0.50	£0.50

> You should now be able to attempt questions 14.4 and 14.5 at the end of this chapter.

5 | CONTRIBUTION

The *contribution* is calculated by deducting the variable costs from the sales. It is known as the contribution because it represents the amount which initially contributes towards the fixed costs of the business, and when these have been covered, contributes to the profit. Contribution is not profit, because no allowance has been made for the fixed costs of the business.

Sales – Variable costs = Contribution

The *contribution per unit* is calculated by deducting the marginal cost per unit from the selling price per unit. The *total contribution* from a specified level of activity is calculated by deducting the total variable costs incurred from the total sales figure.

Example

	1 penholder £	1,000 penholders £
Sales	2.00	2,000
Variable costs	0.50	500
Contribution	1.50	1,500

> You should now be able to attempt task 14.1 and questions 14.6 and 14.7 at the end of this chapter.

6 | BREAK-EVEN POINT

The level of activity at which a company makes neither a profit nor a loss is known as the *break-even point*. It can be expressed in terms of units, sales value or percentage of capacity and is calculated as follows:

$$\text{Break-even point (units)} = \frac{\text{Total fixed costs}}{\text{Contribution per unit}}$$

Example

Using the *Perth Pens Ltd* data:

$$\text{Number of penholders to break even} = \frac{£1,000}{£1.50} = 667 \text{ approx.}$$

This can be proved as follows:

				£
Sales	667 units	@	£2.00	1,333
Less Variable costs	667 units	@	£0.50	333
= Contribution	667 units	@	£1.50	1,000
Less Fixed costs				1,000
Profit/Loss (Break-even)				nil

$$\text{Break-even point (£s sales)} = \frac{\text{Total fixed costs}}{\text{Contribution}^*} \times \text{Sales}^*$$

* These can be per unit or totals at any particular level of activity.

Example

Using the *Perth Pens Ltd* data:

Sales value required to break-even

$$\frac{£1,000}{£1.50} \times £2 \text{ or } \frac{£1,000}{£1,500} \times £2,000 = £1,333$$

An alternative calculation would be simply to calculate the break-even point in units, and multiply by the selling price per unit:

$$\text{e.g. } 667 \text{ units at } £2 = £1,333$$

If *Perth's* total capacity is 1,000 units, then the break-even point could be expressed as a percentage of capacity:

$$\frac{667 \text{ units}}{1,000 \text{ units}} \times 100 = 66.7\% \text{ of capacity}$$

or, using sales levels:

$$\frac{£1,333}{1,000 \times £2} = \frac{£1,000}{£1,500} \times 100 = 66.7\% \text{ of capacity}$$

7 | GRAPHICAL PRESENTATION OF BREAK-EVEN POINT

In Chapter 3 where the graphical presentation of linear cost behaviour was discussed, it was explained that there were two possible graphical presentations of total cost, either being acceptable. The two presentations are:

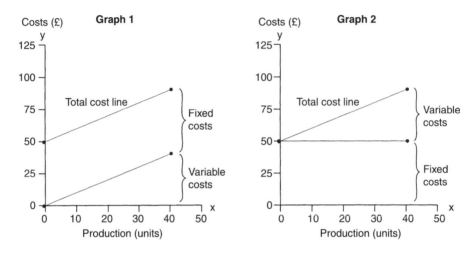

To establish the break-even point all that is now required is to plot a total sales line on either of the two graphs. The total sales line will rise from zero as production rises (here sales and production are always regarded as equal) and where total sales revenue equals total cost, i.e. no profit or loss is made, the break-even point can be read off on the 'x' and 'y' axes. The cost information has been taken from section 4 in Chapter 3, and the selling price is assumed to be £3 per unit produced. The two forms of break-even graph are as follows:

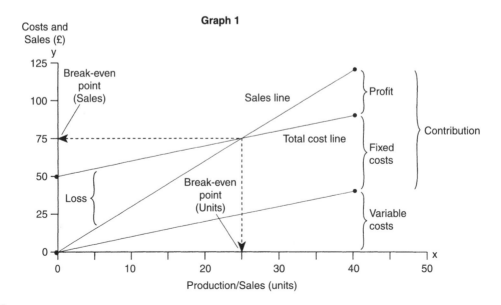

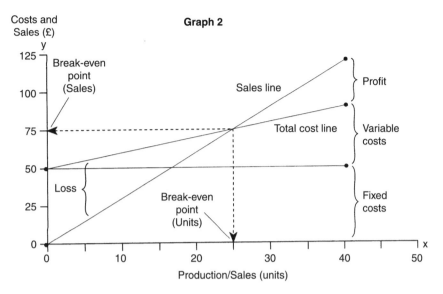

Graph 2

Notice that both charts show the same break-even point, which can be read off both 'x' and 'y' axes depending whether it is desired that the break-even point should be expressed in sales value (y axis), or units or percentage capacity (x axis).

Although we stated in Chapter 3 that the choice of the two graphical approaches depicting costs was a matter of opinion, and either was acceptable, when adding a sales line to the graph so that a break-even point can be determined there is a preferred approach. In Graph 1, where the total cost line is plotted on top of the variable cost line, the *total contribution* can be determined at each activity level when the sales line is added, and this may be regarded as an advantage not available from the other graphical presentation.

Example

Using the *Perth Pens Ltd* data again, the monthly fixed costs are £1,000, the variable costs are 50p per unit, and the selling price is £2 per unit. As all the lines on the graph will be straight lines, we can choose a single level of activity to plot the points for each item. At, say, 1,000 penholders, fixed costs are £1,000, variable costs are £500 and sales are £2,000.

Solution

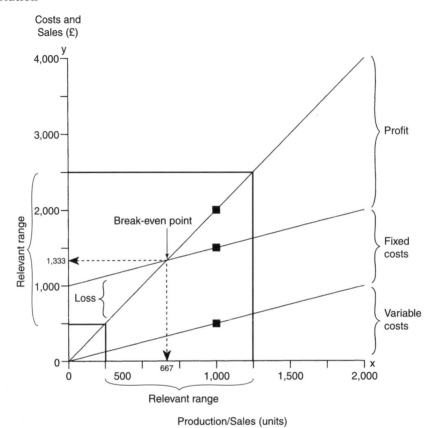

Production/Sales (units)

Using this layout enables the total contribution, i.e. profit plus fixed costs, to be read off at any level of activity, a benefit which is not available from the alternative graph. Although the graph is called a break-even chart because it shows the break-even point, it also shows the costs and profits at various levels of activity, and it is also possible to determine the level of activity required to achieve a particular level of profit.

8 | RELEVANT RANGE

It is realized that the cost structure shown on a straight line break-even graph does not necessarily apply over the whole activity or production range. At higher levels of activity there may be changes in the fixed costs as management is forced to add incremental fixed costs which accompany increased capacity. Similarly, at the lower levels of activity management is forced to reduce its fixed costs in order to move the break-even point downwards to the left to ensure that profits are made at a level where previously losses might be experienced. There may also be changes to the total variable costs.

There may, however, be a range of activity levels where the cost structure does hold good. This range of activity levels is known as the *relevant range*. For example, in *Perth Pens Ltd's* break-even chart (see above), it may be considered that the cost structure shown holds good between, say 250 units and 1,250 units, in which case that would be the relevant range. The elements of the graph above and below those points would not be regarded as a reliable reflection of cost behaviour. The relevant range can also be expressed on the y-axis, and in this case would be between sales of £500 and £2,500.

9 │ MARGIN OF SAFETY

The *margin of safety* is the difference between a given level of sales at which the firm is operating, or planning to operate, and the level of sales at which the firm breaks even. It may be expressed in units of production or sales, sales value (turnover), or it may be expressed as a percentage of the sales value. The margin of safety represents the fall in sales which must take place before the company hits break-even point and losses are incurred if sales continue to fall. The expression of the margin of safety as a percentage of sales value enables organizations of different sizes to be compared.

Example

Paphos Pillars Ltd breaks even at 10,000 units which are sold for £20 each. It is planning to produce 12,500 pillars next year. Calculate the company's margin of safety if the planned level of production and sales is achieved.

Solution

	Units	£
Planned sales	12,500	250,000
Break-even sales	10,000	200,000
Margin of safety	2,500	50,000

$$\frac{2,500}{12,500} \qquad \frac{50,000}{250,000} \times 100 = 20\%$$

Go back to the example of *Perth Pens Ltd* in section 7. If the actual level of production is 1,000 penholders, what would be its margin of safety?

	Units	£	% of sales
Actual sales	1,000	2,000	
Break-even sales	667	1,333	
Margin of safety	333	667	33.3%

Sales could be allowed to fall by one-third before break-even is reached and thereafter losses would be made. Clearly the higher the percentage margin of safety the less risk of the break-even point being reached when sales fall.

> *You should now be able to attempt tasks 14.2 and 14.3 and question 14.8 at the end of this chapter.*

10	TARGET PROFIT

If a company wishes to know the level of activity it has to achieve to obtain a target profit, the formula is:

$$\text{Required activity (Units)} = \frac{\text{Fixed costs} + \text{Target profit}}{\text{Contribution per unit}}$$

Example

Using the data in the *Perth Pens Ltd* example above, the company wishes to make a profit of £500. How many units must be manufactured and sold to achieve this level of profit?

Solution

The calculation is:

$$\frac{\text{Fixed costs} + \text{desired profit}}{\text{Contribution per unit}} = \frac{£1,000 + £500}{£1.50} = 1,000 \text{ units}$$

This can be proved as follows:

				£
Sales	1,000 units	@	£2.00	2,000
Less Variable costs	1,000 units	@	£0.50	500
Contribution	1,000 units	@	£5.50	1,500
Less Fixed costs				1,000
Target profit				£500

Example

Fixed costs: £1,000
Contribution per unit: £5

What is the break-even point in units?

Solution

$$\frac{£1,000}{£5} = 200 \text{ units}$$

Example

Fixed costs: £4,000
Sales: £10,000
Variable costs: £8,000

What level of turnover is required to break even?

Solution

Sales	£10,000
Less: Variable costs	£8,000
Contribution	2,000

$$\frac{£4,000}{£2,000} \times £10,000 = £20,000$$

Example

Fixed costs: £10,000
Contribution per unit: £2
Target profit: £5,000

How many units are required to be produced to achieve the target profit?

Solution

$$\frac{£10,000 + £5,000}{£2} = 7,500 \text{ units}$$

Example

The *Stirling Bicycle Company* is preparing budgets for next year. They plan to produce and sell four models, ranging from the Aberdeen racing bicycle to the Dundee popular tourer.
The sales director provides the following:

Model	Estimated sales demand Number of bicycles	Wholesale selling price per bicycle
Aberdeen	200	£400
Berwick	300	£300
Cairngorm	400	£200
Dundee	600	£100

The budgeted variable costs of production are as follows:

Model	Parts and materials per bicycle	Labour cost per bicycle
Aberdeen	£190	£60
Berwick	£140	£40
Cairngorm	£90	£30
Dundee	£40	£20

Fixed costs are budgeted at £100,000 for the year.
It is expected that all models produced will be sold immediately.

Required

As assistant to the managing director, you are asked to prepare a marginal costing statement for him showing the contribution from each model, and the total budgeted profit for next year.

Solution

Marginal cost statement
showing contribution from each model and the total budgeted profit for next year

Model	Sales price	Variable costs per unit			Contribution per unit	Production/ Sales	Total contribution
		Material	Labour	Total			
	£	£	£	£	£	(units)	£
Aberdeen	400	190	60	250	150	200	30,000
Berwick	300	140	40	180	120	300	36,000
Cairngorm	200	90	30	120	80	400	32,000
Dundee	100	40	20	60	40	600	24,000
					Total contribution		122,000
					Less fixed costs		100,000
					Budgeted profit		22,000

> *You should now be able to attempt questions 14.9, 14.10 and 14.11 at the end of this chapter.*

11 | PROFIT-VOLUME GRAPH

There is another graphic representation of the break-even point. This is achieved by plotting profits against each level of activity, the loss at zero activity being equal to the fixed costs of the firm. This is known as the profit-volume graph, and plotting the data from *Perth Pens Ltd* it would appear as the accompanying graph. You will see that, although this graph gives the break-even point, fixed costs and the profits at various levels of activity, generally it gives less information than the other forms of the break-even graph.

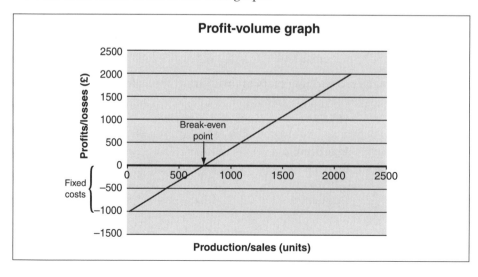

12 | LIMITATIONS OF COST-VOLUME-PROFIT ANALYSIS

As you can see from the graphs which have illustrated cost-volume-profit analysis in this chapter, and from the comments in Chapter 3, the accountant's approach to cost behaviour is essentially one that attempts to treat all costs as linear. Fixed costs in total are treated as being incurred at a level which is maintained over all levels of activity, and variable costs in total increase in sympathy with increases in production, again in a linear fashion. As we have seen earlier in this chapter, the break-even graph is constructed by adding a sales line to the chart which already includes both the fixed and variable cost lines, and the sales line is also treated as a linear function.

The major limitations are therefore:

- *Fixed cost line*

It is unlikely in practice that total fixed costs behave in the manner illustrated by the break-even chart. As activity increases there will come a point where additional resources will be required and incremental elements of fixed cost will be added, giving the fixed costs a stepped function. Where production falls, there will be a tendency for management to shed fixed costs as income falls in an attempt to bring the break-even point downwards to the left, enabling profits to continue to be made at low activity levels. Fixed costs for both increasing and falling activity levels are unlikely to be completely linear.

- *Variable cost line*

The total variable cost line in practice is likely to have curvilinear elements along its length. This is because the marginal cost per unit of production is likely to fall initially as activity increases and the firm is able to benefit from discounts and other reductions which arise from volume purchases of resources. Later, there is likely to be an increase in unit cost as resources become scarce as a result of higher levels of activity.

- *Semi-variable costs*

In Chapter 4 we looked at ways in which attempts are made by accountants to analyse semi-variable costs into their fixed and variable elements. A number of techniques were considered in fitting a cost behaviour line to a *scattergraph*, such as linear regression and the high–low method. Whichever method was adopted, however, the result is only an approximation of cost behaviour, and there is clearly an assumption that all costs can be analysed into fixed and variable components.

- *Activity*

On a break-even chart, activity is shown on the horizontal or x-axis as the independent variable, and cost, the dependent variable, is shown on the vertical or y-axis. This assumes that costs are always a function of activity, and that activity can be expressed by a single measure, both of which are oversimplifications. Discretionary costs, such as advertising or expenditure on research and development, change as the result of managerial decisions and not necessarily activity levels, and there are other cost drivers not necessarily activity-based. There is also more than one way of expressing activity. Aircraft flight costs, for example, may be influenced both by the number of miles flown (fuel) and by the number of take-offs and landings (fuel and landing fees). Indeed, many flight costs are based on time (flying hours), so that the measurement of activity becomes a complex notion.

- *Production and sales*

The approach does not allow for circumstances where production and sales differ, where a change in stock or inventory takes place over the period involved. Production and sales are always assumed to be equal.

- *Profit measurement*

The break-even graph not only shows the point at which neither profit nor loss is made, but estimates of the profits and losses may also be shown by the graph. However, it assumes that profits are measured using a marginal or variable costing basis of profit measurement.

- *Sales*

The sales line is shown as a straight line, thus assuming a constant selling price over the whole range of output and sales. This may not be a reasonable assumption where discounting and other pricing adjustments may need to take place in order to maintain high levels of sales at high activity levels.

- *Single product scenario*

The break-even graph is best applied to a single product firm and only with the application of further assumptions can the approach be applied to a multi-product situation. It is not easy to apply the break-even approach to individual products where a range of products is produced, mainly because of the incidence of general fixed costs which are not product specific.

- *Constant product mix*

Where the break-even graph is applied to a multi-product environment the assumption of a constant product mix is applied. This is because each product is likely to have a different selling price and marginal cost, and a change in the product mix will change the break-even point.

- *Other constant variables*

Production methods and efficiencies are assumed to be constant over the whole range of output and therefore the analysis is essentially a short-term approach. In the longer term, there are likely to changes in these factors.

- *Relevant range*

It is recognized that although the linear relationships do not necessarily apply over the whole range of activity, the cost relationships may well apply between two levels of activity. The production levels between which the relationships apply is known as the *relevant range*.

- *Optimal profits*

Because of the straight line nature of the traditional break-even graph it follows that the optimal profit appears to be made at the highest level of activity. This may not be the case in practice, as higher levels of activity may only be achieved by incurring more than proportionately higher levels of cost. The optimal profit, therefore, may be achieved at lower levels of activity.

saloon. What do you need to define carefully before you collect your data and complete your calculations?

Task 14.2

Assuming that you are paid expenses of 45p per mile, construct a break-even chart based on the information you have collected for Task 14.1.

Task 14.3

Write a short article for your local newspaper explaining why a business with a relatively high level of fixed costs is more likely to experience financial problems from a downturn in its economic activity sooner than a similar business with high variable costs.

Question 14.4

Decide whether the following costs are *fixed* or *variable*:

	Fixed	Variable
Rent of factory		
Materials used in products		
Managing director's salary		
Depreciation of office equipment		
Wages for employees working on the product		
Supervisors' salaries		
Light and heat in the factory		
Metered power to machines in the factory		
Salesmen's commissions		
Business rates		
Routine repainting of the factory		
Royalties paid for each item manufactured		

Question 14.5

Decide whether the following costs are fixed or variable and compute the total cost for 500 penholders. The first two have been completed for you.

Cost	Total cost for 1,000 penholders	Type of cost (fixed or variable) £	Total cost for 500 penholders £
Rent	5,000	F	5,000
Direct materials	250	V	125
Managing director's salary	1,500		
Depreciation	400		
Business rates	1,000		
Operatives' wages	250		
Storekeeper's salary	250		

13   SUMMARY

Adding a sales line to the graphical presentation of variable, fixed and total ⟨
considered in Chapter 3 enables a *break-even chart* or graph to be construc
The *break-even point* is the level of activity where sales and total costs are eqι
Total profit or loss may also be read off the graph at various levels of producti
or sales. The break-even point in units or sales values may also be obtained ⟨
calculation. The general formula is:

Break-even points:

$$\text{In units} = \frac{\text{Total fixed costs}}{\text{Contribution per unit}}$$

$$\text{In sales value} = \frac{\text{Total fixed costs}}{\text{Total contribution}} \times \text{Total sales}$$

The level of activity required to achieve a desired or target profit is obtained from
the formula:

$$\text{Level of activity} = \frac{\text{Total fixed costs} + \text{Desired or target profit}}{\text{Contribution per unit}}$$

The main difficulties encountered by students are:

- deciding whether a cost is variable or fixed: remember that the decision is based on whether or not the cost varies with the level of activity;
- failing to calculate the contribution: contribution is a most valuable concept, the uses for which will be explained more fully in subsequent chapters;
- forgetting the layout of a marginal costing statement;
- insisting on calculating the *total* cost per unit, and profit per unit; these figures can be misleading if there are changes in levels of activity;
- forgetting the formulae for calculating the break-even point;
- forgetting the principles for constructing the break-even chart or graph.

> You should now be able to attempt the objective test at the end of this chapter.

STUDENT ACTIVITIES (* *denotes questions with answer⟨ at the end of the book*)

Task 14.1

A recent report by a motoring organization suggested that the average
per mile to run an average family car is 38.9 pence. Carry out your own calι
tions, either for your own car or for what you would regard as the average f⟨

Question 14.6

If we know two of the three figures from the formula:

$$\text{Sales} - \text{Variable costs} = \text{Contribution},$$

it is always possible to calculate the third figure.

Fill in the missing figures in the following table. The first example has been calculated for you, where the answer is in square brackets.

Example	A	B	C	D	E	F
Sales	[6]	3	5	84	?	64
Variable costs	4	?	2	27	12	?
Contribution	2	1	?	?	15	16

Question 14.7*

Arbroath Hotels Ltd owns a hotel on the promenade at the seaside. It has rooms for 30 guests, and the annual fixed costs are estimated as follows:

	£
Depreciation of furniture	1,000
Business rates	1,200
Repairs and redecorations	1,400
Other annual costs	400
Staff (permanent)	6,000
	10,000

The variable costs, per guest, per week, are estimated as follows:

	£
Food, consumables	20
Domestic staff (part time, occasional)	20
Heating, lighting, laundry, etc.	20
	60

The charge, per guest, per week, is £110, and a normal season lasts for 20 weeks of the year.

Required

i) Calculate *Arbroath Hotels Ltd's* annual profit if all rooms are occupied.

ii) In marginal costing terms, what is the contribution per guest-week?

Question 14.8

Draw up a break-even chart or graph on graph paper using the data on *Perth's* business in the example in section 14.3. Read off from your graph the break-even point in units and sales value, the approximate level of profit or loss at 500 units of output or sales, and the level of activity to achieve a profit of £500.

Question 14.9

i) From the following data, calculate the break-even point in units:

Selling price per unit: £7

Variable costs per unit: £5

Fixed costs: £10,000

ii) From the following data, calculate the break-even point in terms of turnover:

Selling price per unit: £25

Variable costs per unit: £18

Fixed costs: £7,000

iii) From the following data, calculate what turnover (£s of sales) is necessary to achieve the target profit?

A company aims for £20,000 profit next year.

Its fixed costs are budgeted at £40,000.

Selling price per unit: £100

Variable costs per unit: £75

Question 14.10

Using the data from Question 14.7

i) How many guest-weeks has *Arbroath Hotels* to rely on in order to break even?

ii) How else could this break-even point be expressed, other than in terms of 'guest-weeks'?

iii) Draw a break-even chart or graph to represent Arbroath's costs and sales, and indicate the break-even point.

iv) What is Arbroath's margin of safety?

Question 14.11

Montrose Ltd manufactures high-quality soft toys, and has three products: rabbits, dogs and bears. Each of the products goes through the same process and uses the same quality of materials; the only difference arises from the different sizes of the products.

The manufacturing standards and selling prices set for the products for next year are as follows:

	Rabbits	Dogs	Bears
Budgeted production/sales (units)	4,000	3,000	2,000
Material costs per unit	£11.50	£17.50	£25.00
Labour hours per unit:			
Cutting department	2 hrs	2.5 hrs	3 hrs
Finishing department	2 hrs	1.5 hrs	1 hr
Selling price per unit	£32.50	£40.00	£49.00

Employees in the cutting department will be paid £8 per hour, and in the finishing department £6 per hour. Budgeted fixed overheads are £40,000 for next year.

Required

You are trainee production manager for Montrose Ltd, and you have been asked by the Production Director to produce a statement for him which will show the contribution from each product, and the total budgeted profit for next year.

i) Prepare this statement for him.

ii) Calculate the turnover to achieve break-even next year.

iii) Explain what happens to the break-even point if sales take place in different proportions from those budgeted.

Question 14.12

Reigate Restaurant has been serving a standard meal for £10 to its customers for many years. The meal consists of steak, chips and peas, suitably garnished. During the past three months the restaurant has suffered the effects of competition. Previously the restaurant had been running at full capacity serving 3,000 meals per month, but customers have been attracted to a new restaurant nearby and trade has fallen.

Details of revenues and costs for the last three months show the effect of the competition:

	September £	October £	November £
Revenues	24,600	21,900	19,500
Costs:			
Provisions and garnishes	7,380	6,570	5,850
Labour	6,920	6,380	5,900
Overheads	5,500	5,230	4,990
Total costs	19,800	18,180	16,740

The current month, December, looks even worse and the manager estimates that the restaurant is only working at 58 per cent capacity. However, he is aware that the competition is about to close down because of problems with the lease and he expects Reigate Restaurant will return to full capacity in January and remain trading at that level for the rest of the year.

All costs are likely to rise by 5 per cent from 1 January. To compensate for this, the price of the standard meal will be raised from £10.00 to £10.50.

Required

i) Calculate the anticipated profit for the month of December.

ii) Calculate the likely profit for the whole of next year.

iii) Calculate the break-even point of the restaurant for next year expressed as a percentage of full capacity.

Question 14.13

Gloucester Grofits Ltd has developed a new, improved, fluorescent plastic grofit which will be sold to the car industry where they are fixed to widgets by means of spiflicator pins. The company has a present production capacity for 4,500 grofits per annum, after which level of production additional investment in space, personnel and production facilities will be required which will cause higher fixed costs to be incurred. Yet more investment will be required at 8,500 units if higher production levels are required. Although the unit price of grofits tends to fall in order to achieve the higher levels of sales, no savings on unit variable costs are achieved from the higher levels of production.

The following information on sales, costs and profits for next year has been prepared for the managing director of *Gloucester Grofits Ltd* by the accountant:

Number of grofits (units)	Fixed costs £	Variable costs £	Total costs £	Sales £	Profit revenue £	Loss £
0	5,000	0	5,000	0	–	5,000
1,000	5,000	2,000	7,000	4,500	–	2,500
2,000	5,000	4,000	9,000	9,000	0	0
3,000	5,000	6,000	11,000	13,000	2,000	–
4,000	5,000	8,000	13,000	17,000	4,000	–
5,000	9,000	10,000	19,000	20,000	1,000	–
6,000	9,000	12,000	21,000	23,000	2,000	–
7,000	9,000	14,000	23,000	26,000	3,000	–
8,000	9,000	16,000	25,000	29,000	4,000	–
9,000	13,000	18,000	31,000	31,000	0	0
10,000	13,000	20,000	33,000	33,000	0	0

Required

i) Construct a break-even graph from the above budgeted figures.

ii) Assuming that the best estimate of the demand for grofits next year is likely to be around 7,000 or 8,000 grofits, advise *Gloucester Grofits Ltd* of the production and sales strategy to be adopted.

OBJECTIVE TEST* (tick the appropriate box)

i) When activity is increasing, the total variable costs:

a) increase ☐

b) decrease ☐

c) stay the same ☐

d) sometimes increase, sometimes decrease ☐

ii) When activity is decreasing, the variable cost per unit:

a) increases

b) decreases ☐

c) stays the same ☐

d) sometimes increases, sometimes decreases ☐

iii) When activity is increasing, the fixed cost per unit:

a) increases ☐

b) decreases ☐

c) stays the same ☐

d) sometimes increases, sometimes decreases ☐

iv) When activity is decreasing, the total fixed cost:

a) increases ☐

b) decreases ☐

c) stays the same ☐

d) sometimes increases, sometimes decreases ☐

v) If the selling price per unit is £27.00 and the variable costs per unit are £13.00, the contribution per unit is:

a) £40.00 ☐

b) £14.00 ☐

c) £13.00 ☐

d) none of these ☐

vi) If the total sales figure is £5,000, and the total variable costs are £3,000 for 1,000 units, the contribution per unit is:

a) £5.00 ☐

b) £2.00 ☐

c) £3,000 ☐

d) £2,000 ☐

vii) If the variable costs per unit are £6.00, and 500 units have been sold for £5,000, the total contribution is:

a) £4,000 ☐

b) £2,000 ☐

c) £3,000 ☐

d) £8,000 ☐

viii) If the contribution per unit is £2.00, and the total variable costs for 100 units is £300, the total sales figure for those 100 units is:

a) £200 ☐

b) £500 ☐

c) £700 ☐

d) £100 ☐

ix) If the total fixed costs are £12,000, the selling price per unit is £12, and the variable costs per unit are £8.00, the break-even point is:

a) 12,000 units ☐

b) 3,000 units ☐

c) 1,500 units ☐

d) 4,500 units ☐

x) If the break-even point is 3,000 units, and the contribution per unit is £3, total fixed costs must be:

a) £1,000 ☐

b) £9,000 ☐

c) £6,000 ☐

d) none of these ☐

xi) If fixed costs are £16,000, sales are £50,000, and variable costs are £30,000, the turnover required to break-even is:

a) £40,000 ☐

b) £26,667 ☐

c) £9,600 ☐

d) none of these ☐

xii) If fixed costs are £80,000, and contribution per unit is 50 pence, units to be sold to achieve a target profit of £50,000 are:

a) 60,000 ☐

b) 260,000 ☐

c) 600,000 ☐

d) 200,000 ☐

CHAPTER 15

Limiting factors

1 OBJECTIVES

At the end of this chapter you should be able to:

- understand what limiting factors are;
- explain the importance of limiting factors in budgeting;
- explain the importance of limiting factors in decision making;
- calculate how to rank products using limiting factors in marginal costing;
- calculate how to maximize profits using limiting factors.

2 INTRODUCTION

Many factors must combine to enable a business to operate. Land and buildings, plant and machinery and other assets are necessary to form the fixed assets or capital resources which the business uses; materials, labour and overhead resources are also necessary in order to carry out the buying, manufacturing and selling processes.

At any particular point in time it may be possible to identify at least one factor, which, if in short supply, prevents the business from achieving higher levels of activity and profitability. This factor is known as the *limiting factor*.

Examples are:

- shortage of skilled labour;
- shortage of production capacity, such as machinery;
- lack of customer demand for particular products;
- shortage of raw materials;
- shortage of factory space.

3 REDUCING THE EFFECTS OF LIMITING FACTORS

Having identified the limiting factor, the business must take action to reduce the effect of this particular constraint in order to improve the levels of activity and profitability. Each time the effect of a limiting factor is reduced, a new limiting factor comes into effect, constraining the operations of the business. In this way a limiting factor or constraint always exists, even if it is ultimately represented by a shortage of capital. In the examples of limiting factors given in section 2, the business may pursue the following strategies in order to mitigate their effects.

- *Shortage of skilled labour* – Recruit skilled labour by giving incentives for skilled labour to move to the company. For example, increase rates of pay or encourage personnel to move from elsewhere by advertising vacancies there and perhaps paying removal costs.

- *Shortage of production capacity, such as machinery* – Purchase additional production machinery or sub-contract some work to outside companies.

- *Lack of customer demand for particular products* – Increase sales levels by price changes, advertising campaigns or giving sales incentives to staff and/ or customers.

- *Shortage of raw materials* – Search for additional sources of raw materials or reduce dependency on a particular raw material by changing the product design and therefore raw material requirements.

- *Shortage of factory space* – Increase factory space by building an extension, purchasing an additional factory, or sub-contracting work to outside companies.

> *You should now be able to attempt task 15.1 at the end of this chapter.*

4 | PRINCIPAL BUDGET FACTOR

The concept of the limiting factor is particularly important in the budgeting process and the operation of the system of budgetary control. The identification of the limiting factor enables both the planning of higher levels of profitability and the co-ordination of the factors of production and sales, once its effect has been minimized. In budgeting this factor is known also as the *principal budget factor* as there is essentially no difference between this and the limiting factor considered in this chapter.

Example

The sales manager of *Neath (Compact Discs) Ltd* has budgeted sales for the next year at 200,000 units, but the manpower budget allows a maximum of 400,000 labour hours for skilled labour, the limiting factor. It takes 2.5 hours of skilled labour to manufacture a disc.

Required

Calculate the maximum number of discs which may be produced by the company.

Solution

The limit on the number of skilled labour hours available means that a maximum of 160,000 units of production may be achieved, thus:

$$\frac{\text{Skilled labour hours available}}{\text{Skilled labour hours per unit}} = \frac{400,000}{2.5} = 160,000 \text{ units}$$

Among the solutions which may be considered by Neath are to:

- increase the skilled labour hours available by 40,000 units × 2.5 hours = 100,000 labour hours;
- sub-contract the work;
- change the product design or production processes in order to reduce the need for skilled labour.

Each solution may have a different time scale attached to it, but any decision which affects the availability of this resource will affect other parts of the master budget.

5 | PRODUCT RANKING

When a number of different products are produced, it is common for each product to use different amounts of the resources of material, labour and plant and machinery. In order to maximize profits, it is necessary to select the most profitable products and concentrate on the production and sale of these, first of all producing as many units as possible of the most profitable product, then the next most profitable and so on, until the scarcity of the limiting factor makes it impossible to produce further output. Each product must therefore be *ranked* in order of profitability.

In Chapter 14 we saw that the contributions which each product makes initially towards the general fixed costs of the business, and when these are covered, to the profits of the business, are used to determine product profitability. However there are four ways, or levels, in which the *contribution* can be used to rank products in terms of their contributions to profitability.

6 | RANKING ACCORDING TO THE SIZE OF THE UNIT CONTRIBUTION

Level 1 uses the basic approach that the product with the largest contribution from each unit sold is the most profitable product on which the company should concentrate production.

Example

Neath (Compact Discs) Ltd produces two discs, Longplay and Shortplay. The selling prices and marginal costs per unit are as follows. Fixed costs are £45,000 per annum.

	Longplay	*Shortplay*
	£	£
Selling prices	10	6
Marginal costs	6	3
Unit contribution	4	3

Required

Determine the product on which Neath should concentrate production.

Solution

In selling a unit of Longplay a contribution of £4 is made towards the general fixed costs of the business, whereas selling a unit of Shortplay contributes £3 to those same overheads. Therefore, if it is as easy to sell a unit of Longplay as a unit of Shortplay, notwithstanding the higher selling price of the former, then Longplay is to be preferred because of its higher unit contribution. The fixed costs need not be considered in determining the most profitable product because they remain unchanged irrespective of the volumes of Longplay or Shortplay produced.

> You should now be able to attempt question 15.4 at the end of this chapter.

<table>
<tr><td>7</td><td>

RANKING ACCORDING TO THE SIZE OF THE PROFIT-VOLUME RATIO

</td></tr>
</table>

Level 2 recognizes that ranking by the size of the unit contribution which was adopted by the level 1 ranking method does not take into consideration the size of the contribution in relation to the revenue per unit of sales. Some products may have a very small contribution relative to the selling price, and this should be an important factor when ranking products. This approach expresses the contribution as a percentage of the selling price and is known as the *profit-volume ratio* (PV ratio). An alternative name for the profit-volume ratio is the *contribution-margin ratio* or the *contribution-to-sales ratio*. It is obtained by applying the following formula:

$$\text{PV ratio} = \frac{\text{Contribution} \times 100}{\text{Sales}}$$

Notice that the PV ratio is the same percentage whether it is calculated per unit or in total. Thus if Neath (see the example in the previous section) sells 100,000 units of Longplay, the PV ratios are:

$$\text{Per unit} = \frac{£4 \times 100}{£10} = 40\%$$

$$\text{In total} = \frac{£4 \times 100{,}000}{£10 \times 100{,}000} = 40\%$$

Example

Continuing to use the example in the previous section, calculate the PV ratios for the two products and determine the preferred product using this method.

Solution

	Longplay	Shortplay
Profit-volume ratios	$\dfrac{£4}{£10} \times 100 = 40\%$	$\dfrac{£3}{£6} \times 100 = 50\%$

The PV ratio of Shortplay is greater than that for Longplay. Therefore, if it is as easy to sell £1's worth of Shortplay as it is to sell £1's worth of Longplay, then Shortplay is to be preferred because of its higher profit-volume ratio.

One useful way of considering the PV ratio is to regard the percentage as representing the number of pence contribution obtained from selling £1's worth of each product. Thus Longplay contributes 40 pence per £1 of sales achieved, whereas Shortplay contributes 50 pence per £1 of sales achieved. In these circumstances Shortplay is preferred.

8 | RANKING ACCORDING TO THE SIZE OF THE TOTAL CONTRIBUTION

The example in section 6, using a level 1 ranking according to the size of the *unit contribution*, ignores the fact that different sales volumes may be achievable for each product, so the total contributions may also vary in size. Level 3 ranks according to the size of the *total contribution*.

Example

Continue to use the data in section 15.6, but assume that 20,000 units of Longplay and 100,000 units of Shortplay can be sold.

Required

Calculate the total contribution for each product.

Solution

The total contributions of each product become:

$$\text{Longplay} = £4 \times 20,000$$
$$= £80,000$$
$$\text{Shortplay} = £3 \times 100,000$$
$$= £300,000$$

Although the unit contribution of Longplay is greater than that of Shortplay (see the example in section 6), the total contribution of Shortplay is greater than Longplay. Therefore Shortplay is preferred as the most profitable.

9 · RANKING ACCORDING TO THE EFFECT OF LIMITING FACTORS

If a shortage of a particular resource is identified as the *limiting factor*, or *constraint*, the strategy the business should adopt is to use the scarce resource as effectively as possible so as to maximize profits. The level 4 rule in ranking products according to the use of a limiting factor is to express the contribution per unit of product as a rate per unit of limiting factor used in producing that product.

Example

Neath (Compact Discs) Ltd
Continuing to use the data in Section 6, but assume that the limiting factor is a shortage of skilled labour. In producing a unit of Longplay, 1 hour of skilled labour is used, whereas the production of a unit of Shortplay uses half an hour of skilled labour.

Required

Determine which is the most profitable product on which production should be concentrated.

Solution

The contribution per unit of each product expressed as a rate per unit of limiting factor is as follows:

$$\frac{\text{Unit contribution}}{\text{Limiting factor per unit}}$$

$$\text{Longplay} = \frac{£4}{1 \text{ hour}}$$

$$= £4 \text{ per skilled labour hour}$$

$$\text{Shortplay} = \frac{£3}{0.5 \text{ hour}}$$

$$= £6 \text{ per skilled labour hour}$$

Shortplay is preferred because its production represents a more effective use of the scarce resource of skilled labour. Production of Shortplay gives a contribution of £6 per hour of skilled labour used, whereas Longplay produces a contribution of only £4 per hour of skilled labour used in in its production.

10 OTHER MEASURES OF LIMITING FACTORS

In the example in the previous section the quantity of skilled labour used, expressed in hours, is available and it was possible to express the contribution as a rate per skilled labour hour. However, in some circumstances only the cost of the limiting factor per unit of product is available. In such cases the contribution per £1 of limiting factor per unit of product is used to rank products.

Example

Neath (Compact Discs) Ltd
Using the data in section 6 again, assume that the limiting factor is a shortage of direct material. Longplay uses £3 worth of direct material per unit, and Shortplay uses £1.50 of the same material per unit.

Required

Determine which is the most profitable product on which production should be concentrated.

Solution

The unit contribution per £1 of limiting factor for each product is as follows:

$$\text{Longplay} = \frac{£4}{£3}$$

$$= £1.33 \text{ per £1 of direct material}$$

$$\text{Shortplay} = \frac{£3}{£1.50}$$

$$= £2.00 \text{ per £1 of direct material}$$

Shortplay is preferred as its contribution per £1 of scarce resource (direct material) is higher than Longplay.

11 | TWO CONSTRAINTS

It is possible to use this ranking technique where two constraints exist, in circumstances where one of the constraints is a general constraint on the level of production or sales of a particular product.

Example

Channel Seven Ltd manufactures three perfumes: Silk, Musk and Opia. The selling prices and the marginal costs of each product are as follows:

	Silk £	Musk £	Opia £
Selling prices	15	20	30
Marginal costs	10	14	20
Contribution	5	6	10

The firm's fixed costs are £150,000 per annum. There is a shortage of the raw material called essence which is used in all three products. Silk uses 2 kg, Musk uses 1 kg, and Opia uses 3 kg per unit of output. Only 120,000 kg of essence will be available for the year. In addition, market constraints are expected to restrict the production and sales of each product to:

	Units
Silk	40,000
Musk	8,000
Opia	15,000

Required

Calculate the mix of sales which would enable Channel Seven Ltd to maximize profits, and calculate the profit which is achievable at that sales mix.

Solution

To rank the products according to their desirability having regard to the effect of the direct material constraint, calculate the contribution per kg of essence:

	Silk	Musk	Opia
$\dfrac{\text{Contribution}}{\text{Kilos per unit}}$	$\dfrac{£5}{2\text{ kg}} = £2.5$	$\dfrac{£6}{1\text{ kg}} = £6$	$\dfrac{£10}{3\text{ kg}} = £3.33$
Ranking:	3rd	1st	2nd

Because Musk produces the largest contribution per kilo of essence (the scarce resource), in the absence of any other constraints, profit would be maximized by using all the available essence to produce Musk. The number of units of Musk which would be produced under those circumstances would be:

$$\frac{\text{Number of kg of essence available}}{\text{Number of kg of essence per unit of Musk}}$$

$$= \frac{120,000}{1}$$

$$= 120,000 \text{ units}$$

However, the market constraint restricts the production of Musk to 8,000 units only, the production of which would not use all the available quantity of essence. It would only use:

$$8,000 \text{ units} \times 1 \text{ kg per unit} = 8,000 \text{ kg of essence}$$

Moving to the next most attractive product, Opia, the production of the maximum possible level of this product according to the market constraint at 15,000 units would use:

$$15,000 \text{ units} \times 3 \text{ kg per unit} = 45,000 \text{ kg of essence}$$

The production of the maximum possible number of units each of Musk and Opia have so far used 53,000 (8,000 + 45,000) kg of essence, leaving 67,000 kg available for the production of Silk. Because Silk uses 2 kg of essence per unit, its production will be restricted to:

$$\frac{67,000 \text{ kg of essence}}{2 \text{ kg per unit of Silk}} = 33,500 \text{ units of Silk}$$

A summary of the production, use of constraint and maximum profit achieved is as follows:

Ranking	Overriding constraint	Essence kg	Production units	× Contribution per unit £	= Total contribution £
1 Musk	Market	8,000	8,000	6	48,000
2 Opia	Market	45,000	15,000	10	150,000
3 Silk	Material	67,000	33,500	5	167,500
		120,000	Total contribution		365,500
			Less Fixed costs		150,000
			Maximum profit		215,500

You should now be able to attempt tasks 15.2 and 15.3 and question 15.5 at the end of this chapter.

12   THROUGHPUT ACCOUNTING

Throughput accounting has developed as a result of the same changes in manufacturing which have encouraged the introduction of ABC approaches. Direct labour has reduced as a proportion of total cost, whilst fixed costs have increased.

At the same time JIT and value added management philosophies have reduced stocks, which has reduced the importance of stock valuation in accounting systems. Throughput accounting is concerned with providing short-term decisions, and regards all the conversion costs of an enterprise as fixed in the short term, only material is regarded as a variable cost. Conversion costs are those costs incurred by the organization which are incurred in order to change the raw materials into finished goods. Conversion costs exclude material costs.

In throughput accounting the existence of stocks may be regarded as evidence of failure to respond to customer demand in the short term. Theoretically, no stocks would exist if the organization were able to respond immediately to customer requirements directly from production, and just-in-time manufacturing and value added approaches are movements towards this situation where stock levels are minimized.

Throughput accounting applies the same approach to decision making as that used in marginal costing where the contribution per unit of the limiting factor determines the ranking of the products to be produced. In throughput accounting such decisions are made through the use of the *throughput accounting ratio* (TAR). The formula is:

$$\text{TAR} = \frac{\text{Return per factory hour}}{\text{Cost per factory hour}}$$

$$\text{where the return per factory hour} = \frac{\text{Sales price} - \text{material cost}}{\text{Hours on scarce or key resource}}$$

$$\text{the cost per factory hour} = \frac{\text{Total factory cost}}{\text{Total hours available on scarce or key resource}}$$

The cost per factory hour is common to all products produced by the same production facility, and the return per factory hour is essentially the value added per unit of scarce resource. The TAR for each product therefore is a ranking measure, and the products should be ranked according to the size of the TAR.

Although throughput accounting can be used to rank products, it is difficult to see the advantages of this approach over the traditional contribution per limiting factor method of ranking advocated in marginal costing. Throughput accounting is essentially a decision-making technique.

13   SUMMARY

A *limiting factor* is any factor of production and/or sales, the shortage or lack of which restricts the level of activity or profits achievable by a business. The identification and elimination of the limiting effects of any such factor allows higher levels of activity and profitability to be obtained. However, the limiting effects of other factors will come into play so that a limiting factor always exists.

If a range of products is produced it is important to *rank* them according to their relative profitability so that the business can use any scarce resources most effectively and concentrate on the most profitable products in order to maximize profits.

There are four levels of ranking products, each one superseding the previous one. These rank products according to the size of:

1. Unit contribution

2. Profit-volume ratio (or contribution-margin or profit-sales ratio)

3. Total contribution

4. Contribution per limiting factor

If ranking of products according to a limiting factor is used, the general rule is to express the unit contribution of each alternative product as a rate per unit or per £1 of scarce resource or limiting factor. The maximum production of the most profitable product is then carried out until another constraint applies.

> You should now be able to attempt the objective test at the end of this chapter.

STUDENT ACTIVITIES (* denotes questions with answers at the end of the book)

Task 15.1
What do you think is the current limiting factor in your own organization and how could its effect be minimized?

Task 15.2
A local manufacturer has found that his raw material supply has been reduced by 25 per cent because of an industrial dispute. Write a report explaining the techniques which can be applied to ensure that the most profitable products are produced.

Task 15.3
Write a memo to your manager explaining how the simple expedient of dividing the contribution per unit by the limiting factor per unit enables products to be ranked according to their relative profitability and can assist him in decision making.

Question 15.4
Refer to the example in section 15.6. If *Neath* is able to produce either Longplay or Shortplay, but not both, calculate the break-even point in units and sales value when either Longplay or Shortplay are produced. Notice that if Longplay has a larger unit contribution than Shortplay, then its break-even point should be met when fewer units are produced and sold.

Question 15.5

The management of *Tours Bicycles Ltd* is planning next year's production schedules and is considering what its production and sales strategy should be for its range of four models. The following information is available:

Model	Sales demand Units	Selling price £ per unit	Part and materials £ per unit	Labour cost £ per unit
Super	200	400	190	120
Excel	300	300	140	80
GT	400	200	90	60
BMX	600	100	40	40

The labour hour rate will be £10, and the variable overheads will be absorbed at 10 per cent on direct labour cost. Fixed costs are budgeted at £100,000 for the year, and will also be absorbed as a percentage on direct labour cost.

The sales director is of the opinion that, even if extra production capacity were to be made available, the volume of sales of any model could only be increased by a maximum of 25 per cent, and then only at an additional advertising cost of £500 for any one model.

In addition to this limit on sales volume, the other constraint is direct labour.

Required

i) Draw up a schedule showing the budgeted profits for next year based on the planned levels of production shown above.

ii) Advise the management of the company which model(s) and how many units of each model should be produced in order to satisfy the existing demands and to maximize profits if the following total direct labour hours are made available:

a) 10,000 hours

b) 10,500 hours

iii) Calculate the profits which would be made by the company in each case.

Question 15.6

Montrose Ltd manufactures high quality soft toys and has three products: Rabbits, Dogs and Bears. Each product goes through the same process and uses the same quality of materials; the only difference arises from the different sizes of the products. The manufacturing standards set for the products and the selling prices for next year are as follows:

	Rabbits	Dogs	Bears
Budgeted production/sales	4,000 units	3,000 units	2,000 units
Material costs per unit	£11.50	£17.50	£25.00
Labour hours per unit:			
Cutting department	2 hours	2.5 hours	3 hours
Finishing department	2 hours	1.5 hours	1 hour
Selling price per unit	£92.50	£105.00	£110.00

Employees in the cutting department will be paid £8 per hour and in the finishing department £6 per hour.

The total budgeted departmental overheads are split equally between fixed and variable at the budgeted levels of production.

The overhead absorption rates based on budgeted production are as follows:

> Cutting department   £12 per direct labour hour
> Finishing department   £8 per direct labour hour

Required

You are trainee production manager for Montrose Ltd and you have been asked by the Production Director to:

i) Produce a statement for him which will show the contribution from each product and the total budgeted profit for next year.

ii) Show calculations to indicate which product should be subject to reduced production in the event of material shortages.

iii) Show calculations to indicate which product should be subject to reduced production in the event of labour shortages in the finishing department.

iv) Write a brief explanation of the principles upon which your recommendations are based.

Question 15.7

Radio Products Ltd produces a range of radios known as the intercontinental range. The power rating of each radio is based on the number of wave bands, so they are called the Seven, Eight and Eleven. The costs and selling prices for each model are as follows:

	Seven £	Eight £	Eleven £
Selling price	85	100	120
Marginal costs	65	70	80

Budgeted fixed costs for the year are £600,000.

There is a shortage of skilled labour and therefore the total direct labour hours will be restricted to 200,000 for the year. In addition there is likely to be a limit on the total sales levels for each product. The direct labour hours and anticipated maximum sales levels are as follows:

	Seven	Eight	Eleven
Direct labour hours per unit	3	3	5
Maximum achievable sales	40,000 units	20,000 units	10,000 units

Required

i) Calculate the volume of sales of each model which should be produced and sold in order to maximize profits and state the level of profits which would be achieved.

ii) Calculate the value of total sales at which the company would break even, and the margin of safety. Assume the mix of sales is as put forward in your answer to (i).

iii) If an additional 20,000 hours of direct labour could be made available, how would that affect your answers in (i) and (ii).

Question 15.8

National Business Computers produce three desk models. In budgeting next year's production the management is attempting to make sure that the most profitable mix of sales is produced, assuming that one of each of the following constraints is experienced:

i) a restriction on the sales value achievable;

ii) a shortage of direct material;

iii) a shortage of direct labour.

The costs and sales prices per product are as follows:

	66 £	100 £	120 £
Sales value	500	600	1,200
Direct materials	150	160	250
Direct labour	150	200	600
Other direct costs	50	100	120

Required

Rank each of the models in order of profitability for each constraint which is likely to be experienced in the budget year.

Question 15.9*

BMX Racing Ltd is a company set up by some students who feel that there is a market for specialized cycling accessories. They have produced the following information on their initial range of products and asked your advice on the production and sales policy that they should pursue. The students intend to make the products themselves and have calculated that, after allowing for administrative time, holidays etc, there will be an average of 150 hours per week throughout the year of 52 weeks spent on manufacture. They plan to pay themselves a small sum of £5 per hour for time spent on manufacturing. The estimated data per unit of each product are as follows:

	Knee pads £	Elbow protectors £	Gloves £
Selling price	21.00	25.50	32.00
Direct materials			
Covers	3.00	4.00	5.00
Padding	2.00	2.00	1.00
Agency commission	1.00	1.70	2.10
Production time	2 hours	2.5 hours	3 hours
Potential sales	2,000 units	2,000 units	1,000 units

Variable manufacturing overheads are estimated at 10 per cent of selling price and fixed manufacturing overheads £5,000 per annum.

Required

Write a report to the students advising them of the production policy to be pursued. Your report should include:

i) the contribution per unit for each of the products;

ii) the contribution per unit of limiting factor for each of the products, assuming that direct labour hours is the main constraint;

iii) the quantities of each product to be manufactured bearing in mind the limits of the market and the restriction on direct labour hours available;

iv) the profit or loss which may be achieved if the most profitable product mix is manufactured.

OBJECTIVE TEST* *(tick the appropriate box)*

i) In ranking products, we are mostly concerned with:

  a) the gross profit ☐

  b) the net profit ☐

  c) the total absorption cost ☐

  d) the contribution ☐

ii) The most important way in which to rank products is according to:

  a) some constraint or limiting factor ☐

  b) the size of the unit contribution ☐

  c) the size of the total contribution ☐

  d) the size of the profit-volume ratio ☐

iii) The least important way in which to rank products is according to:

  a) some constraint or limiting factor ☐

  b) the size of the unit contribution ☐

  c) the size of the total contribution ☐

  d) the size of the profit-volume ratio ☐

iv) The formula for the profit-volume ratio is:

  a) profit/sales ☐

  b) profit/fixed costs ☐

      c)   fixed costs/contribution   ☐

      d)   contribution/sales   ☐

  v)   Another name for the profit-volume ratio is:

      a)   contribution-margin ratio   ☐

      b)   contribution-sales ratio   ☐

      c)   neither of these   ☐

      d)   both of these   ☐

CHAPTER 16

Relevant costs and revenues

1 OBJECTIVES

At the end of this chapter you should be able to:

- understand why different costs are necessary for different decisions;
- understand and define what differential and incremental costs and revenue are, and how they are used;
- understand what opportunity costs are and how they are used;
- determine which costs are relevant to different decisions in business.

2 INTRODUCTION

In previous chapters we looked at the ways in which marginal or variable costs and limiting factors are used in making some decisions in business. The relationships between sales revenue and fixed and variable costs were used to work out answers to such questions as what level of production or sales are necessary for the the business to break-even or to make alternative levels of profit. Before you continue with this chapter you may find it beneficial to revise your understanding of the concepts and techniques which were covered earlier in the book.

In addition to the decision about what levels of production and sales should be achieved, there are many other decisions required in business. Managers require information which will enable them to answer such questions as:

- At what prices should output be sold?
- Should an order be accepted at less than full cost?
- Should we manufacture or buy a part which we use in the final product?
- What alternative manufacturing methods should we use?
- Should we close down or suspend production for a while in a particular factory?
- Which branch should we close down when there is a choice?
- Should changes be made to the design of a product and the materials used in its manufacture?

In order to obtain the correct answers to these and other questions and to make the most profitable decisions, financial information is required about how income and costs are likely to change as a result of making the alternative decisions which are possible. The financial information must be relevant to the alternative decisions being considered.

3 GENERAL PRINCIPLES

In deciding which particular costs or revenues should be included in the financial information provided to managers to help them make the correct decision, the basic questions which must always be asked are:

- Which costs and revenues are changed by any of the alternative decisions which could be made?
- By how much are they changed by each decision?

The answers to these questions identify the costs and revenues which should be included when choosing alternative courses of action. These costs and revenues are known as the *relevant costs and revenues*. In other words they are *relevant* to the proposals being considered.

When a manager makes a decision there are usually several alternative actions which he or she can take. There are always at least two alternatives, that is, either make a decision to change or make a decision to continue with the existing way of doing things.

Relevant costs can be costs which behave in a number of different ways. Sometimes the relevant costs are variable costs, sometimes fixed costs or opportunity costs. In some circumstances the relevant costs are a combination of all three types.

4 MARGINAL COSTS AND VARIABLE COSTS

You will remember from Chapter 14 that variable costs are those costs which, in total, change in relation to changes in the level of activity, and marginal costs are the variable costs expressed as a rate per unit of production or sales. For example, total material costs will increase/decrease in direct proportion to changes in production levels because the material costs per unit, part of the marginal costs, remain constant.

Example

Melbourne Publications produces books. The marginal costs (for example, material, labour, power) amount to £2 per book. The total variable costs for various production levels are as follows:

Number of books	1,000	5,000	20,000	30,000
Marginal cost per book	£2	£2	£2	£2
Total variable costs	£2,000	£10,000	£40,000	£60,000

Melbourne's present level of production is 20,000 books per month. They are considering whether to increase production by 50 per cent, and want to know what effect this will have on total costs. The increase in production can be achieved without increasing any of the fixed costs of the factory. What are the relevant costs to this decision to increase production?

Solution

As the total fixed cost will not change, the only part of total cost which will alter will be the variable costs. The variable costs will increase by:

$$50\% \times 20{,}000 \text{ units} \times £2 = £20{,}000$$

These variable costs are the costs which are relevant to the decision.

5 RELEVANT REVENUE

In many cases a particular action or decision will also result in a change in sales revenue, either as a consequence of a price adjustment or as a result of an increase or decrease in the volume of sales, or both. The decision which Melbourne is considering could also result in an increase in sales revenue, and therefore the extra sales revenue could also be relevant to the decision.

Example

Continuing to use the example in section 4, Melbourne expects that the additional 10,000 books (50 per cent of 20,000 units of normal production) will be sold for £6 per book. What is the relevant revenue?

Solution

The resultant change in revenue is:

$$50\% \times 20{,}000 \text{ units} \times £6 = £60{,}000$$

This represents the relevant revenue of this decision.

6 CONTRIBUTION

We have already met the contribution in Chapter 14, and you will remember that the contribution per unit is selling price per unit – the marginal cost per unit. The total contribution is either

$$\text{contribution per unit} \times \text{sales volume in units}$$

or

$$\text{total sales revenue} - \text{total variable costs}$$

In many decisions where both the revenue and the variable costs are relevant factors, the difference between the two, the contribution, may be used instead.

Example

Using the examples in sections 4 and 5, calculate Melbourne's increased unit and total contribution which would result from the proposed 50 per cent increase in production and sales.

Solution

Melbourne's unit and total contributions would be:

		Contributions		
		Unit		Total
		£		£
Selling prices	6	× 10,000 =		60,000
Marginal costs	2	× 10,000 =		20,000
Contribution	4	× 10,000 =		40,000

The financial data relevant to the question of whether to increase production by 50 per cent is summarized above. Both the changes in total costs and revenue which arise because of the increase in activity are relevant. The costs are expected to increase by £20,000, which is less than the increase in the sales revenue of £60,000. Therefore the net increase in contribution and profit of £40,000 means that the proposed change to increase the sales and production should take place.

7   DIFFERENTIAL COSTS AND REVENUE

In each case it is always the *changes* in cost and revenue which arise from a proposed action which are relevant to that action. These changes are sometimes known as *differential costs* and *differential revenue* because we are concerned with the difference which would arise in each of the costs and revenue as a direct result of a particular decision, such as the one to increase production and sales levels.

Sometimes an alternative decision may cause costs and/or revenue to fall, in which case the amounts by which they fall are also called differential costs and differential revenue. Differential costs and revenues which increase are sometimes called *incremental costs* and *incremental revenue*.

In Melbourne's examples the total costs and revenues increase by £20,000 and £60,000 respectively as a result of increasing production and sales. In this case, because increases are involved, these changes are known as incremental costs and incremental revenue. The proposal to increase production and sales is recommended because, as a result, incremental revenue is greater than incremental costs. The incremental contribution is therefore £40,000.

Many alternatives are looked at in this way. They should be pursued if incremental revenue exceeds incremental costs, but rejected if incremental costs exceed incremental revenue.

8   FIXED COSTS

So far we have considered Melbourne's decision to increase production and sales by 50 per cent, and this decision has affected total revenue and variable costs only. As far as the costs are concerned, the *incremental* or *differential* costs are made up of changes to the *variable costs* only.

When some proposals are considered, however, the incremental or differential costs may also include changes in the *fixed costs* of the business. You will remember from Chapter 14 that fixed costs are those costs which, in total, stay the same regardless of changes in the level of activity.

You will appreciate that it is not possible to increase production indefinitely without increasing fixed costs at some stage. In increasing production to a substantially higher level there comes a point where additional factory space is required, and this alone will cause fixed costs such as rent, rates, insurance, cleaning, depreciation and other fixed costs to rise.

The normal definition of fixed costs, therefore, only holds good for certain limited increases in activity, usually described as in the short term, or between two levels of activity known as the *relevant range*.

Example

Using the example in sections 4, 5 and 6, Melbourne wishes to double output from the normal level of 20,000 books per month. The marginal costs will remain at £2 per book, but in order to obtain this level of production an investment in capacity is required which will increase the monthly fixed costs by £45,000.

Required

Calculate the relevant costs and revenue and advise Melbourne on whether the increase in production and sales is justified.

Solution

The relevant costs and revenue are those which change as a direct result of obtaining the increase in production and sales. In this case they are incremental because they increase:

	£
Incremental sales: 20,000 units × £6	120,000
Incremental variable costs: 20,000 units × £2	40,000
Incremental fixed costs	45,000
Total incremental costs	85,000
Incremental profit	35,000

The increase in production and sales is justified as there is a net increase in profits of £35,000. The incremental revenue exceeds the incremental costs.

Example

Now Melbourne plans to double capacity, with the consequent increase in fixed costs, but is only able to increase production and sales by 50 per cent.

Required

Calculate the relevant costs and revenue, and advise Melbourne on whether the planned increase in capacity is justified.

	£
Incremental sales: 10,000 units × £6	60,000
Incremental variable costs: 10,000 units × £2	20,000
Incremental fixed costs	45,000
	65,000
	(5,000)

In this case the increase in production capacity is not justified if this lower level of sales is achieved, as the incremental revenue is less than the incremental costs.

> *You should now be able to attempt task 16.1 and question 16.4 at the end of this chapter.*

9 | OPPORTUNITY COSTS

An *opportunity cost* is a way of measuring the cost of doing something in terms of the income or benefit that has been sacrificed by not being able to do something else at the same time. An opportunity cost arises because many resources are in limited supply and if used to carry out one course of action cannot be used for another. One factor or resource that is in short supply, both in business and in personal life, is time.

The fact that you are studying this subject at the moment itself has an opportunity cost. Instead of studying you might have been able to carry out a part-time paid job, possibly decorating a room or working behind a bar for which you could be paid £50. In this case the opportunity cost of studying is the income you would otherwise have earned and have therefore forgone by not working in the part-time job, the studying and the job not both being possible due to the scarcity of time. The opportunity cost of studying for a day is, therefore, £50.

In deciding alternative courses of action in business opportunity costs are particularly important where there are scarce resources featured in the decision.

Example

Betts Transport runs a transport business with five trucks. The present net income from truck operations in which the trucks are fully employed throughout the year is £85,000. Betts has been approached by a manufacturer with the proposal that the trucks should be leased to it at a rate of £20,000 per annum per truck. All other costs would be borne by the manufacturer.

Required

Assess Betts Transport's opportunity cost of continuing to operate the trucks itself.

Solution

The trucks are a scarce resource, and they cannot be both operated by Betts and leased to the third party. If Betts continues to operate the trucks then it forgoes or sacrifices the income it would have earned from leasing. The opportunity cost of operating the trucks is therefore the leasing income forgone:

$$5 \text{ trucks} \times £20,000 \text{ per truck} = £100,000 \text{ per annum.}$$

Notice also that there is an opportunity cost relevant to leasing. If Betts leases the trucks to the manufacturer it cannot also operate them. Operating them creates an income of £85,000 per annum, which is therefore the opportunity cost of leasing the trucks, because this would be the income forgone if Betts changed to leasing.

As the opportunity cost of operating the trucks (£100,000) is greater than the opportunity cost of leasing them (£85,000), then it is preferable to lease the trucks to the manufacturer.

> *You should now be able to attempt task 16.2 at the end of this chapter.*

10   MUTUALLY EXCLUSIVE DECISIONS

The use of opportunity cost is particularly important where the alternative actions available are *mutually exclusive*. These actions are where carrying out one action eliminates the possibility of another action taking place simultaneously. For example, the availability of a plot of land will enable either an office block or a factory to be built to occupy the site, but not both. If a mixture of a factory and an office is built, then that becomes a third alternative, all three alternatives being mutually exclusive.

11   OPPORTUNITY COSTS AND OTHER COSTS

As we have seen earlier in this chapter and in Chapter 14, the costs that are most often relevant to decision making in the short term are the incremental variable or marginal costs. In the longer term when further investment in capital expenditure such as plant and machinery, land and buildings, and fixtures and fittings may be necessary, then incremental fixed costs may also be relevant.

Example

Sidney Engineering Ltd has to decide whether to manufacture a part which is incorporated in the final product, or sub-contract its manufacture. The parts cost £1.50 per unit if manufactured outside, or a marginal cost of £1.00 if made internally. The fixed costs amount to £50,000 per annum, and 400 units are required per month. There is adequate spare capacity available for its internal manufacture.

Required

Advise Sidney Engineering on whether to purchase or manufacture.

Solution

This is a typical make or buy problem which is often faced in a manufacturing business. The fixed costs of £50,000 per annum are not relevant to this decision because they continue to be incurred whether the parts are purchased or manufactured. The decision must be based on the variable cost of manufacture compared to the cost if purchased:

	£ per month
Cost of purchase from outside supplier:	
400 units × £1.50	600
Variable cost of internal manufacture:	
400 units × £1.00	400
Advantage of internal manufacture assuming spare capacity	200

If there is no spare capacity available to manufacture the spare part internally, then it can only be made internally by ceasing to manufacture some other product in order to release enough capacity to manufacture the part.

In this case, not only are the variable costs relevant to the decision whether to make or buy, but also the income which is forgone or sacrificed by not being able to manufacture and sell some of the other product. As explained earlier, this income forgone is the opportunity cost of making the part.

Example

Use the above example again of *Sidney Engineering*, but in order to produce the parts internally assume that there is a shortage of manufacturing capacity. In order to manufacture 400 parts, Sydney would have to cease manufacturing some of the other product which takes 30 machine hours per month and makes a contribution, on average, of £10 per machine hour to the fixed costs of the business.

Required

Advise Sidney Engineering on whether to purchase or manufacture the part.

Solution

In this case both variable costs and opportunity costs are relevant to the decision because of the existence of scarce resources, i.e. production capacity. The alternatives now become:

	£ per month
Variable cost of internal manufacture:	
400 units × £1	400
Add	
Income forgone (opportunity cost of manufacturing the part internally):	
30 hours × £10	300
	700
Cost of purchase from outside supplier:	
400 units × £1.50	600
Advantage of purchase assuming no spare capacity	£100

There is an advantage in purchasing the part because the production of the part can only be achieved by transferring some capacity to its production. Its cost, therefore, is the addition of the actual cost of production, in this case the variable costs, and the income forgone by not being able to produce the product which was previously manufactured by the 30 hours of machine time. As this is greater than the purchase price, it is better to buy.

Notice that the effect of the scarce resource may be calculated by expressing the income forgone, usually the contribution, as a rate per unit of scarce resource. In the above example this amounts to £10 per machine hour. The opportunity cost is then the number of units of the scarce resource transferred to the production of the alternative product (30 hours of machine time) at the rate per unit of scarce resource.

> *You should now be able to attempt question 16.5 at the end of this chapter.*

---

12   ACCOUNTING INFORMATION

In most cases *financial information* used in decision making is available from the accounting system. For example, fixed costs and variable costs, differential and incremental costs and revenues may all be recorded in the books of the accounting system because they are accompanied by an actual payment or receipt. Opportunity costs, however, represent income forgone and are not recorded in the accounts. For this reason, opportunity costs are often disregarded by some accountants and managers when considering alternative courses of action. You will now appreciate that the correct decisions cannot be made unless opportunity cost is taken into consideration, particularly where there are scarce resources.

In other cases the historical costs incurred in acquiring an asset may not be relevant in decision making, even though they represent the costs which will appear in the accounting records. For example, if material purchased remains in stores and has no alternative use, its opportunity cost is zero and should be treated as such in summarizing the costs for decision making. Similarly, if items are in store which have a general use in the organization, and their cost has increased since purchase, the replacement cost is the relevant cost as far as decision making is concerned. This is because the use of material regularly used will trigger its purchase at replacement cost. This situation may be summarized as shown in the accompanying diagram.

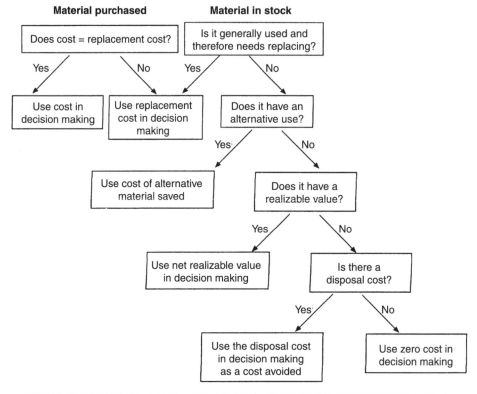

 You should now be able to attempt questions 16.6 and 16.7 at the end of this chapter.

<table>
<tr><td>13</td><td>

ASPECTS OF RELEVANT AND NON-RELEVANT COSTS

</td></tr>
</table>

Because it is the changes in costs which determine whether they are relevant to a particular decision, it is sometimes said that only cost changes which cause an additional *cash outflow* for the business should be considered in decision making.

This definition therefore would describe a cost as relevant based not on whether it is fixed or variable for accounting purposes, but whether it causes additional outflow of cash, either immediately or in the future. Such cash outflows are sometimes known as *cash flow costs* or *out of pocket costs*.

Depreciation is not usually a relevant cost in decision making. You will remember that depreciation is simply the accountant's way of charging a proportion of fixed assets against profits over their estimated useful lives. As no cash movements take place when depreciation is charged, and as it is a policy cost which can vary according to the method of depreciation used and the estimated lives of the assets, it should not be treated as a cost which is relevant to decision making.

When fixed assets are purchased, we have seen that they are capitalized in the balance sheet and written off by depreciating them against profits over their estimated useful lives. At any point in time, therefore, the firm's balance sheet will show each class of asset, for example, plant and machinery, at cost less the accumulated depreciation to date on that class of asset. This net figure is known as the *net book value* (NBV). These NBVs are not relevant to decision making unless they are equal to the realizable or sales value of the asset at the time of the decision.

Example

Adelaide Ltd is considering whether to cease the production of widgets. If it continues to manufacture its annual net cash inflow will be £200,000, whereas it could sell the assets used for widget production for £1 million and invest the proceeds to generate 25 per cent per annum interest. The company is unsure what to do as the assets have a book value of £2.5 million, and any sale would cause a £1.5 million loss.

Required

Advise Adelaide Ltd of the correct decision on purely financial grounds.

Solution

The book value of the plant is irrelevant. Today's true value is £1 million, its realizable value at the time the decision needs to be made. The potential £1.5 million loss on sale is a book loss, and although it may be important to the accountants and the Stock Exchange because it has to be recorded in the accounts, it really represents the result of a bad past decision, and should not affect the current decision. The alternatives are:

	£
Net annual cash flow from investing proceeds from sales of assets	250,000
Net cash flow from continuing the production of widgets	200,000
Advantage from selling assets and investing funds	50,000

Sunk costs are past costs which are irrecoverable at their book values and therefore are also irrelevant for decision making. It is always the *current realizable values* which are relevant, whether they are greater or less than the net book values shown in the balance sheet.

Costs which have already been incurred are seldom relevant in business decision making at those values. For example, £10,000 spent on a consultant's report with a view to obtaining additional information which will enable a decision to be made by the management would not be relevant to the decision as the consultant's fee would be payable whatever decision is ultimately made.

Other kinds of costs which may be relevant in decision making are *notional costs* and *discretionary costs*. *Notional costs* are those costs which may be introduced into the accounts for managerial reasons or for comparison purposes. For example, head offices or group holding companies sometimes charge notional interest to divisions or subsidiaries in order to impose a cost on them for the use of group resources. As these are often notional charges and do not represent an actual cost incurred then they may not be relevant in group decision making.

Discretionary costs are costs which are incurred by a decision of management. For example, expenditure on advertising or research and development may be at a level decided by the management, perhaps as a percentage of budgeted sales. The behaviour of these costs must be considered carefully to decide whether they are relevant to a particular decision.

> *You should now be able to attempt task 16.3 and questions 16.8 and 16.9 at the end of this chapter.*

14 | SUMMARY

In business, managers are concerned with making decisions and they need the type of financial information which will help them choose the most profitable course of action where alternatives are available. For this reason we must make sure that the information provided to managers is relevant to the alternative proposals which they are considering. *Relevant costs* and *revenues* are identified by recognizing those costs and revenues which in total may change as a result of a particular course of action being taken. Those that do not change are usually not relevant to the decision.

When there is a possible change in costs or revenue as a result of a proposal then this change is known as *differential cost* or *differential revenue*. Sometimes costs or revenues may increase as the result of a proposal, and the general term for any increase in such items is *incremental cost* or *incremental revenue*.

Differential or incremental costs are often variable costs, but they may also be fixed costs or semi-variable costs, particularly where additional capital expenditure is involved in a decision alternative. For this reason relevant costs can often be identified as additional cash outflows which arise from a decision. They are often referred to as *out of pocket costs*.

Opportunity costs must also be taken into consideration, in addition to the usual fixed and variable costs, where a scarce resource is concerned. This is because alternative A can only be carried out by not doing alternative B, and therefore the net income which alternative B would have generated is forgone or sacrificed. This is known as the opportunity cost of alternative A. Likewise, the opportunity cost of alternative B is the income forgone by not pursuing alternative A.

Other costs which are seldom relevant in decision making are *sunk costs, notional costs, book values* and *depreciation charges*. They must always be replaced by *current, realizable* or *replacement values*.

> *You should now be able to attempt the objective test at the end of this chapter.*

STUDENT ACTIVITIES (* *denotes questions with answers at the end of the book*)

Task 16. 1

The following is an extract from a letter to a railway magazine:

'I am surprised that you published without questioning the absurd figure quoted by the minister in the House of Commons as the operating cost of a train from Berwick to Edinburgh. I suggest that the true cost of running the train of light weight for the 60 miles would be simply fuel and crew wages (assuming this to be the only revenue-earning work of the day). All the other things like rolling stock and station staff are there anyway.'

A response by another correspondent a month later said:

'May I suggest that the statement . . . was ridiculous? The idea that a train has to pay the cost of fuel, plus crew wages, with a little thrown in for maintenance is stupid. How much rolling stock or how many staff would be there if there were no trains? None! The train in question must help to pay for these and other costs.'

What revenue and costs are relevant to the decision whether to run a particular train or not? Write a memorandum to the manager of the operating company, advising him on how to go about solving this problem.

Task 16. 2

You have been asked by your local school to set an examination question which would test pupils' understanding of opportunity costs. A question that would require them to carry out calculations and solve a specific problem rather than repeating a definition is preferred. Set the question and the model answer.

Task 16.3

Write a report to your manager explaining the concept that different costs are required for different purposes such as pricing, planning and decision making.

Question 16.4

Bendigo Tours Ltd sells special packaged holidays to Europe at £600 each, and they expect to sell 1,000 holidays this year. The variable costs per holiday amount to £400, and the fixed costs of the operation total £100,000. As the holidays are very labour intensive, the company proposes to change to a self-catering holiday next year, which would reduce the variable costs of each holiday to £200 but would have the effect of increasing the fixed costs of the operation to £325,000. A selling price reduction of 5 per cent is planned which is expected to increase the number of holidays by 10 per cent.

Required

Identify the costs and revenues which are relevant to this proposal, and draw up a statement to indicate the financial effects of the proposed changes. Advise Bendigo Tours Ltd whether to make the change.

Question 16.5

Darwin Gates Ltd manufactures a standard line in garden gates for which there is already a heavy demand which the company cannot meet because there is a shortage of skilled labour able to weld the metal gates at the assembly stage. The selling price is £180 each. The variable costs are made up of material costs of £80 and direct labour costs. The skilled workers included in the latter take 10 hours per gate, and are paid £10 per hour.

Darwin Gates Ltd has received an enquiry from a large garden centre for some special gates to their own design. The value of the order amounts to £50,000, and the company calculates that the material cost would be £15,000 and the skilled labour would take 4,000 hours to complete the order.

Required

Advise Darwin Gates Ltd on whether it should accept the order and show the financial advantage of following your advice.

Question 16.6

St Kilda Model Cars Ltd make model cars at a rate of 1,000 cars per week and their latest model of a Super Holden is experiencing heavy demand which cannot be met in full because of a shortage of skilled labour.

Details of a typical week's profit statement are as follows:

	£	£
Sales		4,700
Bought in materials	1,300	
Direct labour		
100 hours @ £10 per hour	1,000	
Variable costs:		
80% of direct labout cost	800	
Fixed costs	1,000	4,100
Weekly profit		600

The company has received an enquiry from *Geelong Stores Ltd* to supply a batch of model trucks. The value of the order would be £2,200, and St Kilda estimates that the variable costs of the order would be:

Materials: £800

Included in the material costs is a special part which could be purchased for £60 or, alternatively, manufactured by St Kilda for £32 materials and 2 hours of skilled labour.

Direct labour: 50 hours

Variable overheads: Based on direct labour hours at normal rates

Required

Prepare calculations and advise the company on whether it should accept an order from Geelong Stores Ltd.

Question 16.7

Heidelberg Golf Club employs Bruce, a skilled craftsman, who makes hand-made sets of golf clubs for the members. The club pays Bruce £120 per week, which is based on a working week of 30 hours at £10 per hour during which time Bruce makes one set of clubs. The club sells the sets at £200 per set. The materials cost £20 per set and Bruce works in a room which has £24 of fixed overheads charged to it by the Club accountant. In addition, the accountant regards the £200 of holiday pay paid to Bruce yearly is also a fixed overhead.

Bruce doesn't work very hard. Having finished his set of clubs for the week he usually lights his pipe, picks up the paper and completes the crossword, in spite of the fact that there is a waiting list for the sets of clubs.

The Club secretary has been asked by a rich American member whether Bruce could make five special putters as Christmas presents for his business contacts. These putters would have special engraved brass plates attached, which Bruce says that he could make himself, or could be purchased for £22 each. If Bruce does make them, each plate would take 1.5 hours to make, engrave and fix, and the brass blank would cost £8. The putters themselves would also take 1.5 hours to make. All other materials required would cost £24 per putter and the American is prepared to pay up to £65 each for the putters. Surprisingly, Bruce indicates that he might be able to make the putters and the plates within his normal working week.

The Club secretary does not want to upset the American member, or the other members who are waiting for Bruce to make their orders for complete sets. He therefore tells everyone involved that he will ask Bruce to make whatever the Club's accounting assistant decides gives the Club the highest profit.

Required

If you were the accounting assistant at *Heidelberg Golf Club*, what would you recommend, assuming that either:

i)   Bruce is able to make the American's order within the normal working week, that is, without affecting the making of one of the complete sets for the other members;

or

ii) Bruce has to work overtime to complete the order for the American;

or

iii) Bruce refuses to work overtime, and the American's order can only be completed by not producing one of the complete sets for the other members.

Provide figures for each alternative.

Question 16.8

The estimating department of *Contractors plc* has spent 200 hours preparing an estimate for a job which a customer wants to be completed very quickly. There is considerable competition for the work, and because failure to obtain this job would mean unused capacity which could not otherwise be filled in the short term, Contractors is anxious to obtain the work. The managing director feels that if he could submit a quotation for less than £200,000, the company is likely to get the job.

The estimate below is prepared on a full-cost basis and the managing director has instructed the estimating department to have another look at the calculations and redraft the estimate using opportunity and relevant cost principles.

Cost estimate	£	
Direct materials – ex stock:		
1. 3,500 kg of material A @ £20 per kg	70,000	(see note 1)
2. 200 kg of material B valued @ FIFO		(see note 2)
50 kg @ £200 per kilo	10,000	
150 kg @ £250 per kilo	37,500	
Direct materials – purchased:		
3. 3,000 kg @ £8 per kg	24,000	(see note 3)
Direct labour:		
4. 3,000 hours of grade A labour @ £10 per hr	30,000	(see note 4)
1,500 hours of trainees @ £4 per hr	6,000	
5. Sub-contract work	35,000	(see note 5)
6. Contact supervision	12,000	(see note 6)
7. Depreciation of fixing machine	5,150	(see note 7)
8. Estimating Department costs	4,000	(see note 8)
Subtotal	233,650	
9. Administration and selling overheads	23,365	(see note 9)
Total costs	257,015	
10. Profit margin	28,557	(see note 10)
Quoted price	285,572	

Notes

1. This material is old stock which would be unused if the contract is not obtained. It has a scrap value of £10,000.

2. This material is regularly used on a variety of contracts. Its current replacement price is £275 per kg.

3. This material would be specially purchased. Its current purchase price is £8 per kg.

4. Both Grade A labour and the trainees would be paid idle time if this contract were not obtained, but 20 per cent of these costs represents overtime which will be worked on the contract.

5. This is the actual cost of the sub-contract work which it would be necessary to place outside the company.

6. This is an apportionment of the fixed general supervision costs of £10,000, plus an allowance for overtime which it is anticipated would be spent on the contract and be paid for.

7. A fixing machine to be used on the contract would incur depreciation for the period used on the contract of £5,150. If not used on the contract it could be hired out for £6,800.

8. This is made up of 200 hours spent preparing the estimate at the hourly rate of £20 per hour. No additional staff were employed.

9. This represents a recovery of these fixed overheads at a rate of 10 per cent of total contract costs.

10. This represents a profit margin based on 10 per cent of selling price.

Required
Prepare the revised estimate based on relevant and opportunity cost principles.

Question 16.9*
Zed-Plan Furniture Company manufactures a standard dining room chair for which there is heavy demand. However, the company cannot meet the demand, mainly because of a shortage of skilled labour. The selling price is £90 per chair. Material costs are £40 and the only other variable cost is direct labour, where a skilled worker takes 3 standard hours to make a chair and is paid £10 per hour.

The chair department has received an enquiry from a large furniture store for some special chairs. The total value of the order is £2,500. Zed-Plan's estimator calculates that the materials would cost £700 and the skilled labour would take 150 hours to complete the order.

Required

Advise Zed-Plan on whether it should accept the order, giving calculations to support your advice.

OBJECTIVE TEST* *(tick the appropriate box)*

i) In deciding the costs which are relevant to a decision, they tend to be:

   a) those costs which remain unchanged by each proposal   ☐

   b) those costs which are changed by each proposal   ☐

    c)   both ☐

    d)   neither ☐

ii) Differential costs are:

    a)   always variable costs ☐

    b)   always fixed costs ☐

    c)   sometimes both of these ☐

    d)   never any of these ☐

iii) Incremental costs are:

    a)   always variable costs ☐

    b)   always fixed costs ☐

    c)   sometimes both of these ☐

    d)   never any of these ☐

iv) Opportunity costs are:

    a)   the costs of not doing something ☐

    b)   the costs of doing something ☐

    c)   the income lost by doing something else ☐

    d)   the income generated by doing something else ☐

v)   To get the total relevant costs, opportunity costs should be:

    a)   added to other relevant costs ☐

    b)   subtracted from other relevant costs ☐

    c)   sometimes considered ☐

    d)   always considered ☐

CHAPTER 17

Payback and accounting rate of return

1 OBJECTIVES

At the end of this chapter you should be able to:

- calculate the payback period for projects;
- calculate the accounting rate of return;
- appreciate the advantages and limitations of these two techniques of project appraisal.

2 INTRODUCTION

A decision which often has to be made in business is whether to invest in a long-term project. At the heart of this kind of decision is the fact that the investment is made now in order to create future returns or profits. The success of such an investment depends on whether the future returns will be adequate to justify the investment. This is done by making estimates or projections of the future returns and using a number of techniques to determine whether the investment is likely to be worthwhile. This process is known as *capital investment appraisal* or *capital budgeting*.

All methods of capital investment appraisal involve predicting *future* costs and revenues and/or cash flows. The relative strength of any particular method of screening projects is therefore dependent upon the ability to predict accurately the future impact of an investment decision in financial terms.

In this chapter we shall be examining two techniques of capital investment appraisal: *payback period* and *accounting rate of return*. Essentially, the payback period is the time it takes a business to get its money back. The accounting rate of return is a simple measure of the return on an investment expressed as a percentage.

3 PAYBACK PERIOD

Payback period is a simple and easily understood technique of appraising the acceptability of projects – hence its popularity with the non-accountant businessman. The project is considered purely from the point of view of its *cash flows*, both in and out, over the life of the project. The objective is to recover the cash outlay in the shortest possible time, therefore the payback period is expressed in years.

Example

We are considering buying an ice cream van and employing someone to operate it. Cash spent on buying the van would be £12,000. For each year the cash flows are estimated as follows:

	£	£
Cash		
Cash received from sale of ice cream		29,000
Cash out		
Cash paid for:		
Ice cream ingredients, cones, wafers, flake chocolate, etc.	5,000	
Wages for driver/salesperson	16,000	
Other expenses: petrol, tax and insurance, repairs, maintenance, etc.	4,000	
Total cash out:		25,000
Net cash flow:		4,000

Note that *depreciation* of the van itself is *not* included. This is because depreciation is *not* a cash flow. The cash flow relative to the van is the cash paid for the van when purchased. This was explained in Chapter 16.

Solution

Year	*Yearly net cash flows* £	*Cumulative net cash flows* £
0	(12,000)	(12,000)
1	4,000	(8,000)
2	4,000	(4,000)
3	4,000	Nil
4	4,000	4,000
5	4,000	8,000

There are several things in this table which need explanation:

- Year 0 is a conventional way of recording the start of year 1, the commencement of the project. Year 1, 2, 3, etc. means end of year 1, 2, 3, etc.

- It is customary to assume that cash flows during a year will be received at the end of that year. This is, of course, not true, but it simplifies the calculation and errs on the side of conservatism, giving a slightly pessimistic rather than optimistic view if the cash flows are positive. It is possible to produce cash flows on a quarterly or monthly basis, but this is seldom done in payback calculations, because forecasting to this degree of refinement is rarely possible or necessary.

- Negative cash flows (cash going out) are shown in brackets, whereas positive ones (i.e. cash coming in) are not.
- A required payback period for projects of this type will be established and if the projected payback period is shorter or equal to this time then the project may be accepted on financial grounds.

You will see that the cumulative cash flows are shown as *nil* at the end of year 3. This means that at the end of year 3 the cash flowing in from the project has reached the figure of £12,000, which is same as the initial cash outflow in payment for the van at the start of year 1. We therefore say that the *payback period* for the project is three years.

Example

What is the payback period for a project, the net cash flows for which have been budgeted as follows?

Year	Annual net cash flows £
0	(18,000)
1	8,000
2	8,000
3	8,000
4	8,000
5	8,000

Solution

Year	Annual net cash flows £	Cumulative net cash flows £
0	(18,000)	(18,000)
1	8,000	(10,000)
2	8,000	(2,000)
3	8,000	6,000
4	8,000	14,000
5	8,000	22,000

The answer lies somewhere between two and three years. Assuming the cash flow is regular throughout the year, it should be easy to see that the answer is 2.25 or 2 years and 3 months. If the figures are not so simple, the way to calculate the part year is:

Year	Cumulative cash flows £
0	(18,000)
2	(2,000)
3	6,000

Add the two cumulative cash flows *ignoring* the fact that the first figure is negative (in brackets):

$$2,000 + 6,000 = 8,000$$

Then divide the earlier figure (2,000) by the total:

$$\frac{2,000}{8,000} = \frac{1}{4} = 0.25 \text{ of a year}$$

Therefore the payback period is $2 + 0.25 = 2.25$ years.

An alternative method is to start adding from year 1 until you get to the total outlay you made in year 0,

	£	£	
Year 1	8,000	8,000	
Year 2	+8,000	= 16,000	2.00 years
Year 3	+2,000	= 18,000	$\frac{2,000}{8,000} = 0.25$ years

> You should now be able to attempt question 17.4 at the end of this chapter.

---

4 ASSESSMENT OF PAYBACK

The main *advantages* of the payback period technique are as follows:

- The technique is very simple to calculate and is understood by managers who may not be very numerate.

- It produces results which are useful for 'risky' projects, e.g. where the prediction of cash flows for more than the first few years is difficult, due, say, to possible changes in the market. For example, changes in technology may make a product obsolete in a year or so, although the current market for it seems assured.

- Some businesses may need to consider short-term cash flows more important than long-term cash flows, perhaps due to lack of capital adequate to sustain long-term objectives. It is not much use aiming for long-term profitability if the business fails in six months' time from lack of cash.

- The technique deals with cash flow projections, unlike accounting rate of return, which considers projections of profit. As cash flows are uninfluenced by accounting policies such as those for the depreciation of assets they may be regarded as a better method of measuring return.

The main *disadvantages* of the payback period technique are as follows:

- Net cash inflows in year 5 are given the same degree of importance as those for year 1. Cash now or soon is worth more than the same amount of cash in five years' time. This is known as the *time value of money*, which payback ignores.

- The technique ignores cash flows after the payback period. In Question 17.4 at the end of this chapter, Project A's cash flows are increasing steadily, whereas those from Project B are decreasing.

- There is a tendency to require very short payback periods for projects to which this approach is applied. Consequently, long-term projects, which might take some time before a return is achieved, might never be considered if payback only is used as a method of appraisal. Such projects as aircraft, shipbuilding, bridge construction, power stations and large infrastructure projects usually have a longer period before payback is achieved.

Despite these disadvantages, this technique is widely used in industry for evaluating investments in long-term projects.

5 | ACCOUNTING RATE OF RETURN

Payback is concerned with *cash flow*. *Accounting rate of return* (ARR) is concerned with *profit* and *average capital*. *Capital invested* means the money that is tied up in the business (all the assets owned by the business, less any money which the business owes) or, in other words, what the business is worth. *Average capital invested* means that if the business is worth £18,000 at the beginning of next year and £22,000 at the end of next year, then the *average capital invested* for next year is £20,000.

$$£$$
$$\underline{£18,000}$$
$$\underline{£22,000}$$
$$\underline{\underline{£40,000}} \div 2 \text{ (years)} = £20,000$$

ARR is calculated as *average profit* (before tax) as a percentage of *average capital invested*:

$$\frac{\text{Average pre-tax profit}}{\text{Average capital invested}} \times 100$$

It should be appreciated that there is more than one formula for the calculation of the ARR. Sometimes average profits are expressed as a percentage of the *original capital invested* rather than *average capital invested* in the project. It is, however, important to maintain a consistent approach in the calculation of the ARR. Clearly the required percentage return necessary before a project may proceed will be dependent on the precise formula used.

Example

Camborne Mines Ltd is contemplating a new project, and there is a choice of two. Details of the forecasts for these projects are:

	Project A £	Project B £
Annual sales	100,000	210,000
Annual cost of sales including expenses	60,000	130,000
Capital required to start the project	190,000	450,000
Extra capital which will need to be introduced during the year	20,000	100,000

What are the respective accounting rates of return for the two projects, and which project do you consider is the better one?

Solution

	Project A £	Project B £
Pre-tax profit:		
Sales less cost of sales	40,000	80,000
Average capital invested:		
Start of year 1	190,000	450,000
End of year 1	210,000	550,000
	400,000	1,000,000
Divide by 2 = average capital invested	200,000	500,000
Pre-tax profit	40,000	80,000
Average capital invested	200,000	500,000
× 100 = ARR	20%	16%

If we rank these projects by their ARR, then project A has the higher ARR of 20 per cent.

However, Camborne would be well advised not to base the decision purely on this method of project appraisal. For example, it would be interesting to know what the payback periods would be. (We cannot calculate them because the information given is inadequate.) Also, you will note that project B requires more capital, but makes more profit (£80,000 compared with £40,000) than project A in absolute terms.

Assuming that the capital required for project B (£450,000 increasing to £550,000) is available for investment, then, since project A requires less than half this amount, what is Camborne to do with the difference? It could be put into a building society, but the return would be likely to be much less than the 16 per cent for project B.

How about investing in two projects of the A type? It could be considered, but it may not be possible. In other words, ARR is too poor a technique to be a satisfactory basis for a decision. It leaves too many questions unanswered.

> *You should now be able to attempt question 17.5 at the end of this chapter.*

6 | DEPRECIATION AND RESIDUAL VALUES

The link between the payback and the ARR techniques can sometimes be established by converting the annual *cash flows* which are projected for a payback calculation into annual *profits* by deducting the depreciation charge for each year. Similarly, to convert profits to cash flows, depreciation should be added back. Remember that depreciation is not a cash flow item so is not included in the projections for a payback calculation.

Some projections may give a value of assets at the end of their effective working lives. This may be a scrap value or a realizable value in the final year of the project. This is known as a *residual value*.

Using the payback method of appraisal this presents few problems as this residual value simply represents a cash inflow in the final year of the investment. When the ARR method is used, however, the residual value clearly affects the average capital invested for the project.

Example

Eden Projects Ltd is considering a new five-year project. Its investment costs and annual profits are projected as follows:

	Year	£
Investment	0	250,000
Profits	1	40,000
	2	30,000
	3	20,000
	4	10,000
	5	10,000

The residual value at the end of the project is expected to be £40,000 and depreciation of the original investment is on a straight line basis. Using average profits and average capital employed calculate the ARR for the project and the payback period.

Solution

Accounting rate of return:

$$\text{Average profits} = £110,000/5 \text{ years} = £22,000$$

$$\text{Average investment} = \frac{£250,000 + £40,000}{2} = £145,000$$

$$\text{ARR} = \frac{£22,000}{£145,000} = 15.2\%$$

Payback

Annual depreciation to be added back:

$$\frac{£250,000 - £40,000}{5 \text{ years}} = £42,000 \text{ per annum}$$

	Profits +	depreciation	= cash flow	Cumulative
	£	£	£	£
0			(250,000)	(250,000)
1	40,000	42,000	82,000	168,000
2	30,000	42,000	72,000	96,000
3	20,000	42,000	62,000	34,000
4	10,000	42,000	52,000	(18,000)*
5	10,000	42,000	52,000	

* = payback year   3 years + 34/52 = 3 years 8 months

Notice that the residual value of the investment is normally added to the investment before the average investment is obtained. This has the effect of lowering the ARR where a residual value exists.

7 | ADVANTAGES AND DISADVANTAGES OF ACCOUNTING RATE OF RETURN

The main *advantages* of the accounting rate of return technique are as follows:

- Calculations are very simple.

- The entire life of the project is taken into account, unlike the payback method.

- One of the major ratios in assessing corporate performance is *return on capital employed*. This expresses the firm's profit before interest and taxes as a percentage of capital employed. ARR is a very similar measure applied to individual projects, and there is therefore a degree of consistency in screening projects using a measure which is similar to the way in which corporate performance is ultimately measured.

The main *disadvantages* of the accounting rate of return technique are as follows:

- The timing of profit flows is completely ignored.

- There are a number of different definitions of accounting rate of return and various ways of calculating it which can lead to confusion.

- The crucial factor in investment decisions is cash flow and the accounting rate of return uses profits.

- The technique takes no account of the time value of money.

- It takes no account of the incidence of profits.

- Averages can be misleading. This is demonstrated in question 17.5 at the end of this chapter.

8 GENERAL PROBLEMS WITH PAYBACK AND ARR

The simple nature of the calculations required for the more traditional methods of appraisal such as payback and ARR, and their lack of mathematical rigour, cause some difficulties when applying these techniques to more complex projects. In particular:

- Projects do not always conform to a typical standard cash flow pattern of an investment at the beginning (year 0), followed by a stream of returns over time. Some projects are more complex and have net investments over a number of years, and further net investments part way through the projects' lives.

- Investment in projects is not only made up of capital expenditure in buildings, plant and machinery and fixtures and fittings, but also in working capital such as debtors and stocks. Working capital may have a more cyclical nature than the investment in fixed assets, with both increases and reductions over the life of the project. The traditional approaches of investment appraisal have more difficulty in accommodating this aspect in the calculations.

- Government taxation policies are often designed to influence the investment strategies of firms. Taxation, therefore, is an important element of investment appraisal and should be included in any capital investment appraisal calculation. Both traditional techniques experience some difficulty in incorporating taxation into project appraisal calculations.

9 SUMMARY

Two traditional techniques of project appraisal are *payback period* and *accounting rate of return*. The payback period technique is concerned with cash flows and calculates the time it will take to recover the cash invested in the project. The accounting rate of return is concerned with profit and expresses this as a percentage of the average capital employed in the project.

Both techniques have the advantage of simplicity, but their disadvantages are significant. Therefore, more sophisticated techniques are required for effective decision making. These are explained in the next chapter.

> *You should now be able to attempt tasks 17.1, 17.2 and 17.3, question 17.6 and the objective test at the end of this chapter.*

STUDENT ACTIVITIES (* denotes questions with answers at the end of the book)

Task 17.1
A friend of yours has just started a new business, and is considering purchasing some new machinery. This machinery is the most advanced of its kind, and it will

replace his existing machinery. Your friend intends to use the accounting rate of return method of project appraisal in order to evaluate this investment. Write a letter to him, stating why you think the payback method of project appraisal is preferable.

Task 17.2

The publisher of a new textbook on project appraisal wishes to include a diagram which clearly shows how the payback method of project appraisal operates. Draw such a diagram.

Task 17.3

Using any of your possessions, such as a bicycle, car, surfboard or stereo system, calculate the monthly rental you would have to charge to give a payback period of 30 months.

Question 17.4

Truro Ltd wishes to decide between two alternative projects, the cash flows for which have been projected as follows:

Year	Project A £	Project B £
0	(24,500)	(25,500)
1	8,000	12,000
2	9,000	11,000
3	9,000	11,000
4	10,000	9,000
5	12,000	8,000

Calculate the respective payback periods for Projects A and B, and comment on the figures.

Question 17.5*

Bude Hotels Ltd has the choice of buying one of two guest-houses as going concerns. Details of forecasts provided by the accountant are as follows:

	Guest-house A £	Guest-house B £
Capital required (likely to be static over the next three years)	200,000	200,000
Pre-tax profits for the next three years:		
Year 1	30,000	50,000
Year 2	40,000	40,000
Year 3	50,000	30,000

Guest-house A is in an area where holidays are increasing in popularity, whereas the area where guest-house B is situated is apparently decreasing in popularity.

Required

Calculate the average annual pre-tax profits and the respective accounting rates of return, and comment briefly on your figures.

Question 17.6

Tintagel Investments Ltd wishes to invest in buying a business in Cornwall. There are two businesses available. The purchase prices for each are the same, £50,000. Business A is a newsagency and sweet shop which is in a very good commercial position. Net cash flows are expected to start at £8,000 per annum and increase steadily thereafter. Business B is a gift shop which has done well in the past, but due to redevelopment and competition in the area is expected to go downhill and reach a level of cash flow of £8,000 per annum. Details of the anticipated cash flows for the two businesses for the first 10 years are given below:

	Business A £	Business B £
Year 1	8,000	12,000
Year 2	9,000	11,000
Year 3	10,000	10,000
Year 4	11,000	9,000
Year 5	12,000	8,000
Year 6	13,000	8,000
Year 7	14,000	8,000
Year 8	15,000	8,000
Year 9	16,000	8,000
Year 10	17,000	8,000

It can be assumed that in both businesses the investment of £50,000 covers the purchase price of the business, both assets and stock, and that the value of the assets and stock will remain constant at about £50,000 throughout the 10 years.

Required

Calculate the respective payback periods for businesses A and B, and also the accounting rates of return. Use the results of your calculations (if you consider they are relevant) to advise *Tintagel* which of the two businesses should be purchased.

OBJECTIVE TEST* (tick the appropriate box)

i) Payback period is the time, in years, which it takes for cash inflows of a project to equal:

a) the average capital employed ☐

b) the cost of capital employed ☐

    c) the cash overdraft limit agreed with the bank   ☐

    d) the cash outflows   ☐

ii) The cash flow figures used for payback calculations should not include:

    a) sales receipts   ☐

    b) payments for wages   ☐

    c) depreciation   ☐

    d) interest on bank overdraft   ☐

iii) A project has a cash outflow in year 0 of £17,100, and cash inflows for the first and subsequent years of £3,600 per annum. The payback period is:

    a) 4 years 3 months   ☐

    b) 4 years 9 months   ☐

    c) 4 years 6 months   ☐

    d) 4 years 7.5 months   ☐

iv) A project has a payback period of 2.5 years. The cash inflows for years 1, 2, 3 and 4 are budgeted £5,000, £5,500, £6,000 and £7,000 respectively. The cash outflow at the start of year 1 is expected to be:

    a) £13,500   ☐

    b) £16,500   ☐

    c) £23,500   ☐

    d) none of these   ☐

v) Which one of the following four projects is to be preferred (using payback as the method of appraisal), the cash flows for which are as follows:

Project	Outflow inflow £	Year 1 inflow £	Year 2 inflow £	Year 3 £	
a)	18,000	8,000	9,000	10,000	☐
b)	18,000	10,000	10,000	9,000	☐
c)	18,000	9,000	10,000	10,000	☐
d)	18,000	12,000	8,000	9,000	☐

vi) Payback may be usefully employed as a first screening method in project appraisal because it is a rough measure of:

    a) viability   ☐

    b) profitability   ☐

    c) liquidity   ☐

    d) none of these   ☐

vii) Accounting rate of return on investment is a measure of:

    a) liquidity   ☐

    b) profitability   ☐

    c) risk   ☐

    d) certainty   ☐

viii) For project X, the average profit, before tax, for the next three years is budgeted at £8,500 per annum. The average capital employed over the three years is budgeted at £50,000. The accounting rate of return is:

    a) 17%   ☐

    b) 58%   ☐

    c) 51%   ☐

    d) 19.33%   ☐

ix) In calculating the profit figure for use in the accounting rate of return calculation, the following is necessary:

    a) tax on profit should be deducted from that profit   ☐

    b) depreciation should be excluded from costs   ☐

    c) depreciation should be included as a cost   ☐

    d) none of these   ☐

x) Which of the following statements is true:

    a) Payback takes account of the time value of money   ☐

    b) Payback is a reasonable indicator of profitability   ☐

    c) ARR at least gives an indication of liquidity   ☐

    d) ARR takes no account of the timing of profits   ☐

CHAPTER 18

Discounted cash flow

1 OBJECTIVES

At the end of this chapter you should be able to:

- understand what is meant by present value;
- understand what is meant by discounted cash flow;
- calculate the present values of future cash flows;
- understand the mathematics of discounted cash flow;
- use discounted cash flow tables;
- understand the use of net present value and internal rate of return;
- understand the profitability index.

2 INTRODUCTION

In Chapter 17 we began to examine the techniques used in business when a decision has to be taken regarding whether to invest in a project which will generate returns in the future. You will remember that this is often decided by projecting the investment and future returns and applying *capital investment appraisal* or *capital budgeting* tests to determine whether the project is likely to be worthwhile. We described two techniques for testing the feasibility of such projects, *payback period* and *accounting rate of return* (ARR). Although both these approaches offer a number of advantages, one of their greatest weaknesses is that that fail to take into account the *time value of money*.

The time value of money is the concept that an amount received or paid today is worth more than an identical sum received or paid at a later date because of the interest which could be earned in the interim period if the money received earlier or paid later is invested. The time value of money, therefore, uses an interest rate which the money could earn if not invested in a project, sometimes called the *opportunity cost of capital*. It should be noted that the concept of £1 received today being worth more than £1 received later has nothing to do with inflation *per se*, although it is possible to include inflation in the calculations if this is considered necessary.

Example

Supposing you receive £100 now, which you invest at 10 per cent per annum in a building society. At the end of the first year the value of £100 would have risen to

£110, since interest of 10 per cent would have been added to the original capital sum.

If you continue to leave the £110 invested, assuming that the compounding was annual (and not half-yearly, quarterly or monthly), then at the end of the second year a further £11 (10 per cent of £110) would have been added to the sum invested and it would now be worth £121. In order to see what the investment would be worth at the end of years 3, 4 and 5, it is more convenient to draw up a table.

Year	Original sum invested £	Factor	Cumulative value of investment £
0	100	1.00	100.00
1	100	1.10	110.00
2	100	1.10^2	121.00
3	100	1.10^3	133.10
4	100	1.10^4	146.41
5	100	1.10^5	161.05

The factors in the above table are for compound interest. If you want to calculate them try the following on your calculator:

Year 1	100×1.1	$= 110$
Year 2	$100 \times 1.1 \times 1.1$	$= 121$
Year 3	$100 \times 1.1 \times 1.1 \times 1.1$	$= 133.1$ and so on.

3 | PRESENT VALUE

From the above example you can see that £100 received now and invested at 10 per cent will be worth £161.05 in five years' time. We could also say that £161.05 to be received in five years' time is worth, at the present time, much less than £161.05. In fact, assuming an annual compound interest rate of 10 per cent, we could say that £161.05 received in five years' time is the same as £100 now. In other words, £161.05 to be received in five years' time during which period the annual compound interest rate is 10 per cent has a present value of £100. The formula for this is the standard compound interest formula:

$$A = P(1 + r)^t$$

where:

A = final amount or compounded sum

P = principal or amount invested

r = annual interest rate, expressed as a decimal (e.g. 10 per cent = 0.10)

t = time expressed in years

Example

Suppose we want to know what £100 received in five years' time is worth now, assuming a compound interest rate of 10 per cent. We can calculate this as follows:

$$£100 \times \frac{£100}{161.05} = £62.09$$

We can check this using compound interest by taking £62.09 as the present value and calculating its growth at 10 per cent per annum interest, as follows.

Year	Principal	Discount factor at 10%	Cumulative value of investment
	£		£
0	62.09	1.00	62.09
1	62.09	1.10	68.30
2	62.09	1.10^2	75.13
3	62.09	1.10^3	82.64
4	62.09	1.10^4	90.91
5	62.09	1.10^5	100.00

4	PRESENT VALUE TABLES

If you have understood the above example, you will appreciate that we can produce another more convenient table which shows the present value of £100 received at the end of each individual year. This table is simply the table in the previous example with the last column in reverse order.

Example

Year	Present value of £100 at 10%
	£
0	100.00
1	90.91
2	82.64
3	75.13
4	68.30
5	62.09

Obviously, the present value of £100 received now in year 0 must be £100. Reading from the table we can see that the present value of £100 received in five years' time is £62.09 when the interest rate is 10 per cent.

Present value tables usually express values as a factor of £1 or simply 1 unit of any currency, thereby serving all other currencies. The following example shows a table for an interest rate of 10 per cent.

Example

Year	Discount factor at 10%
0	1.0000
1	0.9091
2	0.8264
3	0.7513
4	0.6830
5	0.6209

Although this table is to four decimal places, tables to three and even two decimal places are sometimes used and considered sufficiently accurate.

5 | DISCOUNTING

Earlier in this chapter we gave the formula for calculating compound interest as follows:

$$A = P(1 + r)^t$$

The process of finding the present value is called *discounting*. Discounting is the opposite of compounding and the formula is obtained by using the normal rules of algebra to make the P the subject of the equation as follows:

$$P = \frac{A}{(1 + r)^t}$$

In calculating the discount factor tables, A is always treated as 1 unit and therefore this leaves two unknowns: r and t. The present value factors (P) are then calculated by assuming r as 1 per cent for years 1 to n, then 2 per cent for years 1 to n, and so on until the factors for P can be built into a discounted cash flow table as in *Table 1 in the Appendix* at the end of this book. In order to find the present value of any sum received or paid for a given percentage rate, the sum is simply multiplied by the present value factor read off from the table for the appropriate year and percentage rate.

Example

What is the present value of £500 received annually at the end of the next five years, using a 10 per cent discount rate?

Solution

Using the discounted cash flow table (Table 1 in the Appendix), at a 10 per cent discount rate:

Year	Principal £		Discount factor at 10%		Present value £
1	500	×	0.909	=	454.50
2	500	×	0.826	=	413.00
3	500	×	0.751	=	375.50
4	500	×	0.683	=	341.50
5	500	×	0.621	=	310.50
					1,895.00

You should now be able to attempt question 18.6 at the end of this chapter.

6 CUMULATIVE PRESENT VALUE TABLES

Table 2 in the Appendix at the end of this book gives ranges of *cumulative present value factors* for given interest rates and time periods. These represent the cumulative sum of individual year present value factors from Table 1, and are used in discounting when a constant sum of cash is received or paid over a number of years.

Example

Continuing to use the example in the previous section, receiving £500 per annum for five years is a constant annual sum, therefore using the cumulative discounted cash flow table (Table 2 in the Appendix), at a 10 per cent discount rate is a short cut.

Year	Principal £		Cumulative discount factor at 12%		Present value £
1–5	500	×	3.791	=	1,895.50

As you may have noticed, there is a small discrepancy in the results (£1,895.50 in this calculation, compared with £1,895.00 in the previous example) and this is due to rounding. Note also that when you use Table 2, only one year's cash flow is multiplied by the factor.

The receipt or payment of a constant sum year after year is known as an *annuity*, and cumulative discounted cash flow tables can be used as a short cut for calculating the present value of an annuity. Consequently, they are sometimes referred to as *annuity tables*. You may have noticed that these always start from year 1 and go to year n, where n represents the number of years of the annuity. This means that if an annuity does not start at year 1, you must take care when using the tables to establish the present values.

Example

What are the present values of the following amounts, received at the end of each year, using a 12 per cent discount factor?

Years 1, 2 and 3 £2,000 per annum

Years 4, 5 and 6 £3,000 per annum

Solution

Using the cumulative discounted cash flow tables (Table 2 in the Appendix), at a 12 per cent discount rate:

Year	Principal		Cumulative discount factor at 12%		Present value
	£				£
1, 2, 3	2,000	×	2.402	=	4,804
4, 5, 6	3,000	×	1.709*	=	5,127
					9,931

* 1,709 is arrived at as follows:

Cumulative factor for Year 6	4.111
Less Cumulative factor for Year 3	2.402
Cumulative factor for Years 4 to 6	1.709

This is the same as adding the individual factors from Table 1 for years 4, 5 and 6 (0.636 + 0.567 + 0.507 = 1.710). Again, there is a small difference due to rounding.

An *alternative* method is as follows:

Year	Principal		Cumulative discount factor at 12%		Present value
	£				£
1–6	2,000	×	4.111	=	8,222
4–6	+1,000	×	1.709	=	1,709
					9,931

You should now be able to attempt task 18.1, and questions 18.7 and 18.8 at the end of this chapter.

7	**DISCOUNTED CASH FLOW**

So far we have considered discounting and the mathematics of discounting as they are applied to a series of cash flows in order to obtain the present value of those cash flows. *Discounted cash flow* (DCF) is the name given to a number of techniques which use discounting as a basis for determining the returns which may be obtained from investment projects. From these anticipated returns a decision can be made whether to invest in a particular project, or if a number of projects are being considered, to decide which project is likely to give the best return in DCF terms. There are three DCF decision making techniques: *net present value, profitability index* and *internal rate of return*.

As its name implies, DCF considers the cash flows which are likely to arise from the pursuit of a particular project or investment and the *incidence* of those cash flows, when they are likely to arise. Unlike the *accounting rate of return* (ARR) which we examined in the previous chapter, *cash flows* rather than profits are considered. This means that the accountants' practice of differentiating between capital and revenue expenditure is unnecessary for this technique, which is concerned with projected cash inflows and cash outflows of an investment. Moreover, *depreciation* policies become largely irrelevant with this technique because depreciation is a non-cash item.

8 | CHOOSING THE INTEREST RATE

The choice of the discount rate is an important aspect of DCF and there are several alternatives. If a project is assessed using a rate of interest which could otherwise be earned if the funds were invested in an alternative investment such as a bank account or government securities, the required rate would be described as the *opportunity cost of capital*; opportunity cost because it represents the benefit forgone by pursuing the internal project rather than the alternative investment. An alternative takes into consideration the interest rate which would be payable on funds *borrowed* in order to fund a project, in which case this would be regarded as the *cost of capital rate*.

The *weighted average cost of capital* (WACC) approach assumes that each individual organization's sources of capital are unique and it is possible to calculate a WACC from the mix of capital and the returns which each item of capital requires. Although it is outside the scope of this book to determine the return which each type of capital might require, a typical WACC calculation might be as follows.

Example

Penzance & Co Ltd has a source of capital employed of £180,000. This comprises loan capital (or debt) of £60,000, on which interest has to be paid of 13 per cent and ordinary shares (equity) of £120,000 on which the shareholders require a 16 per cent return.

Required

Calculate the WACC.

Solution

The WACC can be calculated in two ways:

i)

$$
\begin{array}{llr}
 & & £ & £ \\
\text{Loan capital} & 60{,}000 \times 13\% = & 7{,}800 \\
\text{Share capital} & \underline{120{,}000} \times 16\% = & \underline{19{,}200} \\
 & 180{,}000 & 27{,}000 \\
\end{array}
$$

$$
\text{WACC} = \frac{£27{,}000 \times 100}{£180{,}000} = 15\%
$$

ii)

	Rate	Weights	WACC %
Loan capital	$13\% \times \dfrac{60}{180}$	(33.3%) =	4.33
Share capital	$16\% \times \dfrac{120}{180}$	(66.7%) =	10.67
			15.00

The calculation of WACC can be a complex process and the example above is simplified. One other aspect which could be taken into consideration is that interest on loan capital is deductible from profits before any taxation charge is calculated, loan interest being described as 'tax deductible'. In this case the tax effect could be accounted for by multiplying the interest rate by $(1 - t)$, where $t =$ the corporation tax rate, thus reducing the cost of loan capital. In some cases market values may be available for both the debt and the equity, and could be substituted in the calculations.

Any interest rate chosen is really only a guide to the returns which are required by the organization. It should be borne in mind that a discount rate may be adjusted upwards to take into consideration the fact that there may be greater risk associated with some projects, therefore the rate may be increased to a *hurdle rate* to accommodate risk. Similarly, a higher rate of return may be required from those projects which can be assessed in order to compensate for those kinds of corporate investments from which a return may not be quantifiable, such as welfare projects.

> *You should now be able to attempt tasks 18.2 and 18.3 at the end of this chapter.*

9   BASIC ASSUMPTIONS OF DCF

The main basic assumptions inherent in the DCF technique are as follows:

- The cash flows, with the exception of the commencement of the project which is always regarded as taking place at the commencement of year 0, are assumed to take place at the end of the year in question.

- In general, the choice of interest rates assumes that lending rates and borrowing rates are the same, something which does not apply in practice as the interest rate charged on borrowed money is usually higher than that which is earned when it is lent.

- The interest rate is constant throughout the life of the project.

- The annual cash flows are certain. It is possible to bring in calculations which attempt to accommodate risk, but this is outside the scope of this book.

- Inflation is ignored, so that cash flows are assumed at constant values. Again, it is possible to incorporate inflation into the DCF calculations, but this approach is not covered here.

Although these assumptions attempt to simplify the DCF approach, it is still a very powerful and extensively used technique in capital investment appraisal.

10 NET PRESENT VALUE

The *net present value* (NPV) is the difference between the present values of the cash inflows and outflows. This approach to capital investment appraisal is based on the simple notion that, after discounting the projected cash flows, both in and out, an investment is likely to be worthwhile if the present value of the inflows exceeds the present value of the outflows. This condition is a *positive net present value* and indicates that the investment as projected will earn more than the interest rate used to discount the cash flows. In economic terms, the NPV represents the change in the value of the firm if the project is adopted.

If the present value of the outflows exceeds the present value of the inflows, that is the project yields a *negative net present value*, then the investment as projected is earning less than the discount rate and should be rejected. You will note that the discount rate used under this method represents the rate of return required to make the investment worthwhile, hence the accept/reject approach adopted above where respective positive and negative net present values are achieved.

Example

Bodmin Products Ltd is considering buying a machine which will improve cash flows by £30,000 per annum for the next five years, at the end of which period the machine will be worn out and of no value. The machine will cost £75,000, payable in cash, and Bodmins have fixed the required return on such projects at 15 per cent.

Required

Calculate the NPV of the project.

Solution

Year	Cash flows	Discount factor at 15%	Present value
	£		£
0 Purchase of machine	(75,000)	1.000	(75,000)
1–5 Net cash flow	30,000	3.352	100,560
		NPV	25,560

Notes

Purchase of the machine is a negative cash flow (a cash *outflow*) and is shown in brackets. The discount factor is 1.000 because the cash outflow is at year 0, which is the convention in DCF calculations for the commencement of the project.

The discount factor of 3.352 can be found in the cumulative discounted cash flow table (Table 2 in the Appendix) and is used as a short-cut technique to save the effort of multiplying the individual figures from Table 1 for years 1 to 5 inclusive.

The NPV, the difference between the present value of the outflows and the present value of the inflows, is positive at £25,560. This positive figure means that Bodmins are obtaining more than the required return of 15 per cent. If the NPV had been nil, the return would have been exactly 15 per cent, and if the NPV had been negative then the return would have been less than the required 15 per cent and would have been rejected.

The positive NPV of £25,560 could be said to represent the increase in the value of Bodmin's business if this project were undertaken with the result projected above.

Where a number of projects are being considered of which only one can be pursued, otherwise known as *mutually exclusive projects*, then the NPV approach suggests that the project with the highest positive net present value should be pursued. Such projects are said to be ranked according to the size of the net present value.

Example

Redruth & Co Ltd manufacture bricks and is considering whether to undertake one of two mutually exclusive projects, projects X and Y, each of which would require an investment of £100,000 in machinery which would have a realizable or scrap value of £10,000 after four years. Cost of capital is 15 per cent, and the cash flows associated with the two projects are as follows:

		Project X	Project Y
		£	£
Initial investment	Year 0	100,000	100,000
Net cash inflows	Year 1	40,000	80,000
	Year 2	60,000	40,000
	Year 3	40,000	40,000
	Year 4	80,000	40,000
Realizable value	Year 4	10,000	10,000

Required

i) Calculate the NPV for each project.

ii) Advise the management of Redruth which project should be pursued.

Solution

i) NPV

Year	Discount factor at 15%	Project X cash flow £	Present value £	Project Y cash flow £	Present value £
0	1.000	(100,000)	(100,000)	(100,000)	(100,000)
1	0.870	40,000	34,800	80,000	69,600
2	0.756	60,000	45,360	40,000	30,240
3	0.658	40,000	26,320	40,000	26,320
4	0.572	90,000	51,480	50,000	28,600
		NPV for X	57,960	NPV for Y	54,760

ii) The NPV for Project X is higher than that for Project Y and therefore, considering financial grounds alone, Project X should be adopted.

11 | WORKING CAPITAL

One of the consequences of any new project, apart from the cash outlays and the annual cash flow that arise from them, is that *working capital* is often increased. Increased sales mean that debtors increase, as do stocks of raw materials, work in progress and finished goods. Creditors also tend to increase, which reduces working capital, but not usually to the same extent.

Example

Continuing to use the example in the previous section, *Bodmin* finds they had omitted to take into consideration the impact of working capital requirements, which are likely to be:

		£
	Debtors up by	35,000
Add	Stocks up by	20,000
		55,000
Less	Creditors up by	15,000
	Working capital increase	40,000

The increase in working capital is virtually immediate as far as the project is concerned, and lasts the life of the project although it may fluctuate during that time, and is released at the end of the project when debtors pay, the stocks return to nil and the creditors are paid. To bring working capital into the calculations it is necessary to treat any increases in working capital as a cash outflow, whilst reductions in working capital are treated as a cash inflow, in each case in the years in which these changes take place. Taxation flows may also be incorporated in DCF calculations, but this is not covered here.

Example

Revise Bodmin's project appraisal calculations where the investment and dis-investment in working capital of £40,000 take place respectively at the beginning and the end of the project.

Solution

Year	Detail	Cash flows £	Discount factor at 15%	Present value £
0	Purchase of machine	(75,000)	1.000	(75,000)
0	Increase in working capital	(40,000)	1.000	(40,000)
1–5	Net cash inflow	30,000	3.352	100,560
5	Release of working capital	40,000	0.497	19,880
			NPV	5,440

Before adjusting for working capital, the NPV was £25,560 and this has now been reduced to £5,440. The project can therefore be said to be less attractive, but is still acceptable since it still gives a return in excess of 15 per cent.

Calculations which take working capital into account are more realistic since investment in working capital is as much an investment as is capital expenditure itself, and therefore should not be ignored. It has to be financed, a fact which sometimes comes as an unpleasant surprise to entrepreneurs who have over-looked it!

> You should now be able to attempt questions 18.9 and 18.10 at the end of this chapter.

---

12   PROFITABILITY INDEX

The *profitability index* (PI) is a ratio which compares the absolute value of the discounted cash inflows with the original investment. The PI is used to rank mutually exclusive projects, all projects with a PI greater than 1 being worth-while. These profitable projects will then be ranked according to the size of the PI, the greater the PI the more worthwhile the project. Like all ratios, however, care should be exercised in its interpretation. For example, a high PI may be due to the low cost of the original investment, which, unless revealed, could mean that some available capital was not utilized. However, this area of investment appraisal, known as *capital rationing*, is beyond the scope of this book.

Example

We can use the profitability index to rank the two mutually exclusive projects in the previous example of *Redruth & Co Ltd*.

	Project X	Project Y
Present value of inflows	157,960	154,760
Initial investment	100,000	100,000
Profitability index	1.58	1.55

Because the PI for Project X is larger than Project Y then that is the preferred option.

The PI can be used where the cash flows demonstrate a standard cash flow pattern of an investment at Year 0, followed by cash inflows subsequently, but is not satisfactory where a further net *outflow* of cash occurs in subsequent years of a project's life.

13 | INTERNAL RATE OF RETURN

The *internal rate of return* (IRR) is a technique of investment appraisal which is related to the NPV method. Using the NPV approach it is possible to demonstrate that a project which is discounted at, say, a discount rate of 10 per cent will be feasible because it gives a positive net present value. If the discount rates are successively increased, the net present value will steadily fall, go through zero, and then become negative, illustrating that higher discount rates cause fewer projects to be worthwhile. The IRR is the discount rate which applies when the present value of inflows equals the present value of outflows, that is, the net present value is zero.

Computers and some pocket calculators can easily calculate the IRR of a project, but manual calculation of IRR requires some trial and error. However, an understanding of the calculations necessary will help you to understand what IRR is and appreciate its value and limitations. An illustration is sometimes worth a thousand words, so we will look at an example.

Example

We will use the example of *Bodmin* again. The calculations are as follows:

Year	Detail	Cash flows	Discount factor at 15%	Present value
		£		£
0	Purchase of machine	(75,000)	1.000	(75,000)
1–5	Net cash inflow	30,000	3.352	100,560
			NPV	25,560

You will see that at a 15 per cent discount rate the NPV is positive and therefore the investment was regarded as worthwhile. Now we shall recalculate the NPV using discount rates of 20 per cent, 25 per cent and 30 per cent. Will the project be worthwhile at these cost of capital rates?

Solution

Year	Cash flow £	Discount factor at 20%	Present value £	Discount factor at 25%	Present value £	Discount factor at 30%	Present value £
0	(75,000)	1.000	(75,000)	1.000	(75,000)	1.000	(75,000)
1–5	30,000	2.991	89,730	2.689	80,670	2.436	73,080
		NPV	14,730	NPV	5,670	NPV	(1,920)

As you can see, the higher the discount rate, the lower the positive NPV. The project is still worthwhile at 20 per cent and 25 per cent, but not at 30 per cent where the NPV is negative. The higher the discount rate, the smaller the positive NPV becomes, until it eventually becomes negative somewhere between 25 per cent and 30 per cent.

The point at which the NPV changes from positive to negative (that is, where it is zero) lies the *internal rate of return*. The trial and error in calculating the IRR comes about because of the need to find discount rates which give a small negative and a small positive net present value, so that linear interpolation may take place between the two results.

It may help if we now plot the NPVs we calculated in the above example on a graph. The discount rates are marked on the horizontal (x) axis, and the NPVs on the vertical (y) axis.

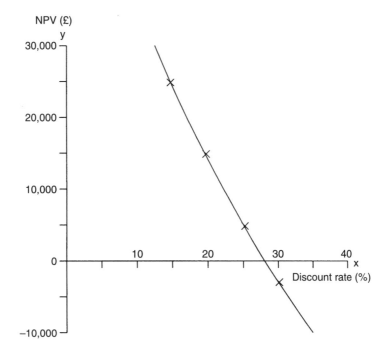

As you can see, the line joining the four points is a slight curve, but for all practical purposes we can assume that it is a straight line provided that the points either side of the x axis are not too far apart. We shall use the data at 25 per cent and 30 per cent discount rates as it is between those two points that the curve crosses the zero line, i.e. the internal rate of return must be between 25 per cent and 30 per cent. The calculation of the precise interest rate at which the NPV = 0 involves *linear interpolation* (linear because it assumes a straight line), and is as follows:

$$25 + 5 \times \left[\frac{5,670}{5,670 + 1,920}\right] = 28.7$$

The figures in brackets represent the *proportion* of 5 per cent (the difference between 25 per cent and 30 per cent) which is required to be added to 25 per cent to give us a point where the curve crosses the horizontal axis:

$$\frac{\text{NPV of 25\% rate}}{\text{NPV of 25\% + NPV of 30\% rate}}$$

We ignore the fact that the NPV of the 30 per cent; rate (£1,920) is negative (i.e. the difference or distance on the curve between *plus* £5,670 and *minus* £1,920 is the total of the two figures). If you find this difficult to understand, the following examples may help.

- If you had £5,670 (a *positive* figure) in the bank yesterday and today you have an overdraft of £1,920 (a *negative* figure), how much money have you drawn out of the bank since yesterday? The answer is £5,670 + £1,920 = £7,590, the *difference* between the two figures!

- The denominator, which is the lower part of the fraction, is the range which is a – b. When b is negative, the range is a – (– b) or a + b. In algebra, multiplying similar signs result in a positive figure; multiplying dissimilar signs result in a negative figure.

Once calculated, the IRR for a project is compared with the target return required by the organization. If it is greater than or equal to the latter, the project is likely to be worthwhile. If it is less than the target return, the project should be rejected. Investments in mutually exclusive projects are ranked according to the size of the IRR.

> *You should now be able to attempt question 18.11 at the end of this chapter.*

14 | COMPARISON OF NPV AND IRR

Net present value and IRR can sometimes give different rankings for mutually exclusive projects, mainly because the inherent re-investment rates for each of the methods vary. For NPV the re-investment rate is the discount rate used, whereas for IRR the re-investment rate is the internal rate of return. The NPV method measures project returns in terms of net present values, which is an *absolute* way of measuring returns. The IRR method measures project returns in terms of a percentage IRR, which is a *relative* way of measuring returns. Where there is conflict between the results of the two methods it is generally regarded that the NPV approach is considered to be more reliable.

It is sometimes possible for a project to have large negative cash flows, not only at the start, but also during its lifetime. This is sometimes known as a non-standard cash flow pattern. This situation could produce multiple IRRs, a distinct IRR for each change of sign where the NPV changes from positive to negative or vice versa. It is very difficult to justify to top management that several rates of return are acceptable for a single project!

Another disadvantage with IRR is that unless other methods of investment appraisal are also taken into consideration, theoretically it would be possible to choose a project X with an initial investment of £1,000, and reject a project Y with an initial investment of £10,000, purely because project X has a higher IRR. This would leave £9,000 uninvested, presumably giving a return equal to the cost of capital. However, the IRR percentage can be regarded as a useful indicator of future returns provided other investment appraisal methods are used in addition to IRR.

Example

In preparing their cash budget for next year *Porlock Ltd* find that they have limited surplus funds, £7,000 of which the managing director wishes to spend on one of two schemes.

Alternative A – Pay £7,000 immediately to a reputable sales promotion agency which would provide extensive advertising and planned 'reminder' advertising over the next 10 years. This is expected to increase net operational cash flows by £2,000 per annum for the first five years and £1,000 per annum for the following five years. Thereafter the effect would be zero.

Alternative B – Buy immediately new labour-saving equipment at a cost of £7,000 which would reduce the operating cash outflows by £1,500 per annum for each of the next 10 years, at the end of which the equipment would be worn out and have no value.

Required

i) Calculate the average ARR per annum for each alternative over 10 years (see Chapter 17).

ii) Calculate the payback periods for each alternative (see Chapter 17).

iii) Calculate the net present value for each alternative using DCF, assuming the minimum desired return to be 18 per cent.

iv) Calculate the internal rate of return for each alternative.

v) Advise the management of the company which alternative should be pursued.

Solution

i) ARR

		A £	B £
Investments		7,000	7,000
Average capital employed (divide by 2)		3,500	3,500
Increase in net cash flows		15,000	15,000
Average increase per annum (divide by 10)		1,500	1,500
Less Depreciation per annum		700	700
Average net income		800	800

Average ARR for both projects:

$$\frac{800 \times 100}{3500} = 22.9\%$$

ii) Payback period

	Year	A £	B £
Investment	0	(7,000)	(7.000)
	1	2,000	1,500
	2	2,000	1,500
	3	2,000	1,500
	4	2,000	1,500
	5	2,000	1,500
Payback period		3.5 years	4.67 years

iii) NPV

Year	Cash flow A £	Discount factor at 18%	Present value £	Cash flow B £	Discount factor at 18%	Present value £
0	(7,000)	1.000	(7,000)	(7,000)	1.000	(7,000)
1–10	1,000	4,494	4,494	1,500	4.494	6,741
1–5	1,000	3.127	3,127			
		NPV of A	621		NPV of B	(259)

iv) IRR

Year	Cash flow A £	Discount factor at 22%	Present value £	Cash flow B £	Discount factor at 16%	Present value £
0	(7,000)	1.000	(7,000)	(7,000)	1.000	(7,000)
1–10	1,000	3.923	3,923	1,500	4.833	7,249
1–5	1,000	2.864	2,864			
		NPVof A	(213)		NPV of B	249

$$18 + 3\frac{621}{621 + 213} \times 44 = 20.98\%; \ 16 + 3\frac{249}{249 + 259} \times 24 = 16.98\%$$

v) Conclusions

The ARR is the same for both projects. Alternative A has the shorter payback period, produces a higher NPV, and also shows a higher IRR which at 22 per cent exceeds the minimum desired return of 18 per cent. Unless there are other factors which should be taken into consideration, alternative A is the more attractive proposal.

> *You should now be able to attempt task 18.5 and questions 18.12 and 18.13 at the end of this chapter.*

15   USING SPREADSHEETS

Most *spreadsheets*, such as *Lotus 1–2–3, Excel* and *QuatroPro*, include a function which will enable you to calculate the NPV and IRR. Therefore the use of discount tables to calculate the NPV or linear interpolation to calculate the IRR is rarely necessary. The precise formulae to be entered in the cells may vary slightly according to the spreadsheet used, but are typically as follows:

- *Net present value* – NPV (interest rate required, cell ranges of cash flows for years 1 to n) minus cell containing cash flow for year 0

- *Internal rate of return* – IRR (cell ranges of cash flows for years 0 to n)

Apart from the speed and accuracy achieved by using a spreadsheet program, it is also possible to test how sensitive a project is to any changes in the variables; for example, the interest rate or the levels and incidence of cash flows. This is achieved by incorporating the changes and obtaining a range of different results. This process is known as *sensitivity analysis*.

16   ADVANTAGES AND DISADVANTAGES OF DCF

The advantages of DCF are as follows:

- The techniques use cash flows rather than the more subjective profits.

- Differentiation between capital and revenue flows is unnecessary.

- Unlike payback, the calculations cover the whole life of the project.

- The time value of money is taken into consideration.

- Discounted cash flow functions are built into computer spreadsheets such as Microsoft Excel.

The disadvantages of DCF are as follows:

- The calculations may be regarded as complex.

- Conflicting results may be obtained between NPV and IRR calculations.

- The IRR method may result in multiple internal rates of return in some circumstances.

- Return on capital employed (ROCE) may be used to measure corporate performance but using DCF to screen alternative investments does not ultimately guarantee maximum ROCE. Discounted cash flow and ROCE are different measures of performance.

17 | SUMMARY

Organizations have to decide whether it is worthwhile investing funds in order to create future returns. There are a number of tests which are applied to projections of the future returns. In Chapter 18 we described how the *payback period* technique and the *accounting rate of return* (ARR) are used. However, both these methods suffer from a major weakness: they fail to take the *time value of money* into account. In this chapter we have examined three techniques which use *discounted cash flow* (DCF) and do take account of the time value of money. The three methods are the *net present value* (NPV), *internal rate of return* (IRR) and *profitability index* (PI) approaches to *capital investment appraisal*.

The NPV and the IRR are related since the latter is the discount rate which causes the present value of inflows to be equal to the present value of outflows. This is where the net present value is zero. The technique of *linear interpolation* may be used to calculate the IRR, but more commonly, spreadsheet programs are used to calculate the NPV and the IRR. Computers may also be used to test the impact on the possible outcomes due to changes in the variables by using *sensitivity analysis*. Although NPV, IRR and PI may be used to rank *mutually exclusive* projects, they do not necessarily all rank projects in the same order and therefore should be used with care. Although there are problems with the DCF techniques, they tend to be more mathematically rigorous than the non-discounted techniques, avoid the necessity to differentiate between revenue and capital items, and also enable working capital and taxation flows to be incorporated into capital investment appraisal.

> You should now be able to attempt the objective test at the end of this chapter.

STUDENT ACTIVITIES (* *denotes questions with answers at the end of the book*)

Task 18.1
Conduct a survey with fellow students or friends to find out how much (hypothetically) they would lend you now for the promise of a payment of £100 in four years' time. Calculate the discount rates they are using and present them either in the form of a bar chart or a line graph.

Task 18.2

You are a trainee accountant in an engineering company. The assistant production manager has asked you for your help. He is contemplating buying a new machine, and does not know which one to select from the three machines which are available. Write him a memorandum specifying the types of information you require so that you can calculate and compare the net present values of the three machines.

Task 18.3

Make a list of what you consider to be the main rules to be applied when working out the net present value of any project.

Task 18.4

You have been asked to give a presentation at a management meeting on linear interpolation. Draft notes for your talk and construct the diagrams you will need to illustrate the points you will make.

Task 18.5

The following letter appeared in the *Financial Times*:

From Mr Isambard Kingdom Brunel

Sir, I am not surprised that British Industry is in the state that it is when we use such poor method for appraising the investments we make. Many businesses are still in the dark ages, and use the Payback Period method with all its short-comings. The only method to use is the Internal Rate of Return. This provides unambiguous results, with no confusion. Using this method there is no need to take into account any other method, since it utilizes the modern principle of discounting future cash flows.

Isambard Brunel, *Engineer*

Write a reply to this letter, stating clearly whether you agree or disagree, and why.

Question 18.6

Assuming a 10 per cent annual rate of interest:

i)   What will £68.30 invested now be worth in 2 years' time?

ii) What will £82.64 invested now be worth in 2 years' time?

iii) What will £62.09 invested now be worth in 4 years' time?

iv) What will £62.09 invested now be worth in 6 years' time?

v)   What is the present value of £100 received in 4 years' time?

vi) What is the present value of £ 75.13 received in 1 year's time?

vii) What is the present value of £ 90.91 received in 3 years' time?

viii) What is the present value of £121 received in 6 years' time?

Question 18.7

What are the present values for the amounts indicated, received annually, for the stated number of years and discount rates? Answer to the nearest £1.

	Amount received annually (£)	Years	Discount rate %
i)	140	5	12
ii)	200	4	8
iii)	300	10	15
iv)	590	3	20
v)	999	9	9

Question 18.8

What are the present values of the following cash inflows:

	Years	£ per annum	Discount rate
i)	1, 2 and 3	1,000	8%
	4 and 5	1,500	
ii)	1 and 2	5,000	10%
	3, 4, 5 and 6	7,500	
iii)	1, 2 and 3	8,000	16%
	4, 5 and 6	10,000	
	7, 8 and 9	12,000	

Question 18.9

Liskeards runs a secretarial agency, and is considering buying a computer System. Their accountant has produced a five-year budget, which shows that their cash flows are likely to diminish in the first two years (due to setting-up costs, etc.), but will show positive results thereafter. The figures are as follows:

		£
Year 0:	Purchase of computer and software	(10,000)
Net cash flows:	Year 1	(4,000)
	Year 2	(1,000)
	Year 3	3,000
	Year 4	8,000
	Year 5	10,000

Required

Calculate the NPV of this project, using a discount rate of 12 per cent. Comment on whether you think Liskeards would be advised to go ahead with this project.

Question 18.10

Peter Polperro, currently employed as a part-time waiter, is considering setting up a small pottery to produce, in his spare time, souvenirs for the tourist trade. He estimates that a kiln and other equipment will cost £6,000 at the start of this enterprise, and that working capital of £3,000 will be required for the life of the project. He is hesitant to budget the life of the project beyond a five-year period, at the end of which he assumes that the working capital will be released and that he could sell his kiln and other equipment for £2,000.

He also estimates that net cash inflows arising each year from the project will be £3,000, and has been advised by his bank manager, who is willing to finance the project, to use a discount rate of 16 per cent for the purpose of project appraisal.

Required

Calculate the NPV of this project and state whether you think it is worthwhile.

Question 18.11

Terry Tavistock is considering buying a taxi for £20,000, which will, he hopes, last for five years before it becomes scrap (assume nil value).

Net cash flows (cash receipts less all costs, including a driver but excluding depreciation) are estimated at £7,000 per annum.

Required

Calculate the NPVs of this project using discount rates of 15 per cent and 25 per cent, and calculate the IRR to the nearest whole number percentage.

Question 18.12

Tintagel Investments Ltd in Question 17.6 in Chapter 17, considered two investments. If you attempted that question, you may remember that you were required to advise which of the two businesses (Business A, a newsagent and sweet shop, or Business B, a gift shop) should be purchased. The techniques of appraisal available to you at that time were payback period and accounting rate of return.

At present Tintagel favours Business A, the newsagents and sweet shop, but currently has the £50,000 invested in an account which is producing a return of 16 per cent, and wishes to know whether, on the basis of the anticipated cash flows for the next 10 years, Business A will show any improvement on that return.

It can be assumed that the investment of £50,000 covers the purchase price of the business, both lease and stock, and that the value of these assets will remain constant at about £50,000 throughout the 10 years, with a zero value at the end of the period. Details of the anticipated cash flows for the first 10 years are given below:

	Business A £
Year 1	8,000
Year 2	9,000
Year 3	10,000
Year 4	11,000

	£
Year 5	12,000
Year 6	13,000
Year 7	14,000
Year 8	15,000
Year 9	16,000
Year 10	17,000

Required

Calculate the net present value of Business A, using a discount factor of 16 per cent, and also calculate the internal rate of return. (Tip: Interpolate, using a discount factor of 20 per cent.)

Question 18.13*

This question follows on from Question 18.12. *Tintagel Investments Ltd*, though impressed with your calculations concerning Business A, is not convinced that the newsagents and sweet shop is the right kind of business to acquire, since a newsagency necessitates early mornings and long hours of work. The gift shop, on the other hand, could be open at more congenial hours, and could close for long periods off-season. Perform for the gift shop calculations similar to those which you prepared for the newsagents and sweet shop.

It can be assumed that the investment of £50,000 covers the purchase price of the business, both lease and stock, and that the value of the assets and level of stock will remain constant at about £50,000 throughout the 10 years, with a zero value at the end of that period.

Details of the anticipated cash flows for the first 10 years are given below.

	Business B
	£
Year 1	12,000
Year 2	11,000
Year 3	10,000
Year 4	9,000
Year 5	8,000
Year 6	8,000
Year 7	8,000
Year 8	8,000
Year 9	8,000
Year 10	8,000

Required

Calculate the net present value of Business B, using a discount factor of 16 per cent, and also calculate the internal rate of return for Business B, using a suitable second discount rate for interpolation. Advise Tintagel Investments Ltd.

| **OBJECTIVE TEST** * *(tick the appropriate box)* |

i) The value of £100 invested at 12 per cent per annum, compound
after 5 years is:

   a) £176.23

   b) £161.05

   c) £157.35

   d) £160.00

ii) The present value of £1 to be received in 5 years' time, using a 17 per cent ra
of discount, is:

   a) £0.654 ☐

   b) £3.199 ☐

   c) £0.456 ☐

   d) £0.436 ☐

iii) The present value of £753 to be received in 10 years' time, using a 15 per cent
rate of discount, is:

   a) £185.99 ☐

   b) £247.00 ☐

   c) £179.97 ☐

   d) £179.96 ☐

iv) The present value of £1,000 to be received in 20 years' time, using an 18 per
cent rate of discount, is:

   a) £ 38.00 ☐

   b) £380.00 ☐

   c) £ 37.00 ☐

   d) £ 3.70 ☐

v) The present value of £100 to be received at the end of each year for the next 5
years, discounted at 12 per cent is:

   a) £360.50 ☐

   b) £886.30 ☐

   c) £ 56.70 ☐

   d) £ 55.70 ☐

vi) Project X has the following cash flows:

Year	Cash flows £
0	(20,000)
1	10,000
2	10,000
3	10,000

Using a 15 per cent discount rate, the NPV is:

a) £22,830 ☐

b) £2,830 ☐

c) £283 ☐

d) (£2,830) ☐

vii) Project Y has the following cash flows:

Year	Cash flows £
0	(20,000)
1	8,000
2	10,000
3	12,000

Using a 15 per cent discount rate, the NPV is:

a) £22,416 ☐

b) £2,416 ☐

c) £242 ☐

d) (£2,416) ☐

viii) Referring to (vi) and (vii) above, it is correct to say:

a) Project X has a lower NPV than Project Y ☐

b) Project Y is to be preferred to Project X ☐

c) Project X is to be preferred to Project Y ☐

d) Both projects have the same net present values ☐

ix) If £5,000 of working capital is needed for Project X (Question (vi) above), for the life of the project, the NPV of Project X alters to:

a) £1,120 ☐

b) (£2,170) ☐

c) £6,120 ☐

d) (£4,717) ☐

x) If £5,000 of working capital is needed for Project Y (Question (vii) above), for the life of the project, the NPV of Project Y alters to:

a) £ 706 ☐

b) £5,706 ☐

c) (£2,584) ☐

d) £2,584 ☐

xi) Internal rate of return is:

    a) the method used to calculate the cost of capital ☐

    b) the discount rate which results in an NPV of nil ☐

    c) the mean of positive and negative NPVs ☐

    d) a sophisticated development of the ARR technique ☐

xii) IRR can be calculated by:

    a) taking the mean of positive and negative NPVs ☐

    b) plotting the cash flows on a graph ☐

    c) trial and error, using interpolation ☐

    d) reading the co-ordinates in an IRR table ☐

xiii) Project X has the following cash flows:

Year	Cash flows £
0	(20,000)
1	1,000
2	1,000
3	1,000

The IRR of this project is:

    a) 21% ☐

    b) 22% ☐

    c) 23% ☐

    d) 24% ☐

xiv) The quickest way to solve the previous question would be:

    a) calculate the NPV at 20 per cent and 25 per cent, and interpolate ☐

    b) look up Table 2 and look along the line for year 3 for the nearest factor to 2.000 ☐

    c) plot two NPVs on a graph, draw a line between the two points and read off where the line crosses the x (discount rate) axis ☐

    d) learn how to use a computer program which calculates IRR ☐

xv) The most reliable method of investment appraisal is:

    a) payback period ☐

    b) NPV ☐

    c) IRR ☐

    d) a combination of these ☐

ASSIGNMENT

Aussie Woollen Products Ltd

You are an assistant in the marketing department of Aussie Woollen Products Ltd, and the company is considering the production and marketing of a new range of woollen products which uses a new type of wool. Because of their specialized nature, it is intended to market them through an agency which charges a fee per garment. There are three products in the range, a pullover, a sweater and a smoking jacket. The projected figures for each product are as follows:

	Pullover £	Sweater £	Smoking jacket £
Selling price	210	255	320
Direct materials	50	60	60
Agency fee	10	17	21
Direct labour time	[10 hours]	[12.5 hours]	[15 hours]
The market potential – maximum units per month	[2,000 units]	[2,000 units]	[1,000 units]

Other information is:

Rate of pay per hour £8

Variable production overheads are 50 per cent of direct labour costs.

Fixed overheads are expected to be £50,000 per month.

A special curing process requires skilled labour which is in short supply and the number of direct labour hours required for this process, per garment, is:

Pullover	2	hours
Sweater	2.5	hours
Smoking jacket	4	hours

The company wishes to know whether the introduction of the new range is financially feasible, and if so, what product mix would give the highest profit.

STUDENT ACTIVITIES

i) Prepare a report to the marketing director of the company, and advise him what strategy should be adopted by the company with regard to production and product mix if the market constraint applies; and either skilled labour in the curing process is limited to 9,250 hours per month or the direct material is in short supply, limited to £250,000 worth per month.

ii) Calculate the break-even point expressed in sales value for each optimal mix of sales you have advised and explain why they differ. How do the margins of safety differ?

FORMAT

A report, with tables of data and supporting calculations. A logically reasoned conclusion should be clearly stated.

OBJECTIVES

The student should show an appreciation and understanding of:

- marginal costing techniques
- relevant costs
- limiting factors
- break-even analysis

REFERENCES

Chapters 3, and 14 to 16.

Wight Mineral Water Co Ltd

CONTEXT

You are assistant to Vic Ventnor, managing director of the *Wight Mineral Water Co Ltd*, a company which has recently experienced a flat-spot in sales. Vic has thought of two alternative courses of action to remedy this situation:

Alternative A

Improved technology which will improve the quality and taste of the product. Investment of £30,000 (payable immediately) in new equipment is expected to improve the cash flows by £9,600 per annum. At the end of five years, it is conjectured that the technology and equipment will be obsolete.

Alternative B

Improved marketing. A reputable agency claims that for £30,000 (payable immediately) and £2,000 per annum (payable at the end of each of the next five years), it will provide extensive advertising and 'maintenance' advertising over the next five years. This is expected to improve the annual net cash inflows (over present levels, and not taking into account the payments of £2,000 per annum to the agency), through increased volume of sales of the existing product, by £14,000 per annum for the next three years, dropping, as the impact of the campaign decreases, to an improvement of £8,000 per annum for the following two years.

Vic wishes to prepare a report which he can present to the next meeting of senior managers. He asks you for a memorandum concerning these alternatives, which will help him prepare his report.

STUDENT ACTIVITIES

Write a memorandum to Vic Ventnor, which will help him write his report, and, hopefully, help you in your career.

Your memorandum should include:

i) In respect of each alternative, calculation of:

- the payback period;
- the accounting rate of return;

- the net present value, assuming a minimum desired rate of return of 20 per cent;

- the internal rate of return.

ii) A clear explanation of what each of the four sets of calculations mean.

iii) Your advice on which alternative you consider to be of greater advantage to the Wight Mineral Water Company.

Ignore taxation, inflation and treat all cash flows as occurring at the end of complete years, except for the initial outlays at the start of year 1.

FORMAT

A memorandum to Vic Ventnor, with tables of calculations and comments suitably appended.

OBJECTIVES

In this assignment the student should show an appreciation and understanding of the use of specific financial techniques for decision making.

REFERENCES

Chapters 17 and 18.

CHAPTER 1

OBJECTIVE TEST 1

i) a   ii) e   iii) e   iv) c   v) e

CHAPTER 2

Question 2.9

Brixham Garden Furniture

	£	£	£
Direct materials			
Sand	1,000		
Cement	5,000		
Paint	200	6,200	
Direct wages			
Operators		10,000	
i) Prime cost			16,200
Factory overheads			
Rent		500	
Rates		300	
Power		700	
Light and heat		2,000	
Maintenance wages		1,500	
Canteen wages		2,500	
Depreciation			
Moulds		2,200	
Fixtures and fittings		800	
Mixer repairs		900	11,400
ii) Production cost		27,600	
iii) Administration overheads			
Office			
Rent		100	
Rates		100	
Light and heat		1,300	
Depreciation on equipment		500	
Salaries		1,800	3,800

continued

	£	£	£
iv) Selling overheads			
Salary and commission		2,200	
Car expenses		1,100	3,300
v) Distribution overheads			
Delivery expenses		500	
Packing		800	1,300
vi) Total cost			36,000
vii) *Add* 50% mark up			18,000
Total sales income required			54,000

Selling price per gnome $\dfrac{£54,000}{2,000} = £27$

viii) Profit margin $\dfrac{£18,000}{£54,000} \times 100 = 33.3\%$

OBJECTIVE TEST 2

i) c   ii) d   iii) c   iv) a   v) d   vi) d   vii) b   viii) d   ix) a   x) a

CHAPTER 3

Question 3.8

Auckland Products

Production/sales levels 2,000 units 5,000 units

| | Total costs | | Cost behaviour | Semi-variable costs | |
| | | | | Fixed | Variable |
	£	£		£	£ per unit
Supervision	20,000	20,000	F		
Direct materials	100,000	250,000	V		
Storage and handling	10,000	17,500	SV	5,000	2.5
Maintenance	30,000	60,000	SV	10,000	10.0
Direct wages	90,000	225,000	V		
Electricity	10,000	19,000	SV	4,000	3.0
Rent	26,000	26,000	F		
Insurance	8,000	8,000	F		
Salesmen's salaries (including commission)	50,000	65,000	SV	40,000	5.0
Packaging	27,500	68,750	V		
Staff salaries	80,000	80,000	F		
Distribution	30,000	52,500	SV	15,000	7.5
Rates	20,000	20,000	F		
Depreciation	40,000	40,000	F		

OBJECTIVE TEST 3

i) d   ii) c   iii) a   iv) b   v) d

CHAPTER 4

Question 4.3

X	y	xy	x^2
2	60	120	4
3	80	240	9
4	70	280	16
5	100	500	25
6	90	540	36
Sum 20	400	1680	90

$$n = 5 \quad b = \frac{(5 \times 1680) - (20 \times 400)}{(5 \times 90) - 20^2}$$

$$b = \frac{8400 - 8000}{450 - 400}$$

$$\underline{b = 400 = 8}$$

substitute in formula for 'a'

$$a - \frac{400}{5} - \frac{8 \times 20}{5}$$

$$a = 80 - 32$$

$$\underline{a = 48}$$

Substitute 'a' and 'b' in formula $y = a + bx$

$$y = 48 + 8(9)$$

$$\underline{y = 120}$$

OBJECTIVE TEST 4

i) b   ii) b   iii) d   iv) b   v) d

CHAPTER 5

Question 5.6

Pan-European Tours Ltd

i) *Rhine Valley Tour – Budget for 20X2*

		£	£	Cost increase £
Sales	$40 \times 20 \times 250$		200,000	
Hire of coach	$£480 \times 1.05 \times 20$	10,080		480
Fuel	$\dfrac{1,200 \text{ miles}}{10} \times £2.1 \times 20$	5,040		240
Driver	$£320 \times 20$	6,400		400
Courier	$£160 \times 20$	3,200		200
Ferries	$£4,000 \times 1.1$	4,400		400
Hotels	$£120,000 \times 1.04$	124,800		–
Excursions	$(40 \times 2 \times £1 \times 20) + £9,600$	11,200	165,120	–
Contribution to HO charge			34,880	
Head office charge			16,800	800
Budgeted profit			18,080	2,520

ii) Some costs will be incurred irrespective of the load factor. These costs are: hire of coach, fuel, driver, courier, head office change and (assuming that the ferry charge is per coach and not per passenger), ferries. With an 80 per cent load factor the income and other costs are:

	20X1 £	20X2 £	
Sales	240,000	200,000	
Hotels and excursions	129,600	136,000	
Margin	110,400	64,000	÷ 40 passengers per tour (80% × 50 seats)
Increases in costs		2,520	Margin per passenger = £1,600
Margin required	112,920		

Number of passengers per tour to achieve the required margin:

$$\frac{£112,920}{£1600} = 70.5$$

As 50 seater coaches are used, this would give a load factor of

$$\frac{70.5 \times 100}{50} = 141\% \text{ Impossible with everyone seated!}$$

OBJECTIVE TEST 5

i) c   ii) b   iii) a   iv) c   v) d

CHAPTER 6

Question 6.7

Durban Production Ltd
Cost centre overheads budget

Cost	£	Basis	Machining £	Fabrication £	Finishing £
Cleaning	10,000	area	4,000	2,500	3,500
Rent and business rates	40,000	area	16,000	10,000	14,000
Building insurance	1,000	area	400	250	350
Indirect labour	12,000	I.L. hours	6,000	3,000	3,000
Machinery depreciation	10,000	cap. vals.	10,000	500	500
Supervision	50,000	no. of pers.	30,000	10,000	10,000
Material handling	22,000	val. of mats.	20,000	1,000	1,000
Power	50,500	HP/hours	50,000	500	–
Canteen	50,000	no. of pers.	30,000	10,000	10,000
Total costs	246,500		166,400	37,750	42,350

Note: alternative bases of overhead cost apportionment may be used, e.g. machinery depreciation may be apportioned on a machine hours basis rather than the horsepower/hours basis used, but this would not take into consideration different sized machines in each cost centre.

OBJECTIVE TEST 6

i) d   ii) b   iii) d   iv) d   v) c

CHAPTER 7

Question 7.13

Princetown Products Ltd

i)   a)   Percentage on direct labour cost rate

Department A

$$\frac{£90,000}{£150,000} = 60\% \text{ on direct labour costs}$$

Department B

$$\frac{£85,000}{£23,375} = 364\% \text{ on direct labour costs (rounded)}$$

b)   Direct labour hour rate

Department A

$$\frac{£90,000}{15,000 \text{ hours}} = £6 \text{ per direct labour hour}$$

Department B

$$\frac{£85,000}{2,125 \text{ hours}} = £40 \text{ per direct labour hour (rounded)}$$

Continued

c) Machine hour rate

Department A

$$\frac{£90,000}{3,000 \text{ hours}} = £30 \text{ per machine hour}$$

Department B

$$\frac{£85,000}{42,500 \text{ hours}} = £2 \text{ per machine hour}$$

ii) a) The percentage on direct labour cost method is relatively easy to use since direct labour cost is often charged to cost units or products and therefore may be used as a basis for attracting overheads to products. However, there are a number of drawbacks. For example, many overheads are incurred on a time basis, and the use of direct labour does not use a time factor only. In addition, when operators are paid different hourly rates of pay, this method results in an inequitable charge of overheads to different products.

b) The rate per direct labour hour is often preferable and would be suitable for Department A which appears to be labour intensive.

c) The rate per machine hour method may be the most appropriate method for use in Department B because it is a machine intensive cost centre.

iii) Calculation of job costs

	Job 1 £	Job 2 £	Job 3 £
Direct material costs	550	750	950
Direct labour costs			
Departments A and B	1,374	2,344	3,698
Overhead recovered or absorbed			
Department A (Direct labour hours × £6)	720	1,200	1,800
Department B (Machine hours × £2)	800	1,000	2,000
Total job costs	3,444	5,294	8,448

OBJECTIVE TEST 7

i) c   ii) e   iii) c   iv) b   v) a   vi) c

CHAPTER 8

Question 8.6

Absorption costing

	Units	Rate	£
Sales	1,900	43.50	82,650
Production	2,200	16.50	36,300
Closing stock	300	16.50	4,950
	1,900	16.50	31,350
Apparent profit	1,900	27.00	51,300
Over-recovery	200	4.00*	800
Absorption profit	1,900		52,100

*Fixed cost absorption rate:

$$\frac{£96,000}{24,000}, = £4 \text{ per unit}$$

Over-recovery of fixed costs:

Recovery 2,200 × £4	8,800
Fixed overheads	8,000
Over-recovery:	800

Marginal costing

	Units	Rate	£
Sales	1,900	43.50	82,650
Production	2,200	12.50	27,500
Closing stock	300	12.50	3,750
	1,900	12.50	23,750
Contribution	1,900	31.00	58,900
Fixed costs		8,000	
Marginal profit		50,900	
Change in stock	300	4.00	1,200
Absorption profit		52,100	

OBJECTIVE TEST 8

i) d   ii) c   iii) b   iv) c   v) b

CHAPTER 9

Question 9.4

Hightec Plc

ABC Rates

Cost drivers	Department 1	Department 2
Staff	£60k/5 = 12k per staff	£400k/40 = 10k per staff
Productive	£80k/£0.5m = £0.16 per £1	£700k/£2m = £0.35 per £1
Mat. Process	£30k/1200 = £25 per order	£60k/800 = £75 per order
I.T.	£40k/1250 = £32 per hour	£40k/2500 = £16 per hour

Continued

ABC profit statement (£'000)

		Product A		Product B	Total
Sales		1,760		1,040	2,800
Material (£10 × 20,000)		200	(£12×10,000)	120	320
Labour (£8 × 20,000)		160	(£12×10,000)	120	280
Overheads:					
Variable (£4 × 20,000)		80	(£5 × 10,000)	50	130
Fixed					
Staff	Dept I (£12k × 2)	24	(£12k × 3)	36	40
	Dept II (£10k × 15)	150	(£10k × 25)	250	400
Productive	Dept I (£0.16 × 0.2)	32	(£0.16 × 0.3)	48	80
	Dept II (£0.35 × 1.2)	420	(£0.35 × 0.8)	280	700
Mat. Process	Dept I (£25 × 300)	7.5	(£25 × 900)	22.5	30
	Dept II (£75 × 400)	30	(£75 × 400)	30	60
I.T.	Dept I (£32 × 350)	11.2	(£32 × 900)	28.8	40
	Dept II (£16 × 1,250)	20	(£16 × 1,250)	20	40
		694.7		715.3	1,410
Other overheads					
General administration		70.0		70.0	140
Marketing and distribution – V		40.0		60.0	100
F		50.0		100.0	150
Research and development		40.0		70.0	110
		200.0		300.0	500
Total overheads		894.7		1,015.3	1,910
Profit/(Loss)		425.3		(265.3)	160

OBJECTIVE TEST 9

i) c   ii) a   iii) b   iv) a

CHAPTER 10

Question 10.6

Standard Processing Ltd

AVCO

	Effective units	Material Cost per unit £	£	Effective units	Conversion Cost per unit £	£	Total £
April							
Opening WIP	10,000	0.64	6,400	8,000	1.235	9,880	16,280
Costs	90,000	0.54	48,600	82,000	1.01	82,820	131,420
	100,000	0.55	55,000	90,000	1.03	92,700	147,700
Closing WIP	12,000	0.55	6,600	2,000	1.03	2,060	8,600
Completed production	88,000	0.55	48,400	88,000	1.03	90,640	139,040

Continued

May

Opening WIP	12,000	0.55	6,600	2,000	1.03	2,060	8,660	
Costs	90,000	0.51	46,000	90,000	0.98	88,000	134,000	
	102,000	0.52	52,600	92,000	0.98	90,060	142,660	
Closing WIP	12,000	0.52	6,188	2,000	0.98	1,958	8,146	
Completed production	90,000	0.52	46,412	88,000	0.98	88,102	134,514	

FIFO

April

Opening WIP	10,000	0.64	6,400	8,000	1.235	9,880	16,280	
Costs	90,000	0.54	48,600	82,000	1.01	82,820	131,420	
	100,000	0.55	55,000	90,000	1.03	92,700	147,700	
Closing WIP	12,000	0.54	6,480	2,000	1.01	2,020	8,500	
Completed production	88,000	0.55	48,520	88,000	1.03	90,680	139,200	

May

Opening WIP	12,000	0.54	6,480	2,000	1.01	2,020	8,500	
Costs	90,000	0.51	46,000	90,000	0.98	88,000	134,000	
	102,000	0.51	52,480	92,000	1.00	90,020	142,500	
Closing WIP	12,000	0.51	6,133	2,000	0.98	1,956	8,089	
Completed production	90,000	0.51	46,347	90,000	0.98	88,064	134,411	

OBJECTIVE TEST 10

i) c   ii) b   iii) a   iv) d   v) c

CHAPTER 11

OBJECTIVE TEST 11

i) d   ii) c   iii) e   iv) c   v) c

CHAPTER 12

Question 12.5

Wooden Toys Ltd

	£	£
Standard cost of actual production		
1,345 units @ £81		108,945
Material price variance		
($£2 \times 11,900$) – £25,320	1,520 (A)	
Material usage variance		
[($1,345 \times 9$) – 11,900] $\times$ £2	410 (F)	
Total material cost variance		
($1,345 \times £18$) – £25,320		1,110 (A)

Continued

Wages rate of pay variance
$(£10.50 \times 8,200 \text{ hours}) - £92,250$ 6,150 (A)
Wages efficiency variance
$[(1,345 \times 6 \text{ hours}) - 8,200] \times £10.50$ 1,365 (A)
Total labour cost variance
$(1,345 \times £63) - £92,250$ 7,515 (A)
Actual cost of production   117,570

OBJECTIVE TEST 12

    i) b   ii) d   iii) c   iv) a   v) b

CHAPTER 13

OBJECTIVE TEST 13

    i) e   ii) c   iii) b   iv) a   v) c

CHAPTER 14

Question 14.7

Arbroath Hotels Ltd

	i) Total £	*ii)* Per guest/week £
Income ($£110 \times 20$ weeks $\times 30$ guests)	66,000	110
Variable costs ($£60 \times 20$ weeks $\times 30$ guests)	36,000	60
Contribution	30,000	50
Fixed costs per annum	10,000	
Annual profit	20,000	

OBJECTIVE TEST 14

    i) a   ii) c   iii) b   iv) c   v) b   vi) b   vii) b   viii) b   ix) b   x) b
    xi) a   xii) b

CHAPTER 15

Question 15.9

BMX Racing Ltd

	Knee pads	Elbow protectors	Gloves
i) Contribution per unit:			
Potential market (units)	2,000	2,000	1,000
Manufacturing time	2 hours	2.5 hours	3 hours
	£	£	£
Selling price	21.00	25.50	32.00
Variable costs:			
Direct labour	10.00	12.50	15.00
Direct materials			
Covers	3.00	4.00	5.00
Padding	2.00	2.00	1.00
Variable overheads	1.50	1.80	2.30
Agency fees	1.00	1.70	2.10
Total variable costs	17.50	22.00	25.40
Unit contribution	3.50	3.50	6.60
ii) Contribution per unit of limiting factor:			
Contribution per unit	£3.50	£3.50	£6.60
Number of direct labour hours	2 hours	2.5 hours	3 hours
	= £1.75	= £1.40	= £2.20
Ranking	2	3	1

iii) The optimal product mix

Ranking	£	Hours
1 Gloves (1,000 units @ £6.60)	6,600	3,000
2 Knee pads (2,000 units @ £3.50)	7,000	4,000
3 Elbow protectors (320 units @ £3.50)	1,120	800 (balance)
	14,720	7,800

Total time available (150 hours × 52 weeks) = 7,800 hours

iv) Abridged profit and loss statement

	£
Total contribution	14,720
Less Fixed costs	5,000
Optimal profit	9,720

OBJECTIVE TEST 15

i) d   ii) a   iii) b   iv) d   v) d

CHAPTER 16

Question 16.9

Zed-Plan Furniture Company

Contribution per standard dining room chair

	£	£
Selling price		200
Variable costs		
Materials	40	
Labour (10 hours @ £10)	100	
Total unit variable costs		140
Contribution per chair		60

Contribution per unit of scarce resource (scarce resource = labour hours)

$$\frac{\text{Contribution per unit}}{\text{Labour hours per unit}} = \frac{£60}{10 \text{ hours}} = £6 \text{ per direct labour hour}$$

This represents the contribution which would be lost if the labour hours are used to produce another product; that is, the opportunity cost.

Enquiry from furniture store:

	£	£
Sales value of enquiry		2,500
Materials	700	
Labour 150 hours @ £10	1,500	2,200
Contribution from accepting the order		300
Less Opportunity cost of order 150 hours @ £6 per hour		(900)
Disadvantage of accepting the order		(600)

Conclusion: the contribution from accepting the order would be £300; therefore, other things being equal, the order would be profitable and should be accepted if there is spare capacity to complete it. However, if the order would require labour to be diverted from producing the existing production, then the company would have to forgo the contribution of £900 which, because it is greater than the contribution of £300 produced by the new order, would mean that profits would fall by £600 if the new order is accepted.

OBJECTIVE TEST 16

i) b   ii) c   iii) c   iv) c   v) a

CHAPTER 17

Question 17.5

Bude Hotels Ltd

	Guest-house A £	Guest-house B £
Average annual profits for 3 years	£40,000	£40,000
Average investment	£200,000	£200,000
	20%	20%

Comments: both guest-houses have the same ARRs. From the cashflow point of view, guest-house B might be preferable since in the first year profit is more (cash can be reinvested). From the long-term point of view, guest-house A might be preferred if profits after year 2 are likely to increase (rather than decrease as seems likely with guest-house B).

OBJECTIVE TEST 17

i) d   ii) c   iii) b   iv) a   v) d   vi) c   vii) b   viii) a   ix) c   x) d

CHAPTER 18

Question 18.13

Tintagel Investments Ltd

Business B

Year	Cash flows £	Discount rate 12% Discount factor	Present value £	Discount rate 16% Discount factor	Present value £
0	(50,000)	1.000	(50,000)	1.000	(50,000)
1	12,000	0.893	10,716	0.862	10,344
2	11,000	0.797	8,767	0.743	8,173
3	10,000	0.712	7,120	0.641	6,410
4	9,000	0.636	5,724	0.552	4,968
5	8,000	0.567	4,536	0.476	3,808
6	8,000	0.507	4,056	0.410	3,280
7	8,000	0.452	3,616	0.354	2,832
8	8,000	0.404	3,232	0.305	2,440
9	8,000	0.361	2,888	0.263	2,104
10	8,000	0.322	2,576	0.227	1,816
	Net present value		3,231	Net present value	(3,825)

$$\text{IRR} = 12 + 4 \times \frac{3,231}{3,231 + 3,825} = 13.83\% \text{ (say) } 14\%$$

The advice given to Tintagel will obviously vary with the assumptions made: 14 per cent is less than 16 per cent, but caveats might include the reliability of the forecasted figures, the uncertainty of the future (particularly for a period as long as 10 years), the dangers of possible redevelopment and competition in the area and the unreliability of the property market.

OBJECTIVE TEST 18

i) a   ii) c   iii) a   iv) c   v) a   vi) b   vii) b   viii) c   ix) a   x) a
xi) b   xii) c   xiii) c   xiv) b   xv) d

Discounted cash flow tables

TABLE 1 – Present Value Factors

Rate of discount

Future Years	1%	2%	3%	4%	5%	6%	7%	8%	9%	10%	11%	12%	13%	14%	15%	16%
1	0.990	0.980	0.971	0.962	0.952	0.943	0.935	0.926	0.917	0.909	0.901	0.893	0.885	0.877	0.870	0.862
2	0.980	0.961	0.943	0.925	0.907	0.890	0.873	0.857	0.842	0.826	0.812	0.797	0.783	0.770	0.756	0.743
3	0.971	0.942	0.915	0.889	0.864	0.840	0.816	0.794	0.772	0.751	0.731	0.712	0.693	0.675	0.658	0.641
4	0.961	0.924	0.889	0.855	0.823	0.792	0.763	0.735	0.708	0.683	0.659	0.636	0.613	0.592	0.572	0.552
5	0.952	0.906	0.863	0.822	0.784	0.747	0.713	0.681	0.650	0.621	0.594	0.567	0.543	0.519	0.497	0.476
6	0.942	0.888	0.838	0.790	0.746	0.705	0.666	0.630	0.596	0.565	0.535	0.507	0.480	0.456	0.432	0.410
7	0.933	0.871	0.813	0.760	0.711	0.665	0.623	0.584	0.547	0.513	0.482	0.452	0.425	0.400	0.376	0.354
8	0.924	0.854	0.789	0.731	0.677	0.627	0.582	0.540	0.502	0.467	0.434	0.404	0.376	0.351	0.327	0.305
9	0.914	0.837	0.766	0.703	0.645	0.592	0.544	0.500	0.460	0.424	0.391	0.361	0.333	0.308	0.284	0.263
10	0.905	0.820	0.744	0.676	0.614	0.558	0.508	0.463	0.422	0.386	0.352	0.322	0.295	0.270	0.247	0.227
11	0.896	0.804	0.722	0.650	0.585	0.527	0.475	0.429	0.388	0.350	0.317	0.287	0.261	0.237	0.215	0.195
12	0.887	0.789	0.701	0.625	0.557	0.497	0.444	0.397	0.356	0.319	0.286	0.257	0.231	0.208	0.187	0.168
13	0.879	0.773	0.681	0.601	0.530	0.469	0.415	0.368	0.326	0.286	0.258	0.229	0.204	0.182	0.163	0.145
14	0.870	0.758	0.661	0.578	0.505	0.442	0.388	0.341	0.299	0.263	0.232	0.205	0.181	0.160	0.141	0.125
15	0.861	0.743	0.642	0.555	0.481	0.417	0.362	0.315	0.275	0.239	0.209	0.183	0.160	0.140	0.123	0.108
16	0.853	0.728	0.623	0.534	0.458	0.394	0.339	0.292	0.252	0.218	0.188	0.163	0.142	0.123	0.107	0.093
17	0.844	0.714	0.605	0.513	0.436	0.371	0.317	0.270	0.231	0.198	0.170	0.146	0.125	0.108	0.093	0.080
18	0.836	0.700	0.587	0.494	0.416	0.350	0.296	0.250	0.212	0.180	0.153	0.130	0.111	0.095	0.081	0.069
19	0.828	0.686	0.570	0.475	0.396	0.331	0.277	0.232	0.195	0.164	0.138	0.116	0.098	0.083	0.070	0.060
20	0.820	0.673	0.554	0.456	0.377	0.312	0.258	0.215	0.178	0.149	0.124	0.104	0.087	0.073	0.061	0.051

Rate of discount

Future Years	17%	18%	19%	20%	21%	22%	23%	24%	25%	26%	28%	30%	35%	40%	45%	50%
1	0.855	0.847	0.840	0.833	0.826	0.820	0.813	0.807	0.800	0.794	0.781	0.769	0.741	0.714	0.690	0.667
2	0.731	0.718	0.706	0.694	0.683	0.672	0.661	0.650	0.640	0.630	0.610	0.592	0.549	0.510	0.476	0.444
3	0.624	0.609	0.593	0.579	0.565	0.551	0.537	0.525	0.512	0.500	0.477	0.455	0.406	0.364	0.328	0.296
4	0.534	0.516	0.499	0.482	0.467	0.451	0.437	0.423	0.410	0.397	0.373	0.350	0.301	0.260	0.226	0.198
5	0.456	0.437	0.419	0.402	0.386	0.370	0.355	0.341	0.328	0.315	0.291	0.269	0.223	0.186	0.156	0.132
6	0.390	0.370	0.352	0.335	0.319	0.303	0.289	0.275	0.262	0.250	0.227	0.207	0.165	0.133	0.108	0.088
7	0.333	0.314	0.296	0.279	0.263	0.249	0.235	0.222	0.210	0.198	0.178	0.159	0.122	0.095	0.074	0.059
8	0.285	0.266	0.249	0.233	0.218	0.204	0.191	0.179	0.168	0.157	0.139	0.123	0.091	0.068	0.051	0.039
9	0.243	0.226	0.209	0.194	0.180	0.167	0.155	0.144	0.134	0.125	0.108	0.094	0.067	0.048	0.035	0.026
10	0.208	0.191	0.176	0.162	0.149	0.137	0.126	0.116	0.107	0.099	0.085	0.073	0.050	0.035	0.024	0.017
11	0.178	0.162	0.148	0.135	0.123	0.112	0.103	0.094	0.086	0.079	0.066	0.056	0.037	0.025	0.017	0.012
12	0.152	0.137	0.124	0.112	0.102	0.092	0.083	0.076	0.069	0.063	0.052	0.043	0.027	0.018	0.012	0.008
13	0.130	0.116	0.104	0.094	0.084	0.075	0.068	0.061	0.055	0.050	0.040	0.033	0.020	0.013	0.008	0.005
14	0.111	0.099	0.088	0.078	0.069	0.062	0.055	0.049	0.044	0.039	0.032	0.025	0.015	0.009	0.006	0.003
15	0.095	0.084	0.074	0.065	0.057	0.051	0.045	0.040	0.035	0.031	0.025	0.020	0.011	0.006	0.004	0.002
16	0.081	0.071	0.062	0.054	0.047	0.042	0.036	0.032	0.028	0.025	0.019	0.015	0.008	0.005	0.003	0.002
17	0.069	0.060	0.052	0.045	0.039	0.034	0.030	0.026	0.023	0.020	0.015	0.012	0.006	0.003	0.002	0.001
18	0.059	0.051	0.044	0.038	0.032	0.028	0.024	0.021	0.018	0.016	0.012	0.009	0.005	0.002	0.001	0.001
19	0.051	0.043	0.037	0.031	0.027	0.023	0.020	0.017	0.014	0.012	0.009	0.007	0.003	0.002	0.001	0.000
20	0.043	0.037	0.031	0.026	0.022	0.019	0.016	0.014	0.012	0.010	0.007	0.005	0.002	0.001	0.001	0.000

TABLE 2 – Cumulative Present Value Factors

Rate of discount

Future Years	1%	2%	3%	4%	5%	6%	7%	8%	9%	10%	11%	12%	13%	14%	15%	16%
1	0.990	0.980	0.971	0.962	0.952	0.943	0.935	0.926	0.917	0.909	0.901	0.893	0.885	0.877	0.870	0.862
2	1.970	1.942	1.913	1.886	1.859	1.833	1.808	1.783	1.759	1.736	1.713	1.690	1.668	1.647	1.626	1.605
3	2.941	2.884	2.829	2.775	2.723	2.673	2.624	2.577	2.531	2.487	2.444	2.402	2.361	2.322	2.283	2.246
4	3.902	3.808	3.717	3.630	3.546	3.465	3.387	3.312	3.240	3.170	3.102	3.037	2.974	2.914	2.855	2.798
5	4.853	4.713	4.580	4.452	4.329	4.212	4.100	3.993	3.890	3.791	3.696	3.605	3.517	3.433	3.352	3.274
6	5.795	5.601	5.417	5.242	5.076	4.917	4.767	4.623	4.486	4.355	4.231	4.111	3.998	3.889	3.784	3.685
7	6.728	6.472	6.230	6.002	5.786	5.582	5.389	5.206	5.033	4.868	4.712	4.564	4.423	4.288	4.160	4.039
8	7.652	7.325	7.020	6.733	6.463	6.210	5.971	5.747	5.535	5.335	5.146	4.968	4.799	4.639	4.487	4.344
9	8.566	8.162	7.786	7.435	7.108	6.802	6.515	6.247	5.995	5.759	5.537	5.328	5.132	4.946	4.772	4.607
10	9.471	8.983	8.530	8.111	7.722	7.360	7.024	6.710	6.418	6.145	5.889	5.650	5.426	5.216	5.019	4.833
11	10.368	9.787	9.253	8.760	8.306	7.887	7.499	7.139	6.805	6.495	6.207	5.938	5.687	5.453	5.234	5.029
12	11.255	10.575	9.954	9.385	8.863	8.384	7.943	7.536	7.161	6.814	6.492	6.194	5.918	5.660	5.421	5.197
13	12.134	11.348	10.635	9.986	9.394	8.853	8.358	7.904	7.487	7.103	6.750	6.424	6.122	5.842	5.583	5.342
14	13.004	12.106	11.296	10.563	9.899	9.295	8.745	8.244	7.786	7.367	6.982	6.628	6.302	6.002	5.724	5.468
15	13.865	12.849	11.938	11.118	10.380	9.712	9.108	8.559	8.061	7.606	7.191	6.811	6.462	6.142	5.847	5.575
16	14.718	13.578	12.561	11.652	10.838	10.106	9.447	8.851	8.313	7.824	7.379	6.974	6.604	6.265	5.954	5.668
17	15.562	14.292	13.166	12.166	11.274	10.477	9.763	9.122	8.544	8.022	7.549	7.120	6.729	6.373	6.047	5.749
18	16.398	14.992	13.754	12.659	11.690	10.828	10.059	9.372	8.756	8.201	7.702	7.250	6.840	6.467	6.128	5.818
19	17.226	15.678	14.324	13.134	12.085	11.158	10.336	9.604	8.950	8.365	7.839	7.366	6.938	6.550	6.198	5.877
20	18.046	16.351	14.877	13.590	12.462	11.470	10.594	9.818	9.129	8.514	7.963	7.469	7.025	6.623	6.259	5.929

Rate of discount

Future Years	17%	18%	19%	20%	21%	22%	23%	24%	25%	26%	28%	30%	35%	40%	45%	50%
1	0.855	0.847	0.840	0.833	0.826	0.820	0.813	0.806	0.800	0.794	0.781	0.769	0.741	0.714	0.690	0.667
2	1.585	1.566	1.547	1.528	1.509	1.492	1.474	1.457	1.440	1.424	1.392	1.361	1.289	1.224	1.165	1.111
3	2.210	2.174	2.140	2.106	2.074	2.042	2.011	1.981	1.952	1.923	1.868	1.816	1.696	1.589	1.493	1.407
4	2.743	2.690	2.639	2.589	2.540	2.494	2.448	2.404	2.362	2.320	2.241	2.166	1.997	1.849	1.720	1.605
5	3.199	3.127	3.058	2.991	2.926	2.864	2.803	2.745	2.689	2.689	2.532	2.436	2.220	2.035	1.876	1.737
6	3.589	3.498	3.410	3.326	3.245	3.167	3.092	3.020	2.951	2.885	2.759	2.643	2.385	2.168	1.983	1.824
7	3.922	3.812	3.706	3.605	3.508	3.416	3.327	3.242	3.161	3.083	2.937	2.802	2.508	2.263	2.057	1.883
8	4.207	4.078	3.954	3.837	3.726	3.619	3.518	3.421	3.329	3.241	3.076	2.925	2.598	2.331	2.109	1.922
9	4.451	4.303	4.163	4.031	3.905	3.786	3.673	3.566	3.463	3.366	3.184	3.019	2.665	2.379	2.144	1.948
10	4.659	4.494	4.339	4.192	4.054	3.923	3.799	3.682	3.571	3.465	3.269	3.092	2.715	2.414	2.168	1.965
11	4.836	4.656	4.486	4.327	4.177	4.035	3.902	3.776	3.656	3.543	3.335	3.147	2.752	2.438	2.185	1.977
12	4.988	4.793	4.611	4.439	4.278	4.127	3.985	3.851	3.725	3.606	3.387	3.190	2.779	2.456	2.196	1.985
13	5.118	4.910	4.715	4.533	4.362	4.203	4.053	3.912	3.780	3.656	3.427	3.223	2.799	2.469	2.204	1.990
14	5.229	5.008	4.802	4.611	4.432	4.265	4.108	3.962	3.824	3.695	3.459	3.249	2.814	2.478	2.210	1.993
15	5.324	5.092	4.876	4.675	4.489	4.315	4.153	4.001	3.859	3.726	3.483	3.268	2.825	2.484	2.214	1.995
16	5.405	5.162	4.938	4.730	4.536	4.357	4.189	4.033	3.887	3.751	3.503	3.283	2.834	2.489	2.216	1.997
17	5.475	5.222	4.990	4.775	4.576	4.391	4.219	4.059	3.910	3.771	3.518	3.295	2.840	2.492	2.218	1.998
18	5.534	5.273	5.033	4.812	4.608	4.419	4.243	4.080	3.928	3.786	3.529	3.304	2.844	2.494	2.219	1.999
19	5.584	5.316	5.070	4.843	4.635	4.442	4.263	4.097	3.942	3.799	3.539	3.311	2.848	2.496	2.220	1.999
20	5.628	5.353	5.101	4.870	4.657	4.460	4.279	4.110	3.954	3.808	3.546	3.316	2.850	2.497	2.221	1.999

INDEX

Abnormal gains   157–8
Abnormal losses   154, 156–7
Absorption costing   106–26, 132
   arguments for use   135–6
   drawbacks   141–4
   effects   130
Accounting information   259–60
Accounting rate of return (ARR)
      269–81
   advantages and disadvantages
      276
Accuracy   9–10
Activity   225–6
Activity variance   115
Activity-based costing (ABC)
      140–53, 144–7
   advantages and disadvantages
      146–7
Actual cost   189
Administration overheads   22–3
Adverse variance   80, 83
Amortizing   17
Annuity tables   286–7
Audit   9
Average capital   273
Average cost (AVCO)   20, 22, 114,
      142, 154–5, 158, 160
Average costing   173

B-index   58, 59–62
Backflush accounting   174
Bank balances   16
Basis of apportionment   97–8, 100
Batch costing   170
Behaviour of costs   32–48, 127–8
   graphical presentation   36–9
Blanket rate   107
Board of Directors   67
Break-even point   216–17, 227
   graphical presentation   218–20,
      224, 227
Budget centre   69
Budget co-ordination   70–72
Budget committee   73
Budget setting process   73–4

Budgetary control   67–88, 177
Budgetary slack   81
Budgeted profit and loss account   70
Business objectives   67
Business plan   67–8
By-product costing   162–3

Capital budgeting   269
Capital expenditure   16, 17, 24
Capital expenditure budget   70
Capital invested   273
Capital investment appraisal   269
Cash balances   16
Cash flow budget   72–3
Cash flows   269–70, 288
Cash in hand   16
Cash outflow   261
Chartered Institute of Management
      Accountants (CIMA)   4
Close down or suspend activity
      decisions   6
Co-ordination   71–2, 80
Common process costs   160–61, 162
Competing products   7
Constant product mix   226
Constant variables   226
Content of statements   8–9
Continuous allotment method   98
Contract costing   170–71
Contribution   134, 213, 216, 253–4
Contribution per unit   216
Contribution-margin ratio
      (contribution-to-sale ratio)
      238–9
Control   5
Control accounts   198
Conversion costs   244
Cost absorbed (cost recovered)
      113–14
Cost absorption   106–7, 116
Cost accounting   4
Cost allocation   91–105
Cost apportionment   95–8
Cost behaviour   32–48, 127–8
   graphical presentation   36–9

Cost of capital rate   288
Cost centres   93–4, 100, 116
Cost classification   15–31
   by product cost   92–3
Cost collection and recording
      196–207
Cost drivers   144, 169
Cost estimation methods   50–63
Cost ledger accounts   199–202
Cost objects   92, 93, 167
Cost pools   144, 169
Cost prediction techniques   49–66
Cost recovered   113–14
Cost units   91–2, 93, 98, 116, 167
Cost-plus pricing   7
Cost-volume-profit analysis (CVP)
      213–34
   limitations   225–6
Costing methods   167
Costs   17–18
   ascertainment   5–6
Cumulative present value tables
      286–7
Current assets   15, 16
Current realizable values   262
Customer demand   236

Debtors   16
Decentralization   81
Decision making   6–7, 80, 129
Definition of management
      accounting   4
Dependent variables   49
Depreciation   17, 261, 270, 288
   and residual values   275–6
Detail   10
Detailed budgets   69–70
Differential cost   41
Differential costs and revenues   254,
      262
Direct charge vouchers (DCVs)   197
Direct cost variances   178
Direct costs   18–19, 94
Direct Data Entry (DDE)   197
Direct expenses   19
Direct labour   19, 141, 168
Direct labour costs   110–11, 128,
      142
Direct labour hours   108–9

Direct material cost   111
Direct materials   17, 18, 19, 39, 168
Direct materials variances   178–9
Direct wages   19, 197
Direct wages costs   39
Direct wages variances   179–81
Discount rate choice   288–9
Discounted cash flow (DCF)
      287–90, 299–300
   advantages and disadvantages
      299–300
Discounted cash flow (DCF) tables
      285, 326–7
Discounting   285–6
Discretionary costs   262
Distribution overheads   23
Divisions   4
Documentation   197–8
Double-entry approaches   196

Effective (Equivalent) units   159–60
Efficiency variance   182
Electricity   17, 39
Engineering approach   50
Excel   53, 73, 299
Exception principle of management
      80
Expenditure variance   115, 116,
      182, 185

Factory space shortage   236
Favourable variance   80, 83, 115
Feed-forward control   80, 82
FIFO (First-in-first-out)   19, 21, 114,
      142, 158
Financial accounting   8–10
   compared with management
      accounting   8–10
Financial budgets   69–70
Financial information   259–60
Finished goods   16, 23, 141–2, 198
   documentation   198
Finished goods stock budget   70
Fixed assets   15, 16, 24
Fixed budgets   74–5, 76, 79, 82
Fixed cost line   225
Fixed costs   33–4, 37, 44, 52, 76–7,
      128, 142, 215–16, 254–6
   definition   35

Fixed overhead absorption rate (FOAR)   185
Fixed overhead variances   184–6
Fixtures and fittings   24
Flexible budgets   75–6, 79, 182
Flow chart for integrated accounting   203
Functional budgets   5, 68–9, 79
Functional (Line) managers   67, 83
Functional organization chart   67, 68
Functions   3, 9, 67
Furniture and office equipment   16

Generally Accepted Accounting Principles (GAAP)   8–9
Goal congruency   81
Goods Received notes (GRNs)   197
Graphical presentation
   of break even point   218–20, 224
   of cost behaviour   36–9, 49

Heating   17
High-low method   41, 52, 56, 78
Historical cost method   50–51

Income, ascertainment   5–6
Increase output decision   6
Incremental budgeting   79, 81
Incremental costs and revenue   254, 262
Independent variables   49
Indirect costs   18
Indirect materials   19
Institute of Cost and Works Accountants (ICWA)   4
Integrated accounts   202–3
Interest rate choice   288–9
Interlocking accounts   199–202
Internal rate of return (IRR)   288, 294–9
   compared with net present value (NPV)   194–7
Invoices   197
Iterative approach   74

Job costing (specific order costing or job order costing)   169–70
Jobbing production   7

Joint product costing   160–61
Just-in-time (JIT) techniques   141, 174, 244

Labour shortage   236
Land and buildings   24
Learning curves   57–63
   definition   57
Least squares method   53–7
LIFO (Last-in-first-out)   20, 114, 142
Lighting   17
LILO (Last-in-last-out)   20, 21
Limiting factors   235–50
   ranking according to effect   240–1
   reducing effects of   235–6
Linear cost function   49
Linear interpolation   296
Linear regression   53–7
Lotus 1–2–3   73, 299
Lowest cost financing decisions   7

Machine hours   109–10
Make or buy decisions   6
Management accounting   3–4
   compared with financial accounting   8–10
Managing Director (Chief Executive)   67
Manufacturing developments   140–41
Margin of safety   221
Margin variances   187–9
Marginal costing   127–39, 213–15
   arguments for use   134–5
   effects   130–31
Marginal costing statement   128
Marginal costs   127–8, 252–3
Marginal (or Variable) costing statement   128–9, 213–14
Mark-up   7
Master budget   70
Materials   19–22, 197
   documentation   197
Materials price variances   178–9
Materials shortage   236
Materials usage variant   179
Measuring production   107
Mechanization   140

Motivation   80, 82
Motor vehicles   16, 24
Mutually exclusive decisions   257
Mutually exclusive projects   291

Negative net present value   290
Net book value (NBV)   261
Net present value (NPV)   288,
     290–2, 296–9
  compared with internal rate of
     return (IRR)   194–7
Non-functional budgets   79
Non-linear cost behaviour   57
Normal losses   154, 155–6
Notional costs   262

Operating costing   173, 174
Opportunity cost of capital   282,
     288
Opportunity costs   256–9, 263
Optimal profits   226
Out of pocket costs   261, 262
Outwork   17
Overhead cost absorption   106
Overhead cost absorption rate
     106–7
Overhead variance analysis   115
Overhead variances   181–2
Overheads (Overhead costs)   18, 19,
     22–3, 129, 168

Partly finished sub-assemblies   18
Parts   18
Payback period   269–73, 277
  advantages and disadvantages
     272–3
Percentage on direct labour cost
     110–11
Percentage on direct material cost
     111
Percentage learning curves   58–9
Percentage on prime cost   112
Piecework   35
Planning   4–5, 80
Plant and Machinery   16, 24
Positive net present value   290
Pre-separation costs   160–61, 162
Premises   16
Present value   283–4

Present value tables   284–5
Pricing   7–8, 81
Prime cost   23, 39, 112
Prime ratio   74
Principle budget factor   236–7
Process costing   154–66
Product costing   168–9
Product costs   18, 24, 92–3
Product direct costs   39, 100
Product indirect costs (Overheads)
     22–3
Product ranking   237
Production, measuring   107
Production capacity shortage   236
Production cost   23
Production cost centres   93
Production line, setting up new   6
Production method change   7
Production overheads   22, 94–8, 197
  documentation   197
Production and sales   226
Profit centres   6
Profit margins   7, 74
Profit measurement   129–30, 226
Profit-volume graph   224
Profit-volume ratio (PV ratio)
     (Contribution-margin ratio or
     contribution-to-sales ratio)
     238–9
Profitability index (PI)   288, 293–4
Profits   273
  calculation   131–3

Quantitative budgets   69–70
QuatroPro   299

Ranking technique with two
     constraints   242–3
Rate per direct labour hour   108–9
Rate per machine hour   109–10
Rate per standard hour   112
Rate per unit of production   107–8
Raw materials   16, 18–19
Raw materials consumed   17
Reciprocal costs   98–100
Relevant costs and revenues   6,
     251–68
Relevant and non-relevant costs
     260–2

Relevant range   220–1, 226
Relevant revenue   253
Repeated distribution method   98, 99
Reporting periods   8
Reporting system   68
Research and development overheads   23
Residual values   275–6
Resources   15, 16
   scarce   7
Responsibility   80
Return on capital employed   74, 276
Revenue expenditure   16–17, 24
Risk   272
Role of management accounting   3–12
Rolling budgets   79
Running expenses   17

Sale margin price variance   188
Sales   226
Sales margin variances   187–9
Sales margin volume variance   188
Sales value at split-off point   161
Scarce resources   7
Scattergraph method   51, 63
Scorekeeping   5
Self-balancing   201
Selling overheads   23
Semi-variable costs   39–43, 44, 77, 225
Sensitivity analysis   299
Separate financial and cost accounting   199
Service cost centres   93–4, 98
Service costing   171–3
Shareholders   67
Short-term planning   5
Simultaneous equations   98, 99–100
Single product scenario   226
Small businesses   67
Small value item   17
Specific order costing   169–70
Spreadsheets   299
SSAP 9   9, 114, 135, 142, 147, 189
Standard costing   177–95
Standard costing profit and loss account   189–90

Standard hours   112, 179
Standard marginal or variable costing   190
Standard rates   182
Statements
   content of   8–9
   recipients of   8
Stock   133, 197
Stock valuation   20, 114, 142
Strategic planning   4–5
Sub-assembly   17
Sub-contract work   17
Sunk costs   262
Synthetic cost construction   50

Target costing   8
Target profit   222–4
Throughput accounting   243–4
Throughput accounting ratio (TAR)   244
Time dimension   9
Time value of money   272
Total budgeted production cost centre overheads   107
Total contribution   216
Total contribution ranking   239–40
Total cost variances   180
Total costs   37
Total fixed overhead cost variance   185
Total sales margin variance   187
Total variable overhead variance   182
Total variance   115, 116

Under-absorption   114
Under-recovery   114
Uniform costing   174
Unit contribution ranking   237–8
Unit costing   174
Unit costs   198
   documentation   198

Value-added approach   141, 244
Variable cost line   225
Variable costing statement   128–9
Variable costs   33, 36, 39, 43–4, 76, 127, 213–16, 252–3
   definition   35

Variable overhead absorption rate
  (VOAR)   182, 183
Variable overhead variances   182–4
Variance analysis   142–4
Variances   5, 80, 83, 115, 116
Visual fit methods   52–3
Volume variance   115, 185

Wages   17
  documentation   197

Wages efficiency variance   180
Weighted average cost of capital
  (WACC)   288–9
Work in progress   16, 23, 154,
  158–9
Working capital   292–3
Writing off   17

Zero-base budgeting (ZBB)   79